# BEFORE JACKIE ROBINSON

# Before Jackie Robinson

## Robinson

The Transcendent Role of
Black Sporting Pioneers

Edited and with an introduction by

## GERALD R. GEMS

University of Nebraska Press
LINCOLN & LONDON

# CONTENTS

# BEFORE JACKIE ROBINSON

# Introduction

**B**efore Jackie Robinson is a cooperative effort to recover a significant part of the past. It attempts to fill a significant hole in the
literature of our American history. Why does that matter? Our
personal histories make us who we are as individuals, and our collective histories provide us with a national identity as Americans.
One of the characteristics of American culture that differentiates it
from so many others in the world is the influence of race in American history. The genre of "new biography" that has emerged in the
twenty-first century places greater emphasis on "the socially con-
tested nature of identity constructions, so that it treats biography as
acts of identity politics in the social struggles of a time," a method
that allows "social groups to reach an understanding about who they
are and who they want to be."[1] This volume makes a distinct attempt
to incorporate the factors of race and race politics over a transitional
period in American history that eventually transformed the nature
of American society and American history.

The choice of subjects provides a sense of chronological change
and the incremental transition in race relations in American culture over approximately a half century. Sports provided a very visible means of that process. While many Americans might be familiar
with Jack Johnson, Joe Louis, and Jesse Owens, all of whom operated on an international stage, we chose to examine the lives of no

less important athletic pioneers, once well known but increasingly forgotten, who pushed the social boundaries on other levels in their quest to dismantle racism.

Slavery commenced with some of the earliest colonial settlers in 1619 and held a central role in the American economy and society for the next 250 years. The Civil War, which pitted Americans and even families against one another, is attributed to the enslavement of African Americans. It cost more than six hundred thousand American lives, the greatest disaster in the history of the nation.

With the end of the Civil War and the reorganization of the defeated Confederate states, a period known as Reconstruction, the undertaking offered hope and promise to the newly liberated slaves. That optimistic expectation proved illusory and temporary. When the presidential election of 1876 resulted in a stalemate, the two political parties reached an agreement that gave the presidency to the Republican candidate, Rutherford B. Hayes, but allowed the Democrats to resume their previous control of the southern states. Restrictive suffrage qualifications, complete disenfranchisement, Jim Crow segregation laws, and the sharecropping system quickly returned blacks to a state of peonage, reinforced by widespread lynchings, the ramifications of which still beset the American society today.

A former slave, Booker T. Washington, founded the Tuskegee Institute in Alabama in 1881; it taught vocational skills and provided black teachers for the segregated schools. Rather than social equality Washington preached the acquisition of skills for the workplace. His accommodationist and non-threatening philosophy won him support from white leaders and recognition as the top black spokesperson of the late nineteenth century. Under such guidance athletes found some limited opportunity in the dominant white culture—but not equality. Blacks faced continual denigration and stereotyping and were often depicted as cartoonish minstrels or Sambo figures in the white media, incapable of full inclusion in the white mainstream society.

Jockeys such as Isaac Murphy, Willie Sims, and Jimmy Winkfield won numerous Kentucky Derby races from 1884 to 1902 and earned considerable sums for their skills, but they were only the employees of wealthy owners who garnered the larger prizes and national acclaim.

The black jockeys also suffered the resentment of their white competitors. The jockeys, however, fared better than other athletes. Moses Fleetwood Walker reached the zenith of professional baseball as a catcher for the Toledo team in the American Association in 1884, but white opponents refused to participate in games against him, causing the management to release him and relegating him to the minor leagues thereafter. The white crusade to oust black players from the top echelons of professional baseball continued relentlessly for the remainder of the century. In the South, blacks were completely segregated from interracial competitions in team sports by custom and by law. Any who violated the southern social norms risked beatings, incarceration, and lynching. In the northern states some black football players won recognition for their abilities as individuals who contributed to team success, but they regularly faced the ire of white opponents who sought to injure them. Still William Henry Lewis won All-American honors at Harvard in 1892 and 1893 and eventually rose to the position of assistant U.S. attorney general in Boston, where a local barber had refused to cut his hair.[2] Such black achievements and successes were virtually excluded from presentation at the 1893 World's Fair in Chicago, dubbed the "White City" by the media.[3]

Lewis's ascendance represented a black invasion of the white power structure, but his talents overcame prejudice. Other northern blacks began to test white assumptions of superiority in other forms of sport. Like in horse racing, blacks were expected to serve wealthier golfers as caddies in an employer-employee relationship. When John Shippen, who had learned to play golf as a caddie for whites, entered the sacrosanct U.S. Open in 1896, the other entrants arranged a boycott. Only the courageous efforts of U. S. Golf Association (USGA) president Theodore Havemeyer, who supported Shippen, saved the tournament. Shippen represented a challenge to the white concept of the self-made man, presumably reserved for white males. A loss to a nonwhite could damage the perception of white racial superiority, a basic tenet of the racist society that upheld white privilege. Shippen continued to challenge white hegemony, entering the tournament repeatedly in 1899, 1900, 1902, and 1913. The USGA would eventually adopt a whites-only policy. Such exclusionary tactics resulted in black golfers forming their own parallel organization, and Shippen became a golf instructor, eventually employed at Shady Rest Golf and Country Club, a black enterprise established in Scotch Plains, New Jersey, in 1921. He had made a formidable statement in the quest for equality but had little to show for it, dying in poverty and largely forgotten at the age of eighty-nine in 1968.[4]

Cyclist Major Taylor personified another such provocation as his abilities clearly surpassed that of his white opponents as he set numerous world records in head to head competition and won the world championship by 1899. His success fostered the animosity of white cyclists and their collusion to hinder his efforts forced him to seek his fortune abroad, where he earned as much as $10,000 annually. Such physical prowess offered one means of social mobility when other avenues were denied.[5]

Such head-to-head individual competitions challenged the dominant Social Darwinian beliefs in white superiority. Boxers had already confronted that awareness by the late nineteenth century. White perceptions of blacks as physically inferior, weak-willed, cowardly, lacking in toughness and personal discipline, and unable to withstand a stomach punch enabled black fighters to enter the professional ring. White audiences expected to see and enjoyed watching black boxers being pummeled by white opponents. White men organized "battle royals" in which black youth were thrown in a ring, sometimes blindfolded, to fight until the last one standing was awarded with cheers or coins. At the professional level John L. Sullivan, who held the heavyweight championship from 1882 to 1892, instituted a ban on black challengers to ensure that the symbolic title of physical supremacy remained in white hands.

In 1891 Peter Jackson, the top black heavyweight of the era, fought Jim Corbett to a draw after sixty rounds, negating the belief in blacks' limited endurance. The next year Corbett defeated John L. Sullivan to gain the championship, but he never gave Jackson a rematch. On the same program in which Corbett defeated Sullivan, known as the Carnival of Champions, George Dixon thoroughly thrashed Jack Skelly, a white fighter, to claim the featherweight championship. A day after the mauling an editorial appeared in the *New Orleans*

*Times-Democrat* that objected to the interracial bout: "We of the South who know the fallacy and danger of this doctrine of race equality, who are opposed to placing the negro [*sic*] on any terms of equality, who have insisted on a separation of the races in church, hotel, car, saloon and theatre; who believe that the law ought to step in and forever forbid the idea of equality by making marriages between them illegal, are heartily opposed to any arrangement encouraging this equality, which gives negroes false ideas and dangerous beliefs."[6] The color line was enforced in the South thereafter and given legal sanction in the Supreme Court decision in the case of *Plessy v. Ferguson* in 1896, the unsuccessful suit of a New Orleans mulatto who had refused to take a segregated seat in a railway car.

Black boxers might compete at the lower weight classes because the heavyweight title symbolized the top tier of physical superiority, and in 1902 Joe Gans became the first black fighter acknowledged as a world champion when he captured the lightweight crown. In 1906 he added the welterweight title, and his forty-two-round war with Oscar "Battling" Nelson was considered to be the "fight of the century" and elicited the highest purse for a boxing match up to that date. A black newspaper claimed that Gans enjoyed more celebrity than Booker T. Washington, yet Gans suffered bankruptcy and an early death. His success proved to be ephemeral.[7]

By that time W. E. B. Du Bois, a Harvard PhD, had assumed a more militant stance in opposition to Booker T. Washington's accommodationism. Du Bois declared that blacks need not acquiesce because a "talented tenth" of their number could compete equally with whites on a level playing field. In Chicago a young multisport star, Sam Ransom, proved that assertion in the high school ranks. He was accorded unbiased recognition by the more liberal Chicago media but did not receive a remuneration in the form of college scholarships offered to his white teammates. In 1903 Dubois asserted that "submission to civic inferiority . . . is bound to sap the manhood of any race in the long run."[8] Ransom would assume a more deliberate engagement in American citizenship and fight for greater rights and recognition of blacks throughout the remainder of his life.

Shortly after Ransom's athletic triumphs, Jack Johnson, king of the black heavyweights, destroyed the myth of white supremacy. When champion Jim Jeffries retired from the ring undefeated, Tommy Burns emerged as the new titleholder, and he embarked on a global tour to maximize the profit of his title. Jack Johnson followed him to Australia, where Burns was coerced to fight Johnson for a magnificent sum. It proved to be a gross mismatch as Johnson toyed with Burns before ending his short reign. As the world champion, Johnson refused to give other top black boxers a shot at his title, so Joe Jeannette, Sam Langford, Sam McVea, and others traveled to Europe to gain fame and fortune, as did many black musicians and the celebrated dancer Josephine Baker in later years.

Johnson proceeded to outrage whites by his flamboyant lifestyle, liaisons and eventual marriages to white women, and the fact that a series of "white hopes" could not dislodge him from his position atop the heavyweight ranks. On July 4, 1910, the previously undefeated Jeffries even came out of retirement to restore the laurels to the white race, but he too tasted an ignominious defeat at the hands of Johnson. Johnson's victory fostered race riots throughout America, a measure of whites' vitriolic backlash at their comeuppance. Films of the fight were banned, and the U.S. government got further involved by charging Johnson with a violation of the Mann Act, involving the transportation of women across state lines for illegal purposes, and Johnson became a fugitive. Despite Johnson's dominance of the heavyweight ranks, or perhaps because of it, D. W. Griffith's popular 1915 movie, *The Birth of a Nation*, continued to portray black men as primitive, oversexed, and immoral savages, less than worthy of full citizenship. Johnson lost the title to Jess Willard in Havana, Cuba, in 1915 (Johnson claimed that he threw the fight), and upon his return to the United States in 1920 he served a year in prison and was never permitted to fight for the championship again.[9]

While the federal government persecuted and prosecuted Johnson, the United States portrayed itself more liberally and democratically in the pluralistic representation of the 1912 Olympic team, which featured the black sprinter Howard Drew, the Hawaiian swimmer Duke Kahanamoku, and Native American Jim Thorpe. Drew became known as "the world's fastest human." Kahanamoku garnered six medals as an Olympian from 1912 to 1932, and Thorpe was dubbed the greatest athlete in the world after winning both the pentathlon and the decathlon, but neither blacks, Hawaiians, nor Native Americans were accorded the full rights of citizenship.[10]

After the turn of the century more southern blacks, like Jack Johnson, who was born in Galveston, Texas, migrated northward for opportunities unavailable in the South and in search of a better life. Between 1915 and 1970 an estimated six million southern blacks sought refuge outside that region. Many traveled to northern cities, where they vied with millions of mostly European immigrants for more plentiful and better-paying jobs. The multitudes of European groups often segregated themselves in urban neighborhoods with countrymen whose language and culture they understood, a choice that allowed for a more gradual assimilation into American culture. Southern black migrants had less choice in their accommodations, as white realtors and property owners conspired to prevent black home ownership in their areas, resulting in the ghettoization of blacks within major cities. Within such neglected communities blacks were forced to largely develop their own resources and institutions. Employers and religious groups, such as the YMCA, even built separate sport and recreational facilities to maintain such exclusion lest blacks and poor whites fraternize in their leisure pursuits and possibly unite in labor unions to oppose their bosses.[11]

Sol Butler, the son of a former slave, emerged as a track star during the World War I years, but the carnage derailed the Olympic Games in 1916. Butler set a new American record in the long jump as a soldier at the Inter-Allied Games, a military Olympics held in Paris in the wake of the war. In the 1920 Games he was injured and unable to capitalize on his athletic fame. Thereafter he managed to make a living as a football and basketball star, a sportswriter, and in movie roles. He parlayed his athletic abilities into coaching positions in Chicago within the black community, helping black youth to develop their athletic talents as his life became more closely intertwined with the popular culture. As is true for many black men today, violence permeated urban neighborhoods and dreams went unfulfilled, and Butler eventually lost his life in a bar shootout.[12]

Violence against blacks continued after the war in the form of race riots and lynchings as returning white and black veterans and hosts of ethnic immigrants competed for jobs. Chicago suffered a major race riot in 1919, ignited when black youth wandered across the dividing line that segregated their separate sections of a public beach. The resultant bloodshed lasted for a week, cost thirty-eight lives and more than five hundred injuries, left more than one thousand homeless, and required the intervention of the National Guard to quell the violence. Rube Foster, another Texas transplant, had moved to Chicago as a pro baseball player—and even partnered with a white co-owner of a team—before acquiring his own baseball club. Foster's early success as an entrepreneur signaled the possibilities of life in the more liberal northern cities, but the continued influx of southern blacks threatened the job security of working-class whites. In the wake of the race riot Foster decided to initiate the Negro National League, as black players were still barred from the white Major League teams. The venture proved so successful that a second pro circuit, the Eastern Colored League, appeared in 1923. Foster provided talented black athletes with a stage to display their skills in a "public ritual of performance" that allowed them to establish their newfound sense of masculinity.[13] Other black entrepreneurs found in baseball another means to engage in the popular culture. Some of them merged their baseball enterprises with the numbers racket, a form of the poor man's lottery in black neighborhoods, where residents constructed an alternative economy to meet their needs.

When Bessie Coleman could not meet her psychological, emotional, and occupational needs, she left the country voluntarily because American flight instructors refused to teach her to fly a plane. She found such tutelage in France and returned as the first black female pilot, extending the perceived limits of feminine possibilities. Coleman pushed both racial and gender boundaries, attempting daring feats in barnstorming air shows and exhibitions until such deeds took her life in 1926. Coleman's escape to Paris in response to the impediments she faced in the United States was not atypical. The French capital had served as a refuge for African Americans since the late nineteenth century.

Henry O. Tanner, a black art student, left the United States in 1891 to study in Rome but became so enchanted with the City of Lights that he stayed in Paris. "At no time was he made to feel unwanted or inferior because of his color, which had not always been so in Philadelphia," where he had studied at the Pennsylvania Academy of the Fine Arts.[14] Peter Jackson, the heavyweight boxer, soon followed Tanner to Paris, and a bevy of black fighters popularized boxing in France after the turn of the century. An American writer claimed, "They earn more in a week there than they used to in many months over here."[15] Jack Johnson, as a fugitive from American prosecutors, also resided in Paris, where he mixed boxing with theatrical performances and became a local celebrity until World War I interrupted his interlude. The French had seemingly obtained a fascination with the black body that paved the way for a multitude of African American jazz age entertainers during the 1920s.[16]

The 1920s are considered the first Golden Age of sport in the United States, as the new technology of the radio, motion pictures, and extensive media coverage of athletic stars brought celebrity, fame, and heroization to champions. The era also produced a black renaissance in sports, literature, art, and music, centered in New York's Harlem and Chicago's Bronzeville neighborhoods, where athletes often carried the banner of racial dignity. Such developments promoted black pride and drew attention to African American culture, accomplishments, and abilities, but these did not gain full acceptance in the dominant white mainstream culture. In New York Marcus Garvey preached black nationalism and black enterprise and team owners subscribed to the latter. As it had with Jack Johnson, the federal government perceived Garvey as a threat. He was incarcerated in 1925 and deported to his native Jamaica two years later.

After Johnson's loss of the championship white successors instituted a color ban on black heavyweights. Harry Wills remained a top contender during Jack Dempsey's reign as champion but never got a shot at the crown despite compiling a record of 68-9-3 with fifty-four knockouts and living an abstemious lifestyle. Wills had also defeated Willie Meehan, a boxer who had only lost once to Dempsey in four fights.[17] At the lower weights Tiger Flowers became the first black to capture the middleweight title in 1926. Flowers lived in a large house in Atlanta, ostentatiously but spotlessly as a church deacon and a philanthropist. He proved acceptable to whites as one "who knew his place" and did not assert the recalcitrant attitude of northern blacks. Flowers's career, however, proved short-lived as he died the following year as a result of surgery around his eyes to remove scar tissue caused by boxing.[18] The same could not be said of Francisco Guilledo, a Filipino who assumed the ring name of Pancho Villa, the revolutionary Mexican bandit who had terrorized the American Southwest during World War I. Villa had learned to box from the American soldiers who still occupied his island country since the Spanish-American War of 1898. After defeating the best of the Americans in Manila, he traveled to the United States, where he won the world flyweight championship and antagonized whites as a smaller version of Jack Johnson. He dressed lavishly, spent his money extravagantly, and cavorted with a bevy of white women, followed by his large entourage. Like other people of color, he was racialized by sportswriters, who rationalized his speed and consequent wins over white opponents as the works of an inhuman demon. He, too, died after a short reign of two years due to blood poisoning after surgery for infected teeth in 1925. His wife claimed his death amounted to a murder, and Filipinos considered it a national tragedy. When his body was returned to the Philippines for burial, one hundred thousand mourners attended his funeral.[19]

Both Jack Johnson and Pancho Villa had become enamored of the vibrant nightlife then permeating urban centers as musicians from the South brought ragtime music and then jazz and the blues to northern climes in their migrations. Chicago became a center for the music and recording industry, and Jack Johnson opened an early black and tan cabaret there where upper-class whites drawn to the new genre went "slumming" with black entertainers and dancers to experience a sensuality absent in their own lives. The musical attractions provided other venues for entrepreneurs as black youth and Filipinos flocked to nightclubs and dance halls in search of excitement deemed immoral by white puritans.[20]

Black athletes also had close ties with the music industry as musicians, singers, talent scouts, and booking agents. Paul Robeson, Fritz Pollard, and Jay Mayo "Ink" Williams gained their initial fame on the football field because civic rivalries that spawned incessant gambling required the best athletes and profit and pride superseded race. Within that competitive environment Pollard became the first black quarterback and the first black head coach in the nascent NFL due to his athletic skills, and he recruited other blacks for his ventures. Robeson joined Pollard on the gridiron but would gain greater stature as a singer, actor, and civil rights activist before being chased out of the United States due to his political convictions. Pollard too turned to the music industry and other ventures, as all blacks were weeded out of the NFL after the 1933 season through the efforts of George Marshall, owner of the Washington franchise. But Pollard's son would contribute to the Americans' rejection of Aryan supremacy at the Nazi Olympics of 1936 when he became a bronze medalist in the 110-meter hurdles race.[21]

Basketball provided more opportunities for athletes to make a living during the 1920s as a burgeoning professional circuit and interracial challenge matches offered income during the winter months. Not only black southerners but also more than 140,000 Caribbean migrants traveled to the United States between 1899 and 1937. Bob Douglas, born in St. Kitts (one of the British Virgin Islands), traveled to New York, where he organized a fully professional unit in 1923 known as the Renaissance Five, a reference to the Renaissance Ballroom, from which they emanated. Sport merged with other elements of the popular culture as intermissions at the popular dance halls featured basketball games, and the Renaissance moniker served to market the dance hall as well as the basketball team. The Rens not only prospered, but they also beat the white professional teams and won the first national pro tournament in 1939. Like the boxing victories of Joe Louis, such successes instilled and maintained black pride and a sense of self-worth.[22]

A similar undertaking occurred in Chicago, where the Savoy Five played at the Savoy Ballroom but soon began barnstorming as the Harlem Globetrotters. They assumed the reference to the New York neighborhood as a tribute to its national influence in black life. Both black teams employed a distinctive style of play, executing sharp, crisp passes; dexterous dribbling; and a fast pace in an entertaining style that sometimes baffled white opponents and spectators. Two of the early Globetrotters' players, Tommy Brookins and Harold "Killer" Johnson, became more deeply involved in the music industry and other more nefarious ventures within the popular culture. Johnson earned his nickname for his deadly shooting skills with a basketball before turning to entertainment management and club ownership. Brookins claimed that he had been swindled out of ownership of the team by booking agent Abe Saperstein, a claim that caused his departure to Europe, where he began his music career. He later owned a Chicago nightclub and retired to St. Maarten in the Caribbean. The Globetrotters would win the second professional basketball tournament in 1940 before achieving international fame as comedic entertainers.[23]

Black female basketball teams also proliferated during the interwar years, sponsored by churches and businesses. Isadore Channels starred for the Olivet Baptist Church team and then joined the famed Roamers, who played interracial matches with white women. Members of such teams crossed both social and economic classes, exhibiting the more cooperative nature of society within the black communities. Another barnstorming team, the Philadelphia Tribunes, featured Ora Washington. Both she and Channels were multisport stars. When blacks were banned from the national white tennis association, they formed their own, the American Tennis Association, in 1916. Channels dominated the national championship during the 1920s, winning four individual titles and one doubles crown. Washington followed suit as the dominant player in the 1930s. Blacks could not play in the USLTA tournament until 1948, and stars such as Althea Gibson and Arthur Ashe then rose to prominence, but pioneers such as Channels and Washington sparked the early interest in tennis in black communities. Such women operated within a complex amalgamation of religious, gender, and class relations that pushed the boundaries of femininity long before Venus and Serena Williams transformed the sport of tennis.

Black male athletes such as Eddie Tolan and Ralph Metcalfe became more conspicuous as members of the U.S. Olympic teams in the 1930s, and the heroics of Jesse Owens in the 1936 Games in Berlin undermined Hitler's assertions of Aryan supremacy. Tidye Pickett, the first African American female to make an American Olympic team, did not enjoy such celebrity but rather endured racist harassment and ostracism in 1932. She persevered to return in 1936, only to suffer another tragic setback before becoming a successful educator in relative obscurity. Pickett's educational attainments defied the stereotype of blacks' mental ineptitude.

While black participation in contact sports such as boxing increased during the 1930s, such activities were associated with the lower classes. French sociologist Pierre Bourdieu claimed that one's upbringing within a particular social class determined one's worldview and lifestyle, but the segregated black communities of urban America harbored residents of all classes, from the homeless to millionaires, exposing inhabitants to a greater variety of cultural possibilities. Blacks aspired to greater socioeconomic mobility but found resistance when they tried to contest with whites in the more genteel sports of tennis and golf. As was the case with tennis, blacks had to form their own professional golf circuit, the United Golfers Association (UGA), because the PGA refused to recognize them until 1961.[24]

Teddy Rhodes, like John Shippen, taught himself to play golf as a caddie, and he dominated the UGA, winning more than 150 tournaments, although the prize money paled in comparison to the white PGA circuit. Rhodes became the personal golf tutor of boxing champion Joe Louis, who also sponsored Rhodes on the black golf circuit. Rhodes and two other golfers sued the PGA for its segregation practices, and he managed to play in the 1948 U.S. Open, still fighting the same battles John Shippen had fought a half century earlier. Illness forced Rhodes's retirement, but he continued to instruct the young black golfers who finally won entry into the PGA in the 1960s, a civil rights progression that eventually produced Tiger Woods. The case of Teddy Rhodes clearly indicated that Jackie Robinson's entry into Major League Baseball, though monumental in its significance, had not produced wholesale racial acceptance in American society. A more extensive civil rights movement and an athletic revolution led by Muhammad Ali and other courageous black athletes remained to accomplish that task.

This book concentrates on popular culture, and more specifically sport, as one aspect of American history during the later years of the nineteenth century and the first half of the twentieth century, with the aim to recover the stories of individuals who helped to change the course of the nation. It consciously avoids the stories of more well-known athletes whose lives are chronicled in full-length biographies. It does so within the framework of popular culture in the form of music and sport, which allowed African Americans a measure of opportunity. Even as slaves they were permitted—even expected—to entertain whites. Popular culture allowed them to do so but also provided avenues for greater independence, personal expression, and slow societal change. While many people are aware of the accomplishments and influence of athletes such as Jack Johnson, Joe Louis, Jesse Owens, Jackie Robinson, and Muhammad Ali, such luminaries of the black sporting experience did not emerge spontaneously. Their rise was part of a gradual evolution in social and power relations in American culture over the course of a half century (ca. 1890–1940s). The freedom of speech and religion that eventually exonerated and allowed for the heroization of Muhammad Ali was built upon the stoicism of Jackie Robinson, who endured the pressures of racism to prove that whites and blacks could cooperate seven years before the United States Supreme Court struck down the separate-but-equal doctrine that endorsed segregation in the *Brown v. Board of Education* case in 1954. Robinson's sacrifices were made possible by the gradual but temporary acceptance of black athletes as national heroes. Both Jesse Owens and Joe Louis personified American ideals and democratic values when the nation needed their physical prowess to destroy the Nazi myth of Aryan supremacy in the 1930s, but once both men had accomplished their task, they were relegated to their former status of second-class citizens. Both suffered bankruptcy, and Louis died a pauper.

This book addresses the stories and hardships endured by those pioneers who paved the way for Jackie Robinson and Muhammad Ali to bring about social change. They too contributed much to the larger story of our collective history by their heroic confrontations with the entrenched racism of their times to bring about the incremental changes that allowed for Jackie Robinson to make his historic breakthrough. They did so by courageously crossing racial, social, political, economic, and cultural boundaries in an expression of human agency in the confrontation of a repressive white domination. Their arduous efforts resulted in a richer, better, and more inclusive American culture. The book follows a chronological order to provide for historical contextualization and to analyze the gradual progress, and at times remission, of the cultural flow. Historian Renee Romano has asserted that "Once a past no longer proves useful, it recedes into the pages of books and archives rather than circulating in the broader culture."[25] This work attempts to rescue the meaningful lives of a handful of athletic pioneers from the dustbin of history and reclaim their significance. It addresses, to some degree, the incomplete story of the nation and the historical amnesia that afflicts many of its inhabitants.

## Notes

1. Volker Depcat, "The Challenges of Biography: European-American Reflections," *Bulletin of the German Historical Institute* 55 (Fall 2014): 39–48 (quote, 46–47).

2. Gerald R. Gems, Linda J. Borish, and Gertrud Pfister, *Sports in American History: From Colonization to Globalization* (Champaign IL: Human Kinetics, 2008), 144, 207, 211; Gerald R. Gems, *For Pride, Profit, and Patriarchy: Football and the Incorporation of American Cultural Values* (Lanham MD: Scarecrow Press, 2000), 114.

3. See Ida B. Wells, "The Reasons Why the Colored American Is Not in the Columbian World Exposition," in *Black Writing from Chicago: In the World, Not of It?*, ed. Richard R. Guzman (Carbondale: Southern Illinois University Press, 2006), 20–28.

4. http://johnshippen.net/john-shippen-biography.html (accessed July 27, 2013).

5. Andrew Ritchie, *Major Taylor: The Fastest Bicycle Rider in the World* (San Francisco: Van der Plas/Cycle Publishing, 2010).

6. Colleen Aycock and Mark Scott, eds., *The First Black Boxing Champions: Essays on Fighters of the 1800s to the 1920s* (Jefferson NC: McFarland, 2011), 32–59; *New Orleans Times-Democrat*, September 8, 1892, 4.

7. Colleen Aycock and Mark Scott, *Joe Gans: A Biography of the First African American World Boxing Champion* (Jefferson NC: McFarland, 2008).

8. Du Bois cited in Martin Summers, *Manliness and Its Discontents: The Black Middle Class and the Transformation of Masculinity, 1900–1930* (Chapel Hill: University of North Carolina Press, 2004), 4.

9. Randy Roberts, *Papa Jack: Jack Johnson and the Era of White Hopes* (New York: Free Press, 1983); Theresa Runstedtler, *Jack Johnson: Rebel Sojourner, Boxing in the Shadow of the Global Color Line* (Berkeley: University of California Press, 2012).

10. Debra A. Henderson, "Howard Drew," in *African Americans in Sports*, ed. David K. Wiggins (Armonk NY: M. E. Sharpe, 2004), 88.

11. Isabel Wilkerson, *The Warmth of Other Suns: The Epic Story of America's Great Migration* (New York: Random House, 2010), 9.

12. James E. Odenkirk, "Sol Butler," in Wiggins, *African Americans in Sports*, 55.

13. Summers, *Manliness and Its Discontents*, 4.

14. David McCullough, *The Greater Journey: Americans in Paris* (New York: Simon and Schuster, 2011), 428.

15. Rudolph Fisher, "The Caucasian Storms Harlem," in *Voices from the Harlem Renaissance*, ed. Nathan Irvin Huggins (New York: Oxford University Press, 1995), 74–82 (quote, 80). See also Gwendolyn Bennett, "Wedding Day," 191–97, in the same collection, for the story of Paul Watson, an African American boxer-musician who also resided in Paris.

16. Runstedtler, *Jack Johnson*, 150, 164–95.

17. http://boxrec.com/search.php?status=all&cat=boxer&first_name=Harry&last_name=Wills&submit=Go&pageID=3 (accessed November 24, 2013); Dennis Gildea, "Harry Wills," in Wiggins, *African Americans in Sports*, 408–9. Wills's record does not include another 19-1-3 record with five more knockouts during the World War I era, when sportswriters rendered the decisions as boxing was officially banned in most states.

18. Andrew M. Kaye, *The Pussycat of Prizefighting: Tiger Flowers and the Politics of Black Celebrity* (Athens: University of Georgia Press, 2004).

19. Gerald R. Gems, *The Athletic Crusade: Sport and American Cultural Imperialism* (Lincoln: University of Nebraska Press, 2006), 61–62.

20. Summers, *Manliness and Its Discontents*, 173–75; Kevern Verney, *African Americans and U.S. Popular Culture* (London: Routledge, 2003), 26–30; Chad Heap, *Slumming: Sexual and Racial Encounters in American Nightlife, 1885–1940* (Chicago: University of Chicago Press, 2009); Paul G. Cressey, *Taxi-Dance Hall: A Sociological Study in Commercialized Recreation and City Life* (Chicago: University of Chicago Press, 1932).

21. John M. Carroll, *Fritz Pollard: Pioneer in Racial Advancement* (Urbana: University of Illinois Press, 1992); Martin Bauml Duberman, *Paul Robeson: A Biography* (New York: Ballantine Books, 1989).

22. Summers, *Manliness and Its Discontents*, 4.

23. http://www.pbs.org/wnet/finding-your-roots/stories/famous-relatives/mu-ancestor-tommy-brookins (accessed July 27, 2013).

24. Pierre Bourdieu, *Outline of a Theory of Practice* (Cambridge: Cambridge University Press, 1972).

25. Renee Romano, "Beyond 'Self-Congratulatory Celebration': Complicating Civil Rights Anniversaries," *American Historian* (November 2014): 29–32 (quote, 30).

# ONE

## Like a Comet across the Heavens

*Isaac Burns Murphy, Horseracing, and the*
*Age of American Exceptionalism*

PELLOM MCDANIELS III

In 1879, when Isaac Burns Murphy was just eighteen years old and quickly becoming known as a dependable jockey and a master of the art of pace—the ability to know how fast a horse was running on the track at all times—he traveled from Frankfort, Kentucky, to Saratoga, New York, to compete on one of horseracing's most lucrative racetracks. Already a veteran of the turf, the polished jockey began his career at the age of thirteen as an apprentice jockey for Owings and Williams Stables in his hometown of Lexington, Kentucky. Murphy's success on the racetrack had elevated his importance to racing fans, gamblers, and the owners of some of the country's most important thoroughbreds. Indeed men of the turf from California to New York, seeking to win lucrative big-stakes races, found in the East and West, vied for the opportunity to have the little jockey pilot one of their horses of distinguished pedigree.

When he arrived in Saratoga in the summer of 1879, Murphy was greeted by the dashing J. W. Hunt-Reynolds, the owner of Fleetwood Farms. A grandson of John Wesley Hunt, the first millionaire west of the Alleghany Mountains, Hunt-Reynolds was one of the founders of the Louisville Jockey Club and maintained as one of his firm objectives the improvement of the breed of horse developed in Kentucky. His farm outside of Frankfort, Kentucky, was proving to be one of the most important studs in the country. Hunt-Reynolds's head trainer, Eli Jordan, was more than a familiar face to Murphy; he was a family friend with whom he shared his victories and disappointments. When Murphy's mother, America, settled in Lexington at the end of the Civil War and needed support, Jordan and his wife Cora took her and the family in. The death of Murphy's father, Jerry Burns, a veteran of the Civil War, left a void in the boy's life that Jordan and other community members helped to fill. The races at Saratoga provided another opportunity for them to bond.

On Saturday, July 19, 1879, the racetrack at Saratoga Springs was in good condition, and the weather was perfect for racing.[1] The sixteenth renewal of the Travers Stakes for three-year-olds, a race of a mile and three-quarters, featured Murphy on Hunt-Reynolds's Falsetto. The call to post elicited an "applause which greeted Spendthrift [which] made the great colt prick his ears"; all the while Murphy trotted his charge out onto the track in a manner that exuded confidence and reassurance to the Kentuckians watching in the stands.[2] In a July 26, 1879, *Spirit of the Times* interview Murphy recalled the race and the details of the decisions he made in the saddle. In the interview the eighteen-year-old's thoughtfulness, intellect, and confidence come shining through. No doubt, it was admirable for his day.

"How did you get between Harold [horse] and the pole on the turn?"

"I didn't intend to go upon the turn, but when we started toward the stretch Harold was tired and unsteady, and he leaned away from the pole and gave me room to go in. I thought it better to run for the position than to have to run around him, so I jumped at the chance and went up between him and the rail. I steadied my horse here a moment to compel Harold to cover more ground on the turn, and beat him good, for he was very tired, and just before we got to the stretch I left him and went off after Spendthrift."

"Where did you catch him?"

"Just after we got straight into the stretch."

"Did you have to punish Falsetto?"

"As I tell, when I went up to Harold at the half mile, I hit him one with the spur. Then when I ran between Harold and the pole I gave it to him again. When I got to Harold, I laid there a little while, and kept touching my colt with the right spur, to keep him from bearing out to Harold, and also to make him hug the pole. He is a long strider, and is inclined to lean out on the turns. I kept the spurs pretty busy in him until I got to Spendthrift. Here Feakes drew his whip, and Spendthrift refused to respond to it. So I stopped and let Falsetto come along, but I kept urging him with the reigns. He moved so strong that I did not have to punish him any more."[3]

In spite of his youth, through the interview Murphy's knowledge and skill related to running races, and his intelligence and politeness come across as unimpeachable. The once timid and precocious boy had matured into a full-fledged man capable of defining his purpose in the world and laying claim to his accomplishments as the result of his hard work and discipline. Murphy's success would continue throughout the 1880s and into the 1890s. He became one of the great black jockeys whose ability and intelligence was unique among jockeys, placing him in a class all his own. While his success in the saddle appeared to most as a natural phenomenon, it was Murphy's upbringing in Lexington, Kentucky, during Reconstruction, and the quality of his manhood, which was influenced by his mother and the progressive black community, that helped give shape to his character, work ethic, and purpose in life.

In the saddle, Murphy's professional approach to racing was cultivated from training his mind as well as his body to take advantage of every aspect of each horse he rode, every course on which he raced, and the competition he faced. Unfortunately his well-documented achievements led many to plot against him, including resentful whites, some newly arrived immigrants who could not appreciate his success, and some white horse owners and jockeys who refused to accept the reality that African Americans could rise above their previous condition as slaves to become exceptional individuals. Furthermore, changing economic, social, and political factors, brought on by the overpopulation of some urban environments and a scarcity of jobs, not only accelerated the indignant attacks by whites on the gains made by African Americans during the years of Reconstruction and beyond but also served to justify the savage violence unleashed against African Americans throughout the 1890s. Supported by Jim Crow policies of exclusion and fearing black economic, social, and political power, white Americans were emboldened to terrorize their black neighbors with impunity. Within this convergence of contexts Isaac Burns Murphy became the top jockey of his day. He was an exemplar for American manhood, masculinity, and citizenship for all, as well as a threat to the stability of white masculinity.

### Becoming Exceptional

Murphy's development as a jockey and individual of exceptional ability began with his birth during slavery. Born Isaac Burns in 1861, at the beginning of the American Civil War in Clark County, Kentucky, and raised by his mother in Lexington during the early years of Reconstruction, his childhood was filled with numerous opportunities to learn lessons from the men and women of his community. As noted, after the death of his father, Isaac's mother migrated with him to a firmly entrenched African American community in Lexington, comprised of former slaves and freeborn people of African descent who represented a range of occupations, including carpenters, barbers, mattress makers, educators, ministers, and laborers. Each supported the development of the community's children through moral training, rudimentary education, and the pursuit of excellence based on a future orientation, whereby the basis of their freedom was secured by the Thirteenth, Fourteenth, and Fifteenth Amendments to the U.S. Constitution and their ability to become orderly and productive would make them citizens.

As early as 1865, long before the Freedmen's Bureau, the American Missionary Association, and other benevolent societies began assisting former slaves in securing their freedom through education, schools across the state of Kentucky were established in and by African American communities with the necessary resolve to teach adults and children to read and write. In Lexington, schools were opened in the most important centers of African American social, political, and economic activity: the black churches.[4] In most instances where children were allowed to learn, they "manifested the same dogged commitment to their education" as adults did to their commitment to being recognized as human beings on par with white men.[5] Black children like Isaac provided the most readily available reason for African American leadership to continue to fight to secure the franchise, no matter how dangerous the consequences or the means by which whites would attempt to deter the progress of the race.

Under the tutelage of his mother and capable teachers, by 1870 nine-year-old Isaac Burns was able to read and write.[6] America must have been extremely happy with his progress and his taking full advantage of the opportunity to exercise his freedom in terms that at first glance seemed to guarantee his life would be filled with marvelous rewards for hard work. An exemplar of the qualities needed to succeed in a post-slavery society, America Burns purchased a new home on Pine Street, began acquiring property throughout the city of Lexington, and in April 1873 opened a savings account with the local branch of the Freedmen's Bank. In an effort to secure her and her son's future, she routinely deposited monies she earned from her work as a washerwoman and laundress and the pension she received from the federal government for Jerry Burns's service as a soldier. In turn Isaac was free to spend his youth developing his mind, free from the pressures of toiling and scraping by to live. All was well in the world for America and Isaac until the Freedmen's Bank collapsed. Within two months of opening her account, she had lost almost everything she owned.

America soon became sick with tuberculosis and no doubt began to fear for her son's future. Should she die, what would happen to her boy? In an attempt to secure his future, America asked her employer, Richard Owings, a partner in the Owings and Williams Stable, if he would consider taking her son as an apprentice jockey. In fact it may have been Eli Jordan who suggested Isaac become an apprentice jockey when he was employed as a trainer for the stable. Owings and Williams gave Isaac a chance to secure his future in one of the occupations African American men and boys in the Bluegrass region had long been accustomed to filling. Before the United States became an independent nation and developed its particular style of democracy, both free and enslaved African Americans participated in the development of the agricultural and industrial prosperity of the colonies.

As with the development of livestock on the hundreds of farms in the South and into the western reaches of the new nation beyond the eastern seaboard, horseracing depended upon the labor, skill, and expertise of African American men and boys, whose hands-on experience made them invaluable to the future of the horse industry.

In the spring of 1874 thirteen-year-old Isaac embarked on a path that few could have imagined would prove fortunate to horseracing. That the little boy from Lexington had the potential to become the greatest representative of the sport that the state of Kentucky—maybe even the country—would produce was not foreseeable. But Isaac first had to prove his ability in the stable and then graduate to exercise boy before becoming a rider.[7] Years after Isaac developed into an extraordinary jockey, Eli Jordan recalled how the quiet boy was "always in his place" and how Eli could always put his "hands on him any time, day or night." Jordan would say that Isaac "was one of the first up in the morning, ready to do anything he was told to do or help others. He was ever in good humor and liked to play, but he never neglected his work, but worked hard summer and winter."[8]

Being a part of the daily routine supporting the development of the horses and their abilities, Isaac watched and learned from the grooms as they brushed and combed the horses to put them at ease, recognizing the proper techniques of those skilled at the craft.[9] As exciting as it seemed, the life of a nineteenth-century jockey was filled with danger, but the rewards, both real and imagined, compelled a few brave souls to choose the saddle and reins, the post and paddock, as a way of life. Learning through trial and error to be fearless, Isaac received the best instruction available from Jordan and James Williams, one of the co-owners of the stable. By the spring of 1875 Isaac began competing on the statewide circuit of horse tracks from Lexington to Bowling Green, Kentucky, just north of the Tennessee border.[10]

Early that May, Isaac secured his first official win in his first official race at the Crab Orchard track aboard the filly Glentina.[11] The oldest circular track in the state, Crab Orchard was a great testing ground for potential stakes-winning horses and reliable talented jockeys.[12] At seventy-four pounds, the impish yet resilient boy rode the filly to victory again on his home track in front of his community of supporters, only this time he was riding under the name of Murphy instead of Burns. It seems that America wanted her son to take his grandfather's, Green Murphy's, last name to honor him.[13] However, he was still untested in races for big stakes. For the inaugural Louisville Jockey Club meeting, he was well on his way to learning all that horseracing had to offer a serious, honest, and hardworking jockey able to focus on one objective: winning. He had also learned from his mother about honesty, disciplined work, and perseverance, all of which would carry him further than any horse could.

Although he would not have a mount in the first Kentucky Derby, Isaac was there to observe the horses and jockeys take the track in preparation for the start of the race. And because African American jockeys were common throughout the South as a result of their role on horse farms during slavery, it would not have been odd for him to notice that thirteen of the fifteen jockeys on the track that day were black. The fourteen-year-old Isaac was no doubt smitten by what he saw and felt. Over the next fifteen years he would compete in eleven Kentucky Derbies, winning three (1884, 1890, 1891) and finishing in the money in three others.

### A World of Changing Possibilities

By 1877 the hard-fought gains as a result of the Civil War and Reconstruction legislation were left unprotected by the federal government after the election of Rutherford B. Hayes as the nation's nineteenth president. In an effort to reconcile with the South, Hayes removed federal troops from the region, providing no protection for the freedmen from their former masters and white men intent on restoring the balance of power in their favor. The reign of terror began first in the rural areas, where African American farmers were forcibly removed from their lands at gunpoint, losing not only their property but also their livestock, surplus, and investment in their families' futures. Others were killed and their property destroyed by fire in an effort to purge the land of the impudence of former slaves—a blood sacrifice to be sure.

Isaac and other black jockeys were still somewhat safe in horseracing. Southern whites still saw jockeys or work in the stalls with animals as "nigger work," and they gladly let the African American men and boys occupy most such positions. Still Isaac would have a major role in the development of jockeyship as a middle-class occupation as it became highly lucrative and therefore highly sought after by whites, who viewed the high salaries of black jockeys as obscene and an affront to "their own" boys who could ride horses too, and Irish immigrant boys fighting hard to claim all the rights and privileges of whiteness in America.

In early May 1877, at the beginning of his third racing season, Isaac journeyed to Nashville with James Williams, now sole proprietor of the Lexington stable, in preparation for the annual Nashville Association meeting.[14] Still working as an apprentice, the youthful jockey rode for several other owners besides Williams. His lone victory came on day three on Williams's Vera Cruz in the Cumberland Stakes for three-year-olds.[15] Each time he took to the track, he learned a little more about his new occupation as a desperate profession that rewarded jockeys for winning and showing well. A few weeks later at the third running of the Kentucky Derby, in a stellar field of eleven capable three-year-olds, Isaac's only advantage was his understanding of his horse and how to ride him. Vera Cruz had been his steed on numerous occasions, and he no doubt thought he knew the horse's temperament. Unfortunately a poor start hurt his chances at success in the premiere race of the day. Isaac finished fourth and out of the money.[16]

By 1877 horseracing in the East had been around longer than the country. Tracks at Saratoga Springs, Jerome Park in Westchester County, New York, and Monmouth Park at Long Branch, New Jersey, were developed as an outgrowth of the need for class affiliation and social status.[17] At Saratoga on August 1, riding atop Williams's Vera Cruz in a dash race of a mile and three-quarters for a $600 purse, Isaac had an excellent start in a race that was slow and steady. It was not until the very end of the race that Isaac let Vera Cruz go to the lead and with the very last jump defeated Big Tom" by a head at the finish line.[18] The sixteen-year-old master in the saddle had captured the attention of everyone at the Saratoga Springs course. He was now making a name for himself by beating the best in the East.

Most important, Isaac began riding for J. W. Hunt-Reynolds's Fleetwood Stud Farm. Reynolds would become one of the most important influences in Murphy's career between 1877 and 1880.

In the 1880s and in the South especially, the lives of black people were of little value. Black men and women died almost daily from the abuses heaped on them by vengeful whites still fuming at the changes after the Civil War and the fact that their former slaves were "not only free, but their political equals."[19] Nationally the African American community's leaders responded to the brutal denials of black rights that were believed to have been secured by the Civil War, amendments to the Constitution, and sacrifices made by the men and women who served the cause of freedom. By organizing public protests, petitioning local and national white politicians for support, and voting into office candidates many thought influential enough to argue their case, these capable men and women aspired to achieve the ideals set by the Declaration of Independence regarding life, liberty, and the pursuit of happiness. However, whites continued to deny African Americans access to hotels and train cars and rejected their basic citizenship and human rights. To add insult to injury, on October 15, 1883, the U.S. Supreme Court ruled that the Civil Rights Act of 1875 was unconstitutional, opening the floodgates to the further abuse of African Americans and initiating the demented southern pastime of lynching.

In his personal life, Isaac Murphy experienced two great losses. In the fall of 1879, at the age of forty-eight, America Murphy Burns died of complications related to cancer of the rectum. America had been responsible for nurturing and instilling in her son the virtues she deemed important for his future. Isaac no doubt knew that he owed a great deal to his mother's resilience and sense of purpose for his life, and he honored her memory by maintaining his dignity and focus in all that he pursued. A year later, in September 1880, J. W. Hunt-Reynolds died from a ruptured blood vessel in his brain.[20] A major contributor to Kentucky horseracing and the development of American thoroughbred horses, he was only thirty-four years old. Isaac, who had benefitted from Hunt-Reynolds's generosity of vision, as well as his indefatigable example of gentlemanly decorum and professionalism, had to process his death in terms of viable choices for his future. At the age of nineteen and in the wake of such tremendous losses, he persevered and found strength in Eli Jordan, his friends, and his community. Between 1881 and 1883 Isaac continued to ride for Fleetwood Farms, now under the ownership of Meta Hunt-Reynolds, the widow of J. W. Hunt-Reynolds. He was also able to expand the number of thoroughbred owners with whom he contracted.

There can be no doubt that Isaac's success inspired an enthusiasm for the future for those black people who saw the polished jockey as an indicator of the possibilities of their achieving great things, even as the nation became consumed by "Negro hatred." By the end of the 1881 campaign, Isaac had won twenty-two of fifty-two races, a feat that made him popular in racing circles that included high-stakes gamblers and owners. In 1882 he won thirty-three out of eighty-eight races, placing second on twenty occasions and third in ten. Overall Isaac won an incredible $33,490 for his employers, a sum that is equal to more than three-quarters of a million dollars in today's economy. The fact that Isaac had arrived as a professional was reflected not only in the number of mounts he received but also in the quality of horses he was provided to ride, and both factors increased his visibility. For 1882 Isaac earned between $2,000 and $4,000, which in 2014 dollars would have been between $46,511 and $93,023. Most important, Isaac was his own man and was able to set his fees and have the owners pay him his worth.

### The Prince of Jockeys

As a hero of the turf, Isaac was acknowledged nationally in newspapers and magazines and by various American tobacco manufacturers whose product lines included cards with the likenesses of the most popular athletes. On the occasion of Isaac's twenty-second birthday, C. J. Foster, the editor of the *New York Sportsman*, nominated him for one of the two awards the publication offered: to the jockey who achieved the most wins during the season and to the jockey who won the most money for his employer. Of Isaac's abilities, Foster wrote, "Murphy is one of the best jockeys in America, being especially strong in knowledge of pace, coolness, and good general-ship. He will soon be too heavy to ride, we fear, in which case Uncle Eli ought to and doubtless will take him in and teach him all he knows about training." To help corroborate his observations, Foster also included a quote from a letter written to the *New York Sports-man* by Meta Hunt-Reynolds. She wrote, "Of course I need not tell you of Isaac's honest and trustworthy nature, for the whole of the American turf must be cognizant of that fact; but no one knows it better than I do."[21]

Clearly both Foster and Mrs. Hunt-Reynolds recognized the special individual that Isaac was. In Foster's analysis two elements are unmistakable. First, Isaac's ability as a jockey was head and shoulders above the competition; his intelligence in the saddle and coolness under pressure were a sight to behold. Second, the successful jockey was on the verge of losing his grip on his future in the saddle as the natural process of physical maturation would influence his options.

Still amid the chaos and excitement of his burgeoning career, Isaac found time to meet his future wife. On January 24, 1883, he married Lucy Carr in a ceremony held at St. John's African Methodist Church in North Frankfort. Exactly when and where Isaac met Lucy is not clear. Chances are the couple met in Frankfort at some social gathering and were immediately attracted to one another. Three months after their wedding and a few months prior to the beginning of the 1883 season, Isaac placed an ad in the March 17 edition of the *Kentucky Live Stock Record* under the title "First Class Jockey." In a bold move, he presented himself as a professional rider who could be contracted to ride at a select number of venues for the spring and fall. "I will make engagements to ride in the stakes for the coming racing season at Lexington, Louisville, Latonia, Chicago and Saratoga. I will be available to ride at 110 (possibly 107) pounds. My address until the beginning of the Lexington races will be care of Fleetwood Stables, Frankfort, Ky. 424 8th. Isaac B. Murphy."[22] The ad is unique in that Isaac published details as to when and where he would be available to ride while leaving the terms of compensation as a negotiable point between him and the prospective employers. Because he was literate, anyone who wished to enter into a contract with Isaac was able to do so through correspondence. In other words, because he was able to read, write, and think critically about what he wanted and how he needed to go about achieving it, Isaac had access to the world of business, which traditionally shut most people out due to a lack of education.

By March 24 a new ad appeared in the *Kentucky Live Stock Record* that "[Isaac] has more engagements than he can fill, and that he can make no new engagements" for the 1883 season.[23] If the first ad had been an experiment to see what he was worth to the racing public, it had worked. The fact that it took only a week for his racing calendar to fill up was a clear indication that he had the skills that thorough-bred owners wanted and were willing to pay for. It is also possible that many of his new mounts came as a result of C. J. Foster's January 1883 article in the *New York Sportsman* boosting the Kentucky jockey as the premiere horse pilot of the age. The article also attracted the attention of a number of individuals who were compelled to acknowledge the significant accomplishments of the black jockey for different reasons.

In the January 27, 1883, edition of the African American newspaper the *New York Globe*, the editor, Timothy Thomas Fortune, who had full knowledge of Isaac and his success as a jockey, recognized his importance beyond the saddle and the track.[24] An adherent to the philosophy of agitation for the sake of the progress of the race, Fortune's columns challenged his readers to think for themselves and urge their elected officials to represent them as citizens of the United States and less as wards of the republic who were unable, if not incapable, of functioning without the guidance of whites.[25] On numerous occasions Fortune argued that the black press was obligated to "fight for the rights of our race" and educate black people about themselves and their place in the world.[26] Indeed noting the achievements of African Americans from the "pulpit, in the schools and the colleges, in journalism, in the law, . . . [and] in the prize ring, in all the life of our civilization, [where] the Afro American is acquitting himself as 'a man and a brother,'" Fortune took every opportunity to praise the "modest and unassuming" Isaac Murphy, elevating the exceptional jockey and therefore his profession into the realm of respectable occupations from which African Americans could create a world of possibility. To Fortune, Isaac Murphy was a prince among the jockeys against whom he competed and the men of the turf for whom he rode.[27]

## The Beginning of the End

From 1883 to 1890 Isaac was recognizably the most successful jockey in America. In a terrific 1883 season he competed in more than 130 races and finished first in 50, second in 30, and third in 15. By the end of the season the Murphys made the decision to move to his home town of Lexington, where they would settle down to start a family. Isaac had proven his ability to generate a significant amount of income, which increased not only their purchasing power but also their freedom to pursue some of the finer things in life. Still the Murphys had to be aware of the challenges that would arise out of the U.S. Supreme Court's 1883 ruling that the Civil Rights Act of 1875 was unconstitutional, thus denying federal protections to African Americans. Not only did the ruling accelerate the already eroding gains made by blacks after the Civil War and Reconstruction era legislation, but it also served to validate and perpetuate the sectional and regional abuses meted out on blacks throughout the nation in general and in the South in particular.

By Christmas 1883 Murphy was secured by Ed Corrigan for the coming season. The midwestern-based breeder extended terms to Murphy that called for a retainer of $5,000 (or $117,084 in 2014 dollars) to guarantee first call at pre-designated Jockey Club meetings, while providing the opportunity for Isaac to ride for other owners at other times not in conflict with the races secured by the contract.[28] Considering that the average annual salary for working-class whites was in the range of $100–$150, this was a tremendous amount of money for anyone, especially a man of African descent. In addition, based on the rules of the American Jockey Club, Isaac would receive the standard $10 for every losing race and $25 for every race won. Also, as noted, Isaac was able to ride for other owners willing to pay his fee of $25 per mount, sums that no doubt added to his bottom line. Based on the media coverage of Isaac's and Corrigan's agreed-upon fee, their negotiations were a significant development in horseracing and the future relations between jockeys and owners.

In the January 1, 1884, edition of the *New York Hour* newspaper, the editorial accounts for the influence of "crooked men" on promising young white jockeys whose desires for wealth without work ruin potentially honorable careers in the pigskin. Nevertheless, horse farm owners nationally were beginning to demand white boys as riders for their stables, relegating black jockeys to positions as groomers or stable boys, based on the quickly circulating lie that "though handy about horses, [black boys] are as a rule too ignorant to learn anything but the merest handiwork."[29] What had been considered "nigger work" less than a decade previously was attracting white boys and men wanting to ride the prized thoroughbreds that black jockeys had been paid so handsomely to ride in high-stakes races.[30] By participating in the denial of any significant access to power to racial "others" through force and coercion, native whites and European immigrants forged relationships. In other words, white capital and white labor colluded to deny African Americans access to economic opportunities, which translated into social mobility and political power, and thus wanted to exclude African Americans from horseracing.

Isaac's contract with Ed Corrigan and the salary he was able to command, although a reflection of his abilities as a quality jockey and signifier of his character as a man, began an assault on black labor in horseracing that would eventually lead to the disappearance of black jockeys from the sport they had helped build into a multimillion-dollar industry. In March 1884 in the Denver *Rocky Mountain News*, Corrigan noted some of the reasons why he had contracted with Isaac Murphy for the upcoming season:

> I have engaged Isaac Murphy to ride for me because I have found out by experience that it is of very little use to have good or fair horses without having skill and honesty in the saddle. I believe I was punished by riders last season as much as any man in the country, and I don't intend to suffer in the same way again if I can help it. Good riders are scarce and high priced, but I made up my mind to get a good one, and got one of the best—some people think the best. My

opinion is that I have as good a rider as anybody. I have my stable heavily engaged for the entire season.[31]

Corrigan's statement was proof, of course, of what honesty and hard work could provide for the professional jockey who was willing to ride to win each time he secured a mount. Still it was the amount of money involved that would become the issue for the white boys who could only hope to compete for the kind of contract that Isaac had secured as a result of his unique skills and expertise with horses and his reputation as an honest jockey.

In the spring of 1884, at the tenth running of the Kentucky Derby, the twenty-three-year-old Murphy rode William Cottrill's Buchanan in the race that Kentuckians believed to be the most important contest for three-year-olds. In dramatic fashion Isaac rode the bay stallion to victory. A few weeks later in Chicago he won the first American Derby at the inaugural meeting of the Washington Park Club. On Ed Corrigan's Modesty, Murphy won close to $13,000 in stake and purse money. Overall in the 1884 season Isaac rode in 132 races and won 51. Walter Vosburgh, the dean of horseracing and sports journalism, wrote about Isaac in a way rarely expressed in white newspapers in relation to the manliness of black jockeys—or black men for that matter. In the *Spirit of the Times* Vosburgh wrote eloquently about Isaac as "an elegant specimen of manhood."[32] The toast of horse breeders, fans of the turf, and an adoring "colored" public from one coast of the country to the other, Isaac certainly could not have imagined the changes the future had to offer.

Between 1885 and 1890 Isaac won hundreds of races hosted by jockey clubs throughout the country. He won three more American Derbies at Washington Park, all on horses owned by the California millionaire E. J. Baldwin (Volante in 1885, Silver Cloud in 1886, and Emperor of Norfolk in 1888). He also secured contracts for first and second calls from Baldwin and Corrigan, and these increased his seasonal base pay to more than $10,000. In the spring of 1890, after winning his second Kentucky Derby on Ed Corrigan's horse Riley (which earned him a $1,000 bonus), Isaac contracted to ride for Kentuckian J. B. Haggin as his number one rider for $15,000 for the rest of the 1890 season.[33] This arrangement meant Isaac's relocating to New York, where Haggin's Stable spent considerable time racing at Saratoga, Monmouth Park, Sheepshead Bay (Brooklyn), and Coney Island. These tracks had been the locations of some of Isaac's most important and most dramatic victories of his career. Unfortunately the proclaimed "Prince of Jockeys" was not prepared for the drama that awaited him back east.

After winning the June 17, 1890, Suburban Handicap at the Coney Island Jockey Club, on June 25 at Sheepshead Bay Isaac, riding on Salvator, was matched up against Ed "Snapper" Garrison, who was riding on David Pulsifer's horse Tenny. Under the hot, sunlit sky with a soft breeze coming from the west, twelve to fifteen thousand spectators turned out to see the match. The race promised to set the record straight with regard to who was the better horse and, by default, who was the better breeder, Pulsifer or Haggin. But the contest had other relevant implications regarding who was indeed the better jockey: Isaac Murphy or Ed Garrison. On the track Murphy knew exactly where the competition was at all times, anticipating his moves like a chess master, meeting his believed equal. Keeping Salvator where he needed him for the race, the Kentucky jockey outrode and outsmarted his white counterpart in a near dead heat. One observer in the stands who could account for the outcome with pinpoint accuracy was John Hemment, a photographer who captured the horses in stride as they reached the finish line. In horseracing's first photo finish, it is clear that Murphy's masterful riding led to Salvator's victory over Tenny. The rush of the two horses had set a new record in the mile and a quarter at 2:05, knocking 1.5 seconds off the time set by the Dwyer Brothers' Kingston, a horse that Isaac had ridden to several victories during the previous season.

Over the course of three months Isaac rode for several other owners, earning thousands of dollars in fees and growing his brand in the East. On August 26 he had another big race at Monmouth Park in the Monmouth Handicap on a prized filly, Firenzi. After a false start Isaac asked permission from the starter to dismount and arrange his saddle girths.[34] Why his saddle would have been loose after his leaving the paddock area (where everything should have been secure before this point in the race) is unclear. However, after Isaac had his equipment readjusted and with some assistance in remounting Firenzi, it became obvious to those watching from the stands, as it should have been obvious to his colleagues around him, that something was wrong. Maybe they questioned what they saw but refused to believe their own eyes. According to several reports, Isaac's face was swollen, his eyes glazed over, and his body slumped in his saddle. Something was terribly wrong.

At the start of the race Isaac and Firenzi got away first, and the pace was fast. After the field had gone only a quarter mile, Isaac began to pull Firenzi for reasons unknown. It seems that Isaac was purposely trying to slow down and allow the other horses to pass him. Why would he do something that he had been against since he started running horses? As the other horses passed him, the veteran jockey tried to maintain some power over the spirited horse, pulling her head left and right, trying unsuccessfully to control her movements. In what seems to have been quick thinking by Isaac to prevent his own death by falling off his horse and into the path of the thundering pack, he pulled Firenzi to the rear to gather his wits and try to finish the race that had already been lost. A spectacle beyond belief, Isaac listed to the left and the right over the track, clinging to his saddle with all that he had.

Upon completion of the race and still holding onto Firenzi, Isaac passed the judges' stand and fell from his saddle into a heap on the ground.[35] According to the *New York Times*, the "helpless jockey was assisted into the saddle and managed to keep his seat until the paddock was reached. Then he forgot to ask the permission of the judge to dismount, and his friends had to put him on Firenzi's back again. He was then conducted to the scale and weighed in, after which he was almost carried to the jockeys' room [by his valet and his friends]."[36] As quickly as they could get Isaac changed and secure a carriage, he was hurried away from Monmouth Park to his living accommodations.

Within a few days the executive committee of Monmouth Park decided to suspend Isaac pending an investigation into the events that had played out on the track and in the paddock area on August

26. In an interview Isaac claimed to have been drugged. He assured the committee that he had not drunk any alcohol before the race but had only had water and ginger ale from the grandstand café before he weighed in. He related everything that occurred that he could remember prior to the start of the race, including a conversation with Mr. Crickmore, the starter, and his sitting in the jockeys' dressing room. He recalled that his "head swam and hummed and felt like a vacuum from the moment . . . he dismounted at the starting post to have his saddle adjusted till he passed the scales after the race."[37] In the interview Isaac also defended himself against rumors that painted him as the "Champagne Jockey," whose insatiable thirst for the expensive beverage was the cause of his behavior during the Monmouth Handicap. "No one that knows me," Murphy exclaimed, "would charge me with drinking champagne. I don't drink it because I don't like it."[38]

After considering the facts and listening to several parties, including Isaac himself, the executive committee concluded that the jockey had not been drunk when he was on the grounds of Monmouth Park. "The evidence is conclusive," Mr. Withers, chairman of the committee and director of the American Jockey Club, would state, "that [Murphy] drank no intoxicating liquor while here." To answer some of the questions with regard to Isaac's being drugged, Withers would only say that he took "no stock in that [theory]." He explained that Isaac "drank his milk punches at home, and the Apollinaris and ginger ale that he drank here were in scaled bottles, opened before his eyes. If that ginger ale was drugged, it was drugged in Belfast."[39] In several newspapers Murphy's strange ride aboard Firenzi was attributed to the clambake thrown by Matt Byrnes for the Salvator Club a few days prior to the race. In the *New York Times* especially, he was cited as having overindulged in "champagne, a habit which has in the past gotten the better of him, but never to lead to quite so sad an exhibition of himself as he made at the track yesterday."[40] The scene is described as a pained exhibition by Isaac, who "disgraced himself in the most shameful manner. . . . He was so drunk that he reeled and rolled in the saddle. He jerked Firenzi all about the track in this wild lurching and tumbling about on her back, ruined all of her chances of winning or getting a place."[41] Still there is the question: what if he in fact had been drugged? Why would someone do this?

Rumors had spread about bookmakers who knew something about the outcome of the race and were willing to take money for Firenzi at 6–5 and even odds and after the race walked away with thousands of dollars. The *Times Picayune* reports that several well-known plungers "won big money on Tea Tray, including Dave Johnson, who was "credited with winning $20,000 on the race."[42] If there was a gambling ring involved in changing the outcome of the race without using the traditional means of drugging a horse or paying a jockey to throw the race, it would make sense that the next best thing would be to drug the jockey who seemed a shoo-in and bribe the other jockeys to allow for the ring's preferred horse—in this case, Tea Tray—to win. This is simple enough, but we need to consider an alternative theory that would be more in line with all the evidence provided—that is, someone or a group of people had planned a coordinated effort to kill Isaac Burns Murphy.

Indeed it is one thing to drug Murphy so that he would lose his focus and concentration and quite another when his saddle is loosened before the race. The fact that he had an issue with his saddle and that he was reeling from the effects of some kind of drug are unavoidable. Had he not noticed the state of his saddle and adjusted it, more than likely he would have fallen from Firenzi and been trampled by the other horses on the track. The possibility that someone may have tried to kill Isaac was never considered in the white press covering the story. In fact Murphy had become a pariah. In his defense black newspapers such as the *Cleveland Gazette* wrote that the "leading New York dailies claim that Jockey Murphy has always possessed a great love for champagne and that some person in whom he had confidence, and who had bet heavily on other horses in the race, took advantage of him, placing a drug in his liquor. He has been suspended pending an investigation. We hope that it will result in his being honorably acquitted, and the punishment of the scoundrel who committed the crime, for we believe that Murphy was drugged."[43]

Shortly after his poisoning, Murphy tried to return to the track but struggled to overcome dizzy spells and the subsequent development of stomach ulcers. After a series of treatments Isaac and Lucy returned to Lexington, where he would convalesce over the winter in the quiet of their home and among friends. Still weak from not being able to eat regularly and having his stomach inflamed to the point that he had to keep it wrapped with a "wide bandage on it all the time" to prevent excessive swelling, the slightest jarring of his body causing considerable pain.[44] Reporters came to call on the celebrated jockey to inquire about his future in the profession. When asked by a reporter if he knew of any efforts to have him reinstated, Isaac answered, "Unless I get very much better than I am I shall never ride again. Still, I dislike to have the stigma of expulsion resting on me[;] . . . I feel that I am wholly innocent of being drunk when I rode Firenzi."[45] The incident would haunt Isaac for the rest of his life.

### Conclusion

Less than a year after being poisoned, a recovered and rejuvenated Isaac Murphy returned to the racetrack ready to regain his previous stature both in the saddle and in society. The time away from the track and away from a brutal public that began to identify him as the "Champagne Jockey" provided him an opportunity to reflect on his future, which included making plans for retirement from the saddle to become a full-time owner, breeder, and trainer. Unfortunately the social, political, and economic changes in the larger society had finally caught up to horseracing, and over the next four seasons Murphy's opportunities would ebb and flow based solely on the whims of others.

In 1891, in one of the highlights of the spring racing season, Murphy brought the stallion Kingman, a horse trained and co-owned by the African American breeder Dudley Allen, across the line to win the Kentucky Derby. The victory represented back-to-back Derby wins for Isaac (who had won in 1884 as well) and the record third Derby victory of his career. A few weeks later he won again on Kingman in the Latonia Derby in Covington, Kentucky, earning an extra $1,000 for his services. While these early victories of the 1891 season proved that he was still capable of bringing home a winner if given the opportunity, his importance had begun to fade from the sport. A year later, after signing with the owners of the Hellgate Stable for $10,000 for first call, Isaac and the owners had a falling out due to rumors about his fading abilities. After a legal battle Murphy was paid his full salary but was not allowed to race for other owners without permission from the stable. As expected, they refused his requests to ride for other owners, a situation that ruined his reputation and marked the beginning of the end of his once glorious career in horse racing.

When Isaac Murphy died on February 12, 1896, his importance as a man of certain potential still resonated with those who knew him. His success in the saddle and his exemplary status proved that African Americans could achieve success under the most extreme circumstances. And like a comet across the heavens, he shined brightly, if only for a moment, demonstrating to the black masses that it was indeed possible to achieve greatness despite the ill intent of whites to uphold the promises of democracy for all except those of African descent.

## Notes

1. "A Triumph for Kentucky," *Baltimore Sun*, July 21, 1879, 1.

2. "Colored Jockey," *Macon Telegram*, November 25, 1879, 2.

3. "Saratoga," *Spirit of the Times*, July 26, 1879, 624.

4. Rev. Edward P. Smith to M. E. Strieby, secretary of the American Missionary Association, October 4, 1865, American Missionary Association Archives 44229-32; Richard D. Sears, *Camp Nelson, Kentucky: A Civil War History* (Lexington: University of Kentucky Press, 2002), 269–71.

5. Ronald E. Butchhart, *Schooling the Freed People: Teaching, Learning, and the Struggle for Black Freedom, 1861–1876* (Chapel Hill: University of North Carolina Press, 2010), 7.

6. The *Ninth Census of the United States*, 1870, *Population*, vol. 1, 56, provides a clear representation of the changes that Emancipation and the Civil War created. The numbers of African Americans living in the rural areas of Kentucky and in the urban environments such as Lexington are clearly defined.

7. "King of the Pigskin Artists: The Successful Career of Isaac Murphy, the Colored Archer of America," *New York Herald*, March 17, 1889, 24.

8. Cited in L. P. Tarleton, "Isaac Murphy," *Thoroughbred Record*, March 21, 1896, 136.

9. In C. R. Acton's *Silk and Spur* (London: Richards, 1935), there is a wonderful section (58–70) on the traditional purpose of apprenticeship in the stables for boys who want to become jockeys.

10. R. Gerald Alvey, *Kentucky Bluegrass Country* (Jackson: University Press of Mississippi, 1992), 135–36.

11. "King of the Pigskin Artists," 24; Betty Borries, *Isaac Murphy* (Berea KY: Kentucky Imprints, 1988), 23.

12. Thomas Clark, *History of Kentucky* (Ashland KY: Jesse Stuart Foundation, 1992), 77.

13. "King of the Pigskin Artists," 24; Borries, *Isaac Murphy*, 23.

14. "Stock Gossip: Messrs. Williams & Owings' Stable," *Kentucky Live Stock Record*, April 14, 1877, 228.

15. "The Turf," *Kentucky Live Stock Record*, May 12, 1877, 291.

16. "King of the Pigskin Artists," 24.

17. Steven Reiss, *The Sport of Kings and the Kings of Crime: Horse Racing, Politics and Organized Crime in New York, 1865–1913* (Syracuse NY: Syracuse University Press, 2011).

18. "Third Day of Second Meeting—A Dead Heat for the Grinstead Stakes between Duke of Magenta and Spartan," *Kentucky Live Stock Record*, August 25, 1877, 115.

19. W. E. B. Du Bois, *Black Reconstruction in America 1860–1880* (New York: Free Press, 1992), 673.

20. "Funeral of Colonel J. W. Hunt-Reynolds," *Lexington Weekly Press*, October 6, 1880, 2.

21. C. J. Foster, "Isaac Murphy, Colored Jockey," *New York Sportsman*, January 20, 1883, 34.

22. "First Class Jockey," *Kentucky Live Stock Record*, March 17, 1883, 170.

23. "Stock Gossip," *Kentucky Live Stock Record*, March 24, 1883, 180.

24. "Sentiment and Doings of Our People," *New York Globe*, January 27, 1883, 2.

25. Emma Lou Thornbrough, *T. Thomas Fortune: Militant Journalist* (Chicago: University of Chicago Press, 1972), 44.

26. Irvine Garland Penn, *The Afro-American Press and Its Editors* (Springfield MA: Willey, 1891), 483.

27. "The Prince of Jockeys," *New York Age*, July 5, 1890, 1.

28. "Sporting Summary," *New Hampshire Patriot*, December 20, 1883, 8.

29. "Professional Jockeys," *Springfield Republican*, January 1, 1884, 8.

30. David Roediger, *The Wages of Whiteness: Race and the Making of the American Working Class* (London: Verso, 2002), 146.

31. "Sprays of Sport," *Rocky Mountain News*, March 24, 1884, 2.

32. Cited in Ed Hotaling, *The Great Black Jockeys: The Lives and Times of the Men Who Dominated America's First National Sport* (Rocklin NY: Forum Prima Publishing, 1999), 253.

33. "Turf Notes," *Philadelphia Inquirer*, May 15, 1890, 6; "Turf Gossip," *Live Stock Record*, May 24, 1890, 326; "Personal," *San Francisco Bulletin*, July 25, 1890, 4.

34. "Isaac Murphy's Mistake," *Kentucky Leader*, August 27, 1890, 1.

35. "A Monmouth Sensation," *New York Times*, August 27, 1890, 3.

36. "A Monmouth Sensation," 3.

37. "Murphy's Strange Illness: Neither Drunk nor Drugged, but in a Very Bad Way," *New York Herald*, August 28, 1890, 2.

38. "Murphy's Strange Illness," 2.

39. "Murphy's Strange Illness," 2.

40. "A Monmouth Sensation," 3.

41. "Track and Boulevard," *Chicago Horseman*, September 4, 1890, 1504.

42. "Sporting: The Turf," *Times Picayune*, August 29, 1890, 2; "Isaac Murphy's Mistake," 1.

43. "Isaac Murphy's Fall," *Cleveland Gazette*, August 30, 1890, 2.

44. "Isaac Murphy Ill," *Chicago Herald*, November 23, 1890, 1.

45. Cited in "Isaac Murphy Ill," 1.

# TWO

# John M. Shippen Jr.

*Testing the Front Nine of American Golf*

SARAH JANE EIKLEBERRY

Perhaps a few elite Americans engaged in their own domestic versions of informal pasture golf as early as the eighteenth century, but by 1890 the modern form captivated many members of the nation's upper crust. This "ancient game from Scotland," with its legends of fairways full of cobblers alongside kings provided anxious capitalists with an antimodern antidote to an ever "confusing world."[1] In an effort to assert American golfers as contenders in an overwhelmingly British sportscape, young men of color were temporarily invited into American fairways. In their efforts to procure employment and learn the game, players such as John Shippen Jr. temporarily upset the Social Darwinian perceptions of white supremacy. Initially limited to the seven-month season of elite country clubs in the Northeast and Midwest, golf's ascent as an American pastime leaned heavily on the availability of young, working-class boys who served as caddies, many of whom eschewed schooling for the meager financial boon incurred through hauling bags and cleaning clubs of the socially elite, a relationship that reinforced their status as a sort of "embryonic proletariat" in Jim Crow America.[2] It is within this setting that the first American-born professional tournament golfers were forged in the vacation paradise in New York state today referred to as the Hamptons. The success of the sinewy son of a preacher offers a glimmer into the symbolic leisurescape buttressed in and by the constraints of Jim Crow America at the close of the Victorian era at the turn of the century. This essay aims to explore the social and historical forces that shaped such a sport and, as a consequence, a bourgeoning profession. An examination of John Shippen's pioneering efforts into the world of American golf elucidates the ideological and structural conditions that allowed for his success and contributed to the breach made by African American players into the racially segregated tournaments and organizations of professional golf by the late 1940s.

John M. Shippen (December 2, 1879–May 20, 1968) was among the first American-born golf professionals and certainly the first African American tournament golfer. Athletically reared by British professionals, employed and sponsored by the members of the insular world of white, elite golf and country clubs, Shippen competed in the second U.S. Open Championship in Southampton, New York, in 1896.[3] Initially schooled as a caddie, Shippen served as a club professional at a variety of Long Island courses, instructed prominent players and lesser learners from the leisure class, constructed handmade golf clubs, supervised caddies, provided turf consultations, worked as a greenskeeper, and toured as a player through 1915. Seeking more stability of income and better quality education for his six children, Shippen and his wife, teacher Maude Elliot Lee Shippen, relocated to Washington DC. In 1921 he exchanged his job in public works for a return to the less pristine fairways outside of the full and allied-member courses of the United States Golf Association (USGA). The back nine of Shippen's golfing career was harbored by African American–owned and managed clubs, associations, and courses in Washington DC, Maryland, and New Jersey.[4] Shippen's entrance into the world of Hamptons country club life, establishment and ascendance in a bourgeoning sport defined by American racism and classism, and retreat into an exclusively African American world of amateur and professional golf depended on a confluence of shifts in labor and leisure practices.

## Laboring in Long Island

Many of the processes shaping the intersections of race and class in Long Island were rooted in exchanges among laboring bodies during the colonial period. Originally thirteen indigenous tribes inhabited the region. Since the 1600s the whaling industry, mainly owned by European settlers, served as a large source of employment to indigenous people in Long Island. Their skills and knowledge offered them considerable financial leverage with whaling outfits. By the end of the seventeenth century the economic prosperity and security of many Native Americans and freemen began unhinging. Sometime during the 1668–73 tenure of colonial governor Francis Lovelace, lobbyists persuaded him to enact NYCD 14:675, a code that severely limited the compensation paid to crew members to "one half share of the season's hunt to be divided among the crew, and a cloth coat for each whaler after every whale killed."[5] Perhaps more damaging to crew workers was the installation of the credit system, a type of "debt peonage" that resembled the lien system used by southern sharecroppers.[6] Still a shortage of laborers provided additional financial support in agriculture and service. In the 1630s and '40s whites began purchasing enslaved Africans as one means of reducing the labor shortage in Suffolk and Peconic Counties. Under the New York Law Code of 1708, "Negro, Indian, mulatto, and mustee slaves were subject to the provisions of the law."[7] In less than fifteen years the city of East Hampton's African population rose from 5 to 20 percent by 1700 and 25 percent by 1750, almost all living as slaves.[8]

By the 1730s the offshore-whaling industry had waned and was replaced by the boom and bust of the deep-water sperm whale fleets. By 1800 haul-seining and agriculture surpassed the importance of the whaling industry. This shift was particularly precarious for Native American groups such as the Montauketts. Some tribes had no formal relationship established with the state of New York or the federal government. Towns such as East Hampton and Southampton were legally positioned to refuse the lease of land to native groups and granted residence rights as a paltry alternative. East End hamlets inflicted further marginalization on the Montaukett by restricting their claims to property or residential status if they married outside their racial or ethnic communities. Shinnecock Indians were "effectively confined" by town proprietors in Southhampton to the west and south in Shinnecock Neck.[9] John Strong argues that intermar-

like Walt Whitman exalted the region's fecund beauty and liberating qualities of the unsullied landscape and seashores. Cory Dolgan argues that the initial waves of vacationers threw their upper-class decorum to the salty winds, albeit temporarily. "Freed from the restraints of civilized, urban life and its restrictive sensibilities," the visitors traversed cliffs and played in their "counterurban landscape where all that symbolized the burgeoning economic and social life of the moneyed metropolis could be stripped away like sweaty clothes all along the sandy shore."[17] The endeavors of famous artists frequenting the "American Barbizon," including the exclusive Tile Club members, politicians, business owners, and socialites, were recorded in *Scribner's Monthly* or *Lippincott's Magazine*.[18] As late as 1898, editor, poet, and critic Charles de Kay described East Hampton as the type of "pensive sojourn" where one could "bathe without caring for looks or asking what is the correct thing in bathing suits."[19] Thomas Moran and his wife, Mary Nimmo, established a studio, and William Merritt Chase established the Shinnecock School of Art.[20] Unfettered views of the Atlantic did not quell the elite's ravenous desire for entertainment. The East End, no longer constrained by a labor shortage, saw a boom in the construction of inns, seasonal services, and amusements. Still the Hamptons resisted some of the trappings of the "highly ritualized aristocratic order of other summer colonies" such as Newport or Long Branch.[21] They maintained the feeling of ruggedness while conforming to what the elite wanted nature to be: inspiring, unsullied, and accessible.[22]

While New York's elite continued developing and planning their summer colony, John Matthew Shippen Sr. considered a career change that would one day bring his family to the East End. Shippen Sr., a descendent of enslaved Africans in Jamaica, married Eliza Spotswood Shippen, a multi-racial woman with African American and Shinnecock heritage, and they raised their family in the Hillsdale section of Washington DC's Anacostia neighborhood. After earning an elementary teaching certificate from Howard University and working in the Washington public school system, Shippen Sr. returned to his alma mater to pursue a degree in theology. The Presbyterian Church relocated the Shippens to posts in Fayetteville, Arkansas, and Florence, Alabama. In 1888 Shippen Sr. accepted the post on the Shinnecock Reservation, one of the oldest Presbyterian posts in the nation. As a young boy, Shippen Jr. played with children from the reservation at school and fished, swam, and rode horses with them.[23] The Shippen family's insular life on the Shinnecock Reservation left little reason for interaction with New York City's elite until "a little group of wealthy men advanced the money . . . to buy up all the sand dunes outside of the old Indian reservation."[24] Such a purchase soon stood to alter the course of the Long Island leisur-escape and Shippen Jr.'s teenage life.

## The American Country Club

Since the founding of our nation, voluntary associations have been central to American life, from the religious institutions founded in the seventeenth century to the moral uplift and reform groups of the antebellum and Reconstruction eras and the commercial associations that evolved on the East Coast at the close of the nineteenth century.[25] The country club movement is an example of community building consistent with the American club movement. The movement was by no means relegated to the elite; immigrants, reformers, women, and many other groups sought to establish community through similar efforts.[26] The concept of the oldest American country clubs to dot the eastern seaboard typically originated not in their bucolic suburban surroundings but in private domestic and social spaces of bustling urban centers. According to Richard J. Moss, the oldest country clubs drew "a line between public and private space and [installed] a collective (the membership) as the lords and ladies of that private domain."[27] Of course the New Englanders that first began to do voluntary work would not have approved of "the somewhat frantic pursuit of leisure" that characterized the first fifty years of the American country club. No longer concerned about an "anathema to the work ethic," Protestant elites enjoyed the spoils of their capitalist ventures.[28] Moss argues that similar to Progressivism and Populism, the country club movement was a response to the demise of Victorian era ideologies and the "nerve-racking pace of change," and country clubs created a space where the upper classes could preserve certain traditions associated with their lives despite the influx of non-English-speaking immigrants, the dramatic rise of the nouveau riche, and the diminishment of the tribalism offered through local geographic and social seclusion.[29] Steve Hardy argues that sporting organizations and clubs tend to moderate and ameliorate changes in the social milieu, but the behaviors that they model or promote may be radically new, traditional, or something in between. Though the elite indeed paid homage to the sporting clubs of Great Britain, outright "Anglomania" was exchanged for the promotion of a medicinal prescription for the maladies of urban and industrial life.[30] Three clubs would come to define "the arc of summer life" for the East End: Maidstone Club, Shinnecock Hills Golf Club (SHGC), and the Bathing Corporation.[31]

Initially riding and fox hunting dominated the interests of many early country club members, but golf, tennis, bowling, and swimming soon followed.[32] Despite anxieties about keeping the club afloat, board members at Maidstone Club in East Hampton invested in land for a golf course in 1891. By 1896 golf generated annual revenues upward of $700 for the East Hampton club.[33] Clubs in the Northeast continued investing in sites that were suitable for golf. Each organization attempted to instill its own version of tribalism through Scottish-inspired dress and varying membership procedures. In 1891 Shinnecock Hills Golf Club in Southampton responded to the club's growing popularity by localizing its membership only to "those identified with the social life and interests of the immediate vicinity."[34] The "fashionable watering-place for New York's socially elect" experienced little difficulty locating shareholders and members willing to foot the dues required to don the club's scarlet jacket.[35] By 1892 the club consisted of seventy-five members.[36] In addition, clubs attempted to distinguish their properties by emphasizing landmarks, features, or anomalies in course layout. Such legacies were advertised through publications such as *Outing*, the *American Golfer*, and the organ of the USGA, *Golfing*.

A club's unique identity was also developed through affiliation with famous professionals, architects, and course designers. Shinnecock Hills Golf Club solicited the renowned Gilded Age architect and Tile Club member Stanford White to design its clubhouse. The "Shingle

Style" structure matched other prominent Southampton constructions such as the William Merritt Chase home and studio and the homes of Samuel Parrish, Francis Key Pendleton, and Charles Atterbury, early settlers and developers of the community.[37] Country clubs such as Shinnecock Hills and the Chicago Golf Club in the Midwest also paved the way for a new standard in the 1890s, the eighteen-hole golf course. Though the plan was never realized, Shinnecock trustees considered creating separate courses for young boys and girls.[38] In order to combat the circumstances of a seven-month golf season, a lack of elite competition, and less than top-notch greens, wealthy golf clubs aggressively recruited professionals from the United Kingdom to teach members to play and to improve their game.[39] In 1891 Shinnecock Hills board members commissioned Willie Davis to design a twelve-hole course. In 1895 W. K. Vanderbilt commissioned Willie Dunn Jr., a member of a Scottish family that had produced a long line of well-known professionals, to expand the club course to eighteen holes, which few could complete in under ninety strokes. The golf course at Shinnecock Hills was constructed by the labor of some 150 Shinnecock Indians. According to Dunn, "The place was dotted with Indian burial grounds and we left some intact as bunkers in front of the greens. We scraped out some of the mounds and made sand traps. It was here that the Indians buried their empty whisky barrels, but we did not find this out until later when playing the golf course. One never knew when an explosion shot in a trap would bring out a couple of fire-water flasks, or perhaps a bone or two."[40]

The unity of American country clubs and golf was further solidified when a group of prominent club leaders laid the groundwork for the formation of the USGA. After two controversial national tournaments, the leaders concluded that they ought to move forward in forming a group that could better execute competitions and forge rules for play. Two representatives each from Brookline, Shinnecock, St. Andrews, and the Chicago Golf Club and one representative from Newport met in New York City and drafted the initial foundational documents in 1894. Theodore Havemeyer of Newport, an extremely wealthy sugar cane entrepreneur, was elected president. In addition to creating uniform rules and organizing tournaments, the group set out to devise a system to determine a standard (rather than a club- or tournament-determined) handicap, chose sites for championships, and served as arbiters of disputes. In 1894 the aforementioned clubs' presidents signed the draft forged in New York City.

This moment codified a complex autocratic system that brokered much power over club memberships, club status, and an individual's amateur standing. In 1898 well-to-do amateur golf enthusiasts in *Outing* fretted that the sport might go the way of *"sloggers* of the commonest prize ring type."[41] Moss argues that the control that the USGA established over golf gave the sport a decidedly upper-class ethos: gentility, manners, and tradition were the rule.[42] Fairway gentlemen took many measures to prevent the "boorish fashion" of the "professional ball player and horse jockey" from adulterating their amateur paradise.[43] Before the USGA clarified its position of paid play, golfers wishing to preserve their liminal amateur status were discouraged from competing in competitions where cash awards were "awarded outright in a sweepstakes plan."[44] What constituted "suitable prizes" was subject to opinion, though one *Outing* writer suggested that it was respectable for participants "among the three making the best net scores" to accept awards of 50, 30, and 20 percent of the entrance fee dividends.[45] Club secretaries wielded considerable gatekeeping power in determining a player's amateur status or admittance to a USGA event. In order to be eligible for a prestigious tournament, a player needed to be represented by a sanctioned club. By 1899 the USGA ruled that a player was a professional if he had received money for any golf-related reason; teaching lessons, building clubs, caddying after age fifteen, competing in an exhibition, or administering or engineering a golf course stood to disbar a player's status as an amateur.[46] Ever the promoter, USGA president Havemeyer wielded his editorial influence in *Golfing* to extoll the practicality and relative affordability of the sport. As early as 1897 he criticized the clubs that invested in the construction of lavish clubhouses, leaving their courses to fray or stagnate from overuse or poor design. Undeniably cut from the upper crust, Havemeyer yearned for the sport he loved to spread beyond "the country club set."[47] In several unsigned *Golfing* editorials arguments were waged for maximum access to public

persisting between exclusive club members and the seasonal employees. In 1897 one *Outing* writer expressed such sentiments: "In the old world a caddie is generally a player himself, and a student of the game. Very often here, the caddie is looked upon as little more than a peripatetic golf bag. This is not as it should be."[50] The author argued that treating caddies with more respect would undoubtedly attract more people to the game and make the sport more popular and profitable. Using the language of reform, he argued that "one need have no scruples on this head either, for golf is already a large industry in this country, and promises to support many men and boys who otherwise would find less wholesome and less honest means of occupying themselves."[51] Benevolent paternalism aside, this embroiled rhetoric of tradition, democracy, and love of the game dissipated by the turn of the century and likely held little currency in the country clubs of the southeastern United States.

Despite the initially hopeful rhetoric, by 1900 *Outing* writers referred to the caddie as a sort of literary punching bag, with Price Collier conceding that "those of us who have not been thus equipped for the game still suffer from their ignorance, indifference, and carelessness."[52] Collier hoped with all of the aristocratic underpinning of his own class position that a caddie would "learn his place in the game and play his part with unswerving attention."[53] In a thoroughly romanticized article, Collier reminisced:

> When golf was in the making, the caddie's position was taken by a friend, and he aided his companion in arms to win the victory. The rules still permit, as a consequence of this, that one's caddie, and he only, may give advice. Then, in the gradual evolution of the game, the caddie came to be a paid assistant. He was still, however, looked upon as a sort of friend-servant. He must be obedient as a servant, but he must also be interested as a friend. Otherwise the whole charm of a real caddie is lost. He ought to be as much interested to see his side win as the players. He ought not to be thinking how little he can do, but how much he can do to bring about this result. Otherwise the caddie only adds another burden to the player's already heavy and nerve-destroying responsibilities.[54]

The revered status of the Scottish caddie certainly did not transfer to African American caddies, particularly as the game's diasporic reach extended to include the southeastern United States. Moreover, the number of amateur tournaments and club-sponsored competitions soared. In addition to creating the need for more caddies, such factors further divided elite country clubs and full-member entities of the USGA from allied members and other non-affiliated courses. Price Collier wrote of the rash of tournaments that lesser clubs hosted. With their using bogeys, handicap systems, or some "subtler arrangement with the Green's Committee . . . it is a pity if everyman is not a champion or a record breaker who wields a club." Collier jested that "there are all sorts of beautiful games for those who merely wish to gamble or for those who wish to see themselves in the newspaper."[55]

Curmudgeons aside, a surge in course construction and subsequent tournament play increased the need for caddies. In time white caddies, such as 1913 U.S. Open champion Francis Ouimet, were more able to use their initial training to climb the ladder in the world of elite clubs and professional golf and to boost "international rivalry."[56] Some courses allowed caddies to play on Mondays, when the courses were typically closed for maintenance. Some black caddies played at white-sponsored caddie tournaments, but most waited another three decades until the mid-1920s, while others began to find avenues for competitions and exhibitions through the African American alternative structure, the United Golf Association (UGA).[57] Calvin H. Sinnette argues that though child labor laws gained traction in many spheres of U.S. industry occupied by white youth, the conditions of the child caddie, often as young as eight or nine years, did not receive the same exigency. Jobs in mills, mines, foundries, and other forms of post-Reconstruction industry often barred young black men from employment, but servile jobs were available in white clubs and golf courses peppering the American South. Haphazardly fed caddies often walked an eighteen-hole course up to three times per day, regularly barefoot, carrying bags weighing between twenty and fifty pounds. Tips were often turned over and redistributed by the caddie master, who wielded the power to assign a caddie to a club member who was known for tipping. Depending on the day of the week, time of season, weather, or event schedules, caddies may have found themselves with enough down time to practice putting or engage in bunker play. Many caddies were known to set course records, often with incomplete sets of hand-me-down clubs.[58] Many caddies were drawn to vices such as drinking, smoking, and gambling to fill down times on courses. Though many caddies only partially completed grade school, they consistently and ardently insisted that their own children pursue their educations with seriousness and diligence.[59]

Generations of Shinnecock residents served as caddies or greens-keepers at Shinnecock Hills Golf Club.[60] The summer of 1896 proved to be a rather exciting time for both the nineteen-year-old Oscar Bunn and sixteen-year-old Shippen Jr. The USGA, led by President Have-meyer, selected Shinnecock Hills as the site of its U.S. Open Championship, a prestigious event for those who could not compete within the narrow definition of amateur. In the first U.S. Open, hosted by Havemeyer's home club in Newport, the sugar cane entrepreneur invested much of his own money. This inaugural event was full of fanfare and designed to attract affluent spectators. Havemeyer sponsored parties and a $1,000 trophy and welcomed thirty-two mostly unskilled white entrants.[61]

Rather than attend the 1896 event as caddies, club members encouraged Shippen and Bunn to enroll in the contest.[62] The night before the competition began, several of the English and Scottish professionals threatened to boycott the event if the two teens competed. Despite what Shippen flippantly described as "a slight objection," Havemeyer "declared that the championship would be played with us included, even if we were the only two who played."[63] By the next morning the boycott was dismantled, and the apathy of gentlemen organizers overruled the bickering and pettiness of the British professionals.[64] Richard Moss notes that the professional tournament was in some ways less distinguished or important to the USGA than the more elite amateur event. Moss argues that "Havemeyer and the USGA leadership tended to look on professionals as akin to hired help and no doubt viewed their demands as inappropriate uppityness."[65] Similar to Havemeyer's approach promoting his sport, *Outing* writers thought it was "not the province of these columns to follow the course of professional play" and placed Shippen as a local signifier of the USGA's attempts to imbue its Open Championship with the Scottish traditions of openness.[66] Six months later one *Outing* writer noted the following:

> Young Shippen is an example of what progress can be made at the game, and at the same time he is a notable instance of the cliquishness of some of our imported professionals, who tried to exclude him from their matches on account of his color. . . . In the meantime we cannot do better for ourselves, or for the game of golf in America, than bring up our American caddies in the way they should go, in the hope that in the not far distant future the game of golf shall be a profitable thing for those who play it, and also for those who are employed to make the playing possible and agreeable.[67]

Moss argues that Havemeyer, the figurehead of the USGA, was not widely criticized by American players or enthusiasts because his actions did little to disrupt "deeply ingrained American attitudes" about racism.[68] In addition, his actions reinforced notions of local pride and the national myth of equal opportunity, which they felt distinguished Americans from their more class-conscious British cousins as the United States began to challenge Great Britain for world leadership by the 1890s.[69]

Despite a tense start, "good golf, good weather, and good fellowship marked the championship contest at Shinnecock."[70] The event brought much excitement to the exclusive club according to one *New York Times* writer: "In the afternoon, when the second round was being played, there was a continuous string of carriages arriving at the clubhouse, and by 3 o'clock there were over 300 ladies on the links, many of whom followed the players over the greater part of the course. The gay costumes of the ladies and the scarlet-coated club members made a very pretty picture, scattered as they were, all over the hills."[71]

Shippen tied for fifth in the event and was declared by the *New York Herald* as "the boy wonder of golf."[72] *Chicago Tribune* reporters wrote, "Anyone who plays Shippen has to forget his boyishness and pay attention to his golf because, all things considered, he is the most remarkable player in the United States."[73] In the morning round of the thirty-six hole tournament he tied his partner, Charles MacDonald, the designer of the Chicago Golf Club and winner of the previous U.S. Open in Newport. By the end of the morning round he shared the first-place lead with a score of 78. McDonald played terribly in the next round but did not abandon his partner and continued to follow him as a scorekeeper. In the afternoon Shippen scored an eleven on the thirteenth hole after getting stuck in a sand trap. In an interview with *Tuesday Magazine*, Shippen recalled:

> It was a little, easy par four. I'd played it many times and knew I just had to stay on the right side of the fairway with my drive. Well, I played it too far to the right and ended up in a sand road. Bad trouble in those days before sand wedges. I kept hitting the ball along the road, unable to lift it out of the sand, and wound up with an unbelievable eleven for the hole. You know, I've wished a hundred times I could have played that little par four again. It sure would have been something to win that day.[74]

Shippen finished seven sandy strokes behind the champion, Chicago's club professional, John Foulis. Sixteen-year-old Shippen finished ahead of three of the most widely successful British professionals in the United States: Scottish professional Willie Dunn, Newport's club pro Willie Davis, and Brookline's Willie Campbell.[75] The sixteen-year-old received a ten-dollar check and was extolled by C. Turner of *Outing* as "a competitor whose reputation and skill were sufficient to give the oldest hands a bad quarter of an hour."[76]

Shippen's performance gave American golf enthusiasts much hope for their potential ascension in the professional game. Though *Outing* writers certainly revered the successes and knowledge of "first-rate" Scottish professionals, imported English and American writers satiated their own nationalist rivalries by referring to the Scots as "crusty" and "old."[77] English import Horace Hutchinson complimented Americans for adopting the joviality of the English and swiftly forming a national governing body.[78] Shortly after the 1896 Open, Shinnecock Hills Golf Club staged an exhibition involving Shippen and the new club professional, R. B. Wilson. Shippen defeated the club pro and was soon offered a commensurate position at the newly renovated and enlarged Maidstone Club.[79] By hiring Shippen, Maidstone Club enhanced its personnel with a knowledgeable golf professional. Though modern club histories tiptoe around racial politics, it seems likely that in the context of such an exclusive and insulated environment, Shippen's presence, like that of other African Americans employed within the service industry, did little to offset the overwhelming gap in social standing between hired help and inordinately wealthy club members. It is certain that the club stood to gain unique notoriety for employing a local, rising celebrity with the talent to garner a consistent Maidstone presence in national open tournaments.[80]

The following year turf writers exalted Shippen as one of the nation's leading professionals, with one *Outing* writer quipping that "his club ought to see that despite his color, he is given every opportunity to show what he can do."[81] Maidstone Club members had faith in their club's professional. Shippen's list of high-profile students included Walter J. Travis, an Australian transplant who went on to claim victory in the 1904 British Amateur; the ultra-rich steel magnate Henry Frick; American diplomat James Cromwell; and former New Jersey governor J. S. Freylinghuysen.[82] Such social contacts were remarkably rare for a young African American man. As a consequence, Shippen was able to compete in four additional U.S. Opens: in Baltimore in 1899, Chicago in 1900, and Garden City in 1902 and 1913. His 1902 finish at Garden City (in Long Island) also resulted in a fifth-place tie. He competed as a touring pro until 1913.[83] Some of Shippen's students provided sponsorship for him.

After his father's post concluded at the Shinnecock Reservation in 1898, Shippen Jr. stayed behind, and the rest of the family returned to Washington DC. Shortly thereafter Shippen married a Shinnecock woman, Effie Walker, who died very suddenly and early in their marriage. In 1901 he married another local Shinnecock woman, Maude Elliott Lee. She raised their six children on the reservation while the itinerant golf pro occasionally traveled to secure work and financial support.[84] Riding the coattails of manufacturer Albert Spalding, Shippen began manufacturing his own handmade golf clubs as early as

1898. Shippen's clubs, like those of other professionals, were identified by a uniform metal stamp; they were an expensive investment nearing ten dollars.[85] Wealthy golf enthusiasts were thrilled to invest in "the pockets of [their] countrymen" and believed such chances "of promotion, and gaining a good living out of golf" would draw more than just those "who now see little in it but an apparently exasperating way of wasting time" into the amateur game.[86] For many black caddies, who were often marginalized in the white capitalist economy, this call to arms, aided by Shippen's example, provided additional opportunities for employment.

Many venues welcomed Shippen's skills as a golf pro. Shippen took a brief sojourn from Maidstone for the pro position at Aronimink Golf Club (near Philadelphia) after 1900. Upon his 1902 return to Maidstone he supervised a number of caddies, including Ken Davis, who recalled, "He was an excellent driver. He could outdrive anyone playing at that time. And remember, those were the days of the solid ball and wooden-shafted clubs. Many a player would bet him a dollar that they could outdrive him. In all those years, until he left Maidstone in 1915, I never saw but one man who outdrove him. Shippen collected many a dollars."[87]

Club histories, however, frame Shippen as a man whose drinking interfered with his duties and interpersonal demeanor, further contributing to his departure in 1913.[88] Between 1913 and 1915 he continued to tutor wealthy players and served as a club pro at Spring Lake Golf and Country Club in New Jersey, as well as in the Marine and Field Club (Dyker Beach Club) in Brooklyn. He returned to Shinnecock Hills Golf Club as a greenskeeper for two years and then moved on to National Capital Country Club in Southampton as a greenskeeper.[89]

### Shippen's Back Nine

Though the rhetoric of democratization permeated much of the early enthusiast literature, the 1916 formation of the Professional Golf Association (PGA) reflected the deep-seated sensibilities of American Jim Crowism. Since its genesis PGA administrators made attempts to preclude non-whites from the membership or PGA events. The PGA retroactively revoked the membership of Dewey Brown, a well-known black caddie and pro shop attendant of the Buckwood Inn in Delaware. The PGA used tournament invitations as another means of maintaining segregation. By drawing invites from the previous year's invitationals, the PGA handily barred players of color in such events until the early 1960s.[90] From 1943 to 1961 the PGA adopted a formal clause stating that "male professional golfers of the Caucasian race, over the age of eighteen (18) years, residing in North or South America, who can qualify under the terms and conditions herein specified, shall be eligible for membership."[91]

Shippen's children recall walking two to three miles to attend their lessons at a one-room schoolhouse. Their college-educated mother grew dissatisfied with the quality of such education, and according to her daughter Clara Johnson, she pushed for a relocation to Washington DC. There Shippen took a job in a federal works department until 1921. Shippen then resigned in exchange for seasonal work on the golf courses in Washington DC. At some point the burden of their unstable income drove Shippen and his wife to separate. Shippen was then estranged from his children for decades.[92] Rather than return to the fairways of Long Island, Shippen remained in the Washington DC area. Though he had managed to penetrate and thrive in the white world of golf for two decades and more African Americans between the Boston and Washington DC corridor and the city of Chicago had taken up drivers and putters in the years preceding World War I, they ultimately failed to fully overcome racial barriers.[93]

Barred from white private clubs, African Americans soon overwhelmed many of the pitted, less lavish municipal courses. Black golfers were met with various reactions, "ranging from indifference to hostility to ridicule," as evidenced by their portrayal in literature, news, and film. The first wave of the Great Migration drew nearly two million African Americans from the rural Southeast into the urban centers of the Midwest and Northeast. In their new homes a "goodly number" of black caddies and interested enthusiasts took to the greens at black-owned courses and municipal fairways such as the Windy City Golf Club in Chicago, Capital City Golf Club in Washington DC, and Shady Rest Golf and Country Club in Scotch Plains, New Jersey.[94]

Following the lead of those in sports such as tennis and base-ball, in the 1920s prominent black leaders and well-known citizens began sponsoring their own golf clubs in their own communities.[95] Black clubs provided middle- and upper-class African Americans an outlet to the game. Concomitantly the university and college golf and tennis scene began to develop in the elite historically black colleges and universities of the Southeast. Most of the schools competed within their own conferences, though the occasional match would be arranged with a neighboring white institution.[96] Private black clubs played a significant role in the creation of a black circuit of tournaments. The UGA was formed in 1925, one year after the International Golf Championship Tournament was hosted by Shady Rest Country Club. This tournament was the forerunner to the UGA's National Open. The UGA was integral in providing an alternate tour to that of the racially segregated PGA. Referred to by many players as "the Chitlin' Circuit," the UGA tour provided an opportunity for men and women to compete at a higher level. Those who played the tour did not experience the benefits of corporate sponsors or large purses. Tournament organizers were known to roll up shop before paying tournament winners, leaving already cash-strapped players no choice but to rely on fellow competitors for transportation and assistance with meals. Several players turned to hustling for additional money between tournaments.[97]

During the 1920s until 1927 Shippen worked as a golf instructor at the black-owned Citizens Golf Club in Washington DC. He also invested in and designed a black-owned and operated golf course in Laurel, Maryland, that buckled under the weight of the Great Depression. By 1931 he took a post at black-owned and -operated Shady Rest Golf Club, though players recall his instrumental involvement in the International Golf Tournament in 1925.[98]

Shady Rest originally operated as the white-owned Westfield Country Club, and an enclave of African Americans resided adjacent to it. Neighbors frequently traversed the greens to visit neighbors, establishing what Sinnette describes as an easement known as "the right to travel." When Westfield owners considered expanding the course, they determined that contesting such a legal establishment would be too onerous a litigation to pursue. Rather they sold the club to a prominent group of African American investors, the Progressive Realty Corporation. Sinnette argues that the club's governance represented "a curious combination of elitism and populism."[99] Shady Rest offered riding facilities in addition to a banquet hall that drew performers such as Ella Fitzgerald and speakers such as W. E. B. Du Bois. Similar to white county clubs, Shady Rest remained a closed, private space by design that allowed prosperous members a place to conduct business and fraternize with members of the black elite. Nonetheless, the club offered reduced admissions to its extensive amenities and supported leisure and recreation opportunities for the black community.[100]

Though one in four white clubs closed during the Great Depression, Shady Rest managed to stay afloat amid the harrowing economic downturn. Shippen arranged for living quarters in the clubhouse as part of his initial contract. He secured additional income by selling and repairing handmade clubs, giving lessons, serving as the caddie master, providing consultations to neighboring courses, and playing in exhibition matches. His participation was often arranged by his continuing contacts in the sport.[101] Eventually Shippen's relations with the clubgoers at Shady Rest became strained. He was not a churchgoer, a situation that exacerbated his isolation from an already insular and tightly knit black community. Even more isolation resulted from his occasional quiet drinking benders. After a battle with kidney disease, Shippen recovered and continued entertaining his passion for golf. After retiring from Shady Rest, he moved in with nearby friends before transitioning to a nursing home. His daughter Clara recalls that her father played golf until he was eighty-six years old. In 2008 Shippen and Bunn, his Shinnecock Hills colleague, were posthumously inducted into the Caddie Hall of Fame by the Professional Caddie Association.[102] Today Shippen's grandchildren maintain the John Shippen Memorial Golf Foundation, which heralds Shippen's love of athletics and his father's and wife's passion for education. Each year the foundation sponsors an annual golf tournament that uses the proceeds to generate scholarships for minority athletes excelling in academics.[103]

American golfers, be they upstart summer colony members or urban enclaves of African Americans, have benefited from Shippen's passion, initiative, and example. Though he was so integral to the rise of golf's popularity in two communities separated by decades, geography, and racial identity, the initial respect he received from both groups never matched his social acceptance. Shippen's early personal and social life remained among the Shinnecock. In his last post he became a beleaguered fixture in the clubhouse. The ascent of professional golf in America left little space for professionals like Shippen. Due to the availability of white American-born professionals, the phenomenon of sporting celebrities, and the PGA's efforts to preserve a white membership and invitation circuit, golf yielded to the Jim Crowism that pervaded so many spheres of American life and continued to define the front nine of American golf. Despite such drawbacks, Shippen left a legacy as a pioneer who challenged racial stereotypes, transcended social boundaries, and exemplified the potential for disruptive performances, even on the more hallowed stages of American sport.

## Notes

1. Richard Moss, *Golf and the American Country Club* (Urbana: University of Illinois Press, 2001), 47.

2. Cory Dolgan, *The End of the Hamptons: Scenes from the Class Struggle in America's Paradise* (New York: New York University Press, 2005), 261.

3. "John M. Shippen, 90, Early Negro Golfer," *New York Times*, May 22, 1968, 47.

4. Peter Aviles, "A Talk with Hanno Shippen Smith, Grandson of John Shippen Jr.," November 28, 2004, http://blackathlete.net/2004/11/a-talk-with-hanno-shippen -smith-grandson-of-john-shippen-jr/ (accessed March 3, 2009); Averill Dayton Gues, *Maidstone Club: The Second Fifty Years, 1941–1991* (Kennebunk ME: Phoenix Publishing, 1991), 96–98; "John Shippen Biography," John Shippen Memorial Golf Foundation, http://johnshippen.net/john-shippen-biography.html (accessed July 12, 2014); Moss, *Golf and the American Country Club*, 39–40; Calvin H. Sinnette, *Forbidden Fairways: African Americans and the Game of Golf* (Chelsea MI: Sleeping Bear Press, 1998), 24–25; Phillip St. Laurent, "The Negro in World History—John Shippen," *Tuesday Magazine*, April 1969, 17; Frank Strafaci, "Forgotten Pioneer Professional," *Golfing*, March 1957, 11.

5. The East End of Long Island was primarily occupied by Manhassett, Montaukett, and Shinnecock Indians; the southern shore by Canarsee, Rockaway, Merrick, Marsapeague, Secatogue, and Unkechaug; and the northern shore by

Matinecock, Nesaquake, Setalcott, and Corchaug tribes. During colonial rule many codes were created, though often not enforced. Strong notes that the economic constraints were in full effect by 1680. Quote from John Strong, *The Algonquin Peoples of Long Island from the Earliest Times to 1700* (Interlaken NY: Empire State Press, 1997), 274, cited in Dolgan, *The End of the Hamptons*, 162.

6. Dolgan, *The End of the Hamptons*, 162.

7. Lynda R. Day, *Making a Way to Freedom: A History of African Americans on Long Island* (Interlaken NY: Empire State Press, 1997), 89.

8. Dolgan, *The End of the Hamptons*, 163.

9. David Goddard, *Colonizing Southampton: The Transformation of a Long Island Community, 1870–1900* (Albany: State University of New York Press, 2011), 47.

10. John Strong, *"We Are Still Here!": The Algonquin Peoples of Long Island* (Interlaken NY: Empire State Press, 1998), 21.

11. Day, *Making a Way to Freedom*, 89.

12. Strong, *"We Are Still Here!,"* 23–26.

13. Dolgan, *The End of the Hamptons*, 163–64; Day, *Making a Way to Freedom*, 107–10.

14. Quote from Brewton Berry, *Almost White* (New York: Macmillan, 1963), 33, in Strong, *"We Are Still Here!,"* 11.

15. Goddard, *Colonizing Southampton*, 47–48.

16. Dolgan, *The End of the Hamptons*, 22.

17. Dolgan, *The End of the Hamptons*, 23.

18. Helen A. Harrison and Constance Ayers Denne, *Hamptons Bohemia: Two Centuries of Writers and Artists on the Beach* (San Francisco: Chronicle Books LLC, 2002), 44.

19. Quote from Charles de Kay, "East Hampton the Restful," *New York Times*, October 30, 1898, 34–35, in Harrison and Denne, *Hamptons Bohemia*, 56.

20. D. Scott Atkinson and Nicolai Cikovsky, *William Merritt Chase: Summers at Shinnecock, 1891–1902* (Washington DC: National Gallery of Art, 1987); Dolgan, *The End of the Hamptons*, 23.

21. Dolgan, *The End of the Hamptons*, 25.

22. Dolgan, *The End of the Hamptons*, 25–26.

23. Sinnette, *Forbidden Fairways*, 17.

24. Edward Lyle Fox, "Country Clubs for Everybody," *Outing* 61, no. 1 (October 1912): 116.

25. Moss, *Golf and the American Country Club*, 6.

26. Moss, *Golf and the American Country Club*, 17–18.

27. Moss, *Golf and the American Country Club*, 5.

28. Moss, *Golf and the American Country Club*, 7.

29. Moss, *Golf and the American Country Club*, 12, 8.

30. Moss, *Golf and the American Country Club*, 19.

31. Goddard, *Colonizing Southampton*, 260–61.

32. Moss, *Golf and the American Country Club*, 21.

33. Gues, *Maidstone Club*, 96–97.

34. Moss, *Golf and the American Country Club*, 25.

35. Quote from James Britton, unpublished autobiography, in Harrison and Denne, *Hamptons Bohemia*, 58.

36. Goddard, *Colonizing Southampton*, 243.

37. Dolgan, *The End of the Hamptons*, 27; Moss, *Golf and the American Country Club*, 25; Helen M. Wetterau, *Shinnecock Hills Long Ago* (East Patchogue NY: Searles Graphics, 1991), 41.

38. Goddard, *Colonizing Southampton*, 246–47; James M. Mayo, *The American Country Club: Its Origins and Development* (New Brunswick NJ: Rutgers University Press, 1998), 72.

39. Price Collier, "Golf in America to Date," *Outing* 29, no. 3 (December 1896): 278. Marvin P. Dawkins and Graham C. Kinloch, *African American Golfers during the Jim Crow Era* (Westport CT: Praeger, 2000), 15; Jerome D. Travers, "First Impressions of Scottish Golf," *American Golfer* 1, no. 8 (1909): 434–35.

40. Quoted in Ross Goodner, *Shinnecock Hills Golf Club, 1891–1966* (Southampton NY: Shinnecock Hills Golf Club, 1966), 8–9, in Mayo, *The American Country Club*, 76; Sinnette, *Forbidden Fairways*, 18.

41. Albion, "Golf," *Outing* 32, no. 5 (August 1898): 539.

42. Moss, *Golf and the American Country Club*, 41.

43. Price Collier, "Golf," *Outing* 37, no. 2 (November 1900): 243.

44. Albion, "Golf," 539.

45. Albion, "Golf," 539.

46. Moss, *Golf and the American Country Club*, 39–40.

47. Moss, *Golf and the American Country Club*, 51–52.

48. Collier, "Golf," 273.

49. St. Laurent, "The Negro in World History," 30.

50. P. C., "Golf," *Outing* 30, no. 1 (April 1897): 97.

51. P. C., "Golf," *Outing* 30, no. 1 (April 1897): 97.

52. Collier, "Golf," *Outing* 37, no. 2 (November 1900): 243.

53. Collier, "Golf," *Outing* 37, no. 2 (November 1900): 243.

54. Collier, "Golf," *Outing* 37, no. 2 (November 1900): 243.

55. Price Collier, "Golf," *Outing* 37, no. 4 (January 1901): 492.

56. Henry Leach, "The U.S. Open Championship," *American Golfer* 10, no. 3 (July 1913): 573.

57. Dawkins and Kinloch, *African American Golfers during the Jim Crow Era*, 132.

58. Sinnette, *Forbidden Fairways*, 37–39; Robert Fernandez and Dan Levinson, directors, *Uneven Fairways*, DVD (New York: Moxie Films and Golf Channel, 2009).

59. Sinnette, *Forbidden Fairways*, 43.

60. Charles McGrath, "Behind the Ropes at Shinnecock, a Deep-Rooted Union Frays," *New York Times*, June 11, 2004, http://www.nytimes.com/2004/06/11/sports /golf-behind-the-ropes-at-shinnecock-a-deep-rooted-union-frays.html (accessed June 10, 2014).

61. Dawkins and Kinloch, *African American Golfers during the Jim Crow Era*, 15.

62. Moss, *Golf and the American Country Club*, 52; Sinnette, *Forbidden Fairways*, 17; Strong, *"We Are Still Here!,"* 23–26.

63. Quoted in St. Laurent, "The Negro in World History," 17.

64. Dawkins and Kinloch, *African American Golfers during the Jim Crow Era*, 15.

65. Moss, *Golf and the American Country Club*, 53; Dawkins and Kinloch, *African American Golfers during the Jim Crow Era*, 14; Sinnette, *Forbidden Fairways*, 18.

66. C. Turner, "Golf," *Outing* 28, no. 6 (September 1896): 141; see also Moss, *Golf and the American Country Club*, 52–54.

67. P. C., "Golf," *Outing* 30, no. 1 (April 1897): 98.

68. Moss, *Golf and the American Country Club*, 54.

69. U.S. economic output surpassed that of Great Britain by 1893, and the United States would soon embark on its own imperial venture in the Spanish-American War of 1898.

70. Turner, "Golf," 141.

71. "Foulis Was Best Golfer," *New York Times*, July 19, 1896, 3.

72. Quoted in St. Laurent, "The Negro in World History," 17.

73. Quoted in St. Laurent, "The Negro in World History," 17.

74. Quoted in St. Laurent, "The Negro in World History," 17.

75. "Foulis Was Best Golfer," 3; Moss, *Golf and the American Country Club*, 53; Dawkins and Kinloch, *African American Golfers during the Jim Crow Era*, 15; Sinnette, *Forbidden Fairways*, 19; St. Laurent, "The Negro in World History," 17.

76. Turner, "Golf," 141; "Foulis Was Best Golfer," 3.

77. Collier "Golf in America to Date," 279.

78. Horace G. Hutchinson, "A Gossip on Golf," *Outing* 29, no. 2 (November 1896): 156–61; Horace G. Hutchinson, "Fifty Years of Golf: The Fourteenth Installment of Golfing Reminiscences of Great Britain's First Amateur Champion," *Golf Illustrated* 3, no. 3 (June 1915): 41.

79. Gues, *Maidstone Club*, 96–97.

80. Gues, *Maidstone Club*, vii.

81. Quote from "Golf," *Outing*, October 1887, in Sinnette, *Forbidden Fairways*, 20.

82. "John Shippen Biography"; St. Laurent, "The Negro in World History," 17; Strafaci, "Forgotten Pioneer Professional," 11.

83. Gues, *Maidstone Club*, 96–98.

84. Aviles, "A Talk with Hanno Shippen Smith"; Sinnette, *Forbidden Fairways*, 23–25.

85. Sinnette, *Forbidden Fairways*, 26; "History Detectives: John Shippen Golf Club, Southampton, Long Island," Public Broadcasting System, http://www-tc.pbs.org/opb/historydetectives/static/media/transcripts/2011-04-22/212_golf.pdf (accessed June 5, 2014).

86. P. C., "Golf," *Outing* 30, no. 1 (April 1897): 97.

87. Phillip St. Laurent, "The Negro in World History—John Shippen," *Tuesday Magazine*, April 1969, 30.

88. Shippen's drinking benders were well known by many members of the Shady Rest Country Club.

89. Sinnette, *Forbidden Fairways*, 20–22.

90. Dawkins and Kinloch, *African American Golfers during the Jim Crow Era*, 8–9, 16–17; Moss, *Golf and the American Country Club*, 112; Sinnette, *Forbidden Fairways*, 30–32.

91. Quoted in Dawkins and Kinloch, *African American Golfers during the Jim Crow Era*, 8; Fernandez and Levinson, *Uneven Fairways*.

92. St. Laurent, "The Negro in World History," 30.

93. Sinnette, *Forbidden Fairways*, 51.

94. Sinnette, *Forbidden Fairways*, 51–57.

95. Dawkins and Kinloch, *African American Golfers during the Jim Crow Era*, 7; Sinnette, *Forbidden Fairways*, 58–59.

96. Sinnette, *Forbidden Fairways*, 58–59; Dawkins and Kinloch, *African American Golfers during the Jim Crow Era*, 27.

97. Dawkins and Kinloch, *African American Golfers during the Jim Crow Era*, 27; Sinnette, *Forbidden Fairways*, 58–59.

98. Dawkins and Kinloch, *African American Golfers during the Jim Crow Era*, 23; Sinnette, *Forbidden Fairways*, 22; St. Laurent, "The Negro in World History," 30.

99. Sinnette, *Forbidden Fairways*, 61.

100. Sinnette, *Forbidden Fairways*, 57–61; Fernandez and Levinson, *Uneven Fairways*; Anthony Venotulo, "Shady Rest in Scotch Plains Was the First African-American Club of Its Kind," *Star Ledger*, February 19, 2009, http://blog.nj.com/ledger archives/2009/02/country_club_life.html (accessed July 15, 2014).

101. "Hutchinson Defeats Shippen," *New York Times*, June 26, 1900, 8; Sinnette, *Forbidden Fairways*, 22–23.

102. "PCA Caddie Hall of Fame," Thecaddieassociation.com, http://thecaddie association.com/pca-caddie-hall-of-fame.php (accessed June 29, 2014).

103. Aviles, "A Talk with Hanno Shippen Smith"; Sinnette, *Forbidden Fairways*, 24–25.

# THREE

## When Great Wasn't Good Enough

*Sam Ransom's Journey from Athlete to Activist*

GERALD R. GEMS

The Emancipation Proclamation of 1863, sanctioned by the Thirteenth Amendment to the Constitution in 1865 promised an end to slavery in the United States. The radical Reconstruction of the South in the aftermath of the Civil War seemingly gave African Americans their long-sought inclusion in the mainstream society. Former slaves gained citizenship, civil rights, and suffrage. Blacks were elected to the U.S. Congress, state legislatures, and local offices throughout the South, but such progress proved short lived. The Ku Klux Klan, founded in 1866, began to impose terror and intimidation on southern blacks as its vigilante operations spread throughout the region. Moreover, the disputed presidential election of 1876 resulted in a political compromise that enabled white southerners to restore their primacy throughout the South, subjecting blacks to peonage as sharecroppers and enacting Jim Crow laws that enforced segregation policies and curtailed suffrage rights. The brief glimpse of equality quickly lapsed into pre–Civil War social, economic, and political patterns of white hegemony and racial oppression.

Free blacks living in the urban centers of the North enjoyed much greater latitude. They established their own newspapers throughout the nineteenth century, and they began urging their southern brethren to seek better lives in northern states, where jobs, education, and opportunities awaited. In Chicago John Jones served on the County

Board of Commissioners as early as 1871, and John Thomas won election to the state legislature five years later. The urban centers of Chicago and New York seemed especially attractive to southern blacks, and many thousands headed northward over the succeeding decades.[1]

Sport, as an integral component of popular culture in the cities, often provided greater opportunity for blacks than the high culture that whites reserved for themselves. Popular culture celebrated physicality, a standard that afforded blacks some roles in both sport and music as long as they did not upset the established social hierarchy. While racial attitudes were not as stringent in the North as they were in the South, most whites held strong beliefs in the tenets of Social Darwinism, which prescribed an inferior place to blacks in the society. Sport allowed blacks to test such convictions. In 1884 Moses Fleetwood Walker and his brother Weldy played major league baseball for the Toledo team in the American Association until Adrian "Cap" Anson, captain of the Chicago White Stockings, objected to the use of black competitors. Major League teams banned blacks from the national pastime thereafter. Black ballplayers continued to compete at lower levels, and contingents of black players formed their own barnstorming and local baseball teams in the East and throughout the Midwest. By the turn of the century black teams such as the Chicago Union Giants and Chicago American Giants dominated play. The teams joined forces to challenge white teams in the Chicago City League from 1901 to 1904. Black baseball teams often used John Schorling's park for their games, near the stadium of the American League Chicago White Sox. Schorling, a white man, would later partner with star black pitcher Rube Foster to found the Chicago American Giants. Such a seemingly relaxed atmosphere relative to the separate race relations in the South portrayed the possibilities for a more harmonious society.[2]

Star black athletes found even greater recognition and reward on the collegiate football fields of the North. George Jewett starred as a running back and kicker for the University of Michigan in 1890, but his outstanding play antagonized rival fans. Purdue fans stood and cheered when Jewett had to be carried unconscious from the field in 1892. A teammate admitted that "he undoubtedly was the best player on the Michigan team of 1890," and when an Indianapolis hotel manager refused him service, his white teammates forced the proprietor to retract the decision. Jewett left Michigan to enter the medical school at Northwestern University, where he continued to play for that team for two more years.[3]

In Massachusetts, Amherst fielded two black stars on its football team in halfback William Tecumseh Sherman Jackson and William Henry Lewis, center and captain. Lewis moved on to Harvard Law School and earned All-American honors at center during 1892 and 1893, becoming the first black player to gain such national distinction. Lewis stated that football enabled him "to regard with indifference trifling insults or severe physical hurts." He then coached the Harvard team for several years before turning to politics as a city councilman, state legislator, and assistant U.S. attorney general. Sport thus provided Lewis with a level of celebrity and an opportunity for education and social mobility.[4]

The new game of basketball, invented at the Springfield, Massachusetts, YMCA in 1891, also afforded urban blacks the opportunity to compete with teams in urban centers such as New York, Chicago, Philadelphia, and Washington DC. Such competitions often included dances and musical accompaniment as sport merged with other elements of the popular culture.

Within the popular culture of the South even slaves had been allowed to entertain whites, and they might even be rewarded lavishly for their efforts. Black jockeys such as the Kentucky Derby winners Isaac Murphy, Willie Sims, and Jimmy Winkfield earned handsome sums as employees of the thoroughbred owners, who won the acclaim and the prize money as victors. The best black heavyweight boxer of the late nineteenth century, Peter Jackson, plied his trade gainfully, as whites expected black fighters to be pummeled by their white opponents for the fans' amusement. Southern white men corralled black youths to engage in "battle royals" in which blindfolded fighters fought to the finish until the last one standing might be rewarded with coins or cheers. But when Jackson fought a sixty-one-round draw with the popular James J. Corbett in 1891, he challenged the notions of white supremacy. After Corbett defeated the seemingly invincible John L. Sullivan for the title a year later, Jackson was subsequently denied any opportunity to garner the world championship that symbolically portrayed racial and masculine supremacy.[5]

In 1896 the U.S. Supreme Court rationalized and legalized southern segregation practices in the case of *Plessy v. Ferguson*, in which a New Orleans mulatto unsuccessfully challenged the separate seating arrangements in a railroad car. Black leaders in the North and South disagreed on the quest for achieving racial equality within the country. Booker T. Washington, founder of the Tuskegee Institute in Alabama, cautioned a slow, accommodationist approach, teaching vocational skills to his black students so that they might acquire jobs in the dominant capitalist economy. W. E. B. Du Bois, a PhD with a Harvard degree, countered Washington's philosophy with his belief that a separation of the races forced blacks to experience a double consciousness as second-class and inferior citizens and that a "talented tenth" (such as William Henry Lewis) of African Americans could compete with whites on equal ground.[6]

African Americans increasingly heeded the voice of Du Bois, many heading north for better life chances. The Ransom family did not wait for such admonitions. They preceded the exodus to the North, traveling to Illinois, where their son Samuel was born on the Fourth of July in 1883. Sammy Ransom entered Hyde Park High School in Chicago in 1899, paying for his expenses by working as a hotel bellhop. At Hyde Park he was a good student but became an exceptional athlete, starring in football, baseball, basketball, and track, yet his success demonstrated the liminal status of blacks in American society at the turn of the twentieth century. Although Ransom labored in the shadow of his white teammate, Walter Eckersall, a future All-American at the University of Chicago, he was lauded as an outstanding talent in his own right. The Chicago newspapers praised his exploits with rarely a mention of his race as the Hyde Park teams claimed the Cook County, regional, and even national championships. A 1904 school publication acknowledged Ransom as "ever reliable . . . attracted favorable criticism from friend and foe."[7]

As a baseball player, Ransom excelled at several positions: pitcher, catcher, and infield, with Hyde Park winning the league championship from 1901 to 1903. In 1901 Ransom caught as Fred Beebe pitched in what was described as the "the best battery ever developed at a Western prep school." They were also the "heaviest hitters." Beebe left school and later turned pro. In 1902 Ransom took up the pitching chores and displayed a strong arm on the mound as the team traveled to Indiana, Michigan, and Wisconsin. Hyde Park engaged both other high schools and college teams in its competitions, and Ransom threw seven innings of shutout ball in defeating the University of Wisconsin team. "Ransom's work as a pitcher in these three games won for him the respect of even the Wisconsin supporters."[8] Against Oak Park High School Ransom played catcher, and after he had made two throws to second base, the opponents abandoned any further attempts to steal a base. In a game at Delavan, Wisconsin, Ransom hit a home run so far that it was never found. When the baseball team was expelled from the city league for an unauthorized game in Michigan, Ransom managed to arrange an unofficial game with the league champion, North Division High School, and Hyde Park prevailed 12–0. In 1903 the team elected him its captain, and it went undefeated in league play. Hyde Park won three of five games against the University of Chicago squads, with Ransom getting two of the three Hyde Park hits and scoring its only run in one of the losses. In the other loss he had three of the five hits. It was clear that he could play at the college level. When the high school team defeated the university freshmen by a score of 10–4, Ransom accounted for three hits as the leadoff batter and stole five bases. The *Inter Ocean* newspaper stated that Sam Ransom "is a colored boy and captain of the (Hyde Park) team. He is a natural-born ball player and knows the fine points of the game from A to Z. He plays at shortstop and covers all the territory between third base and right field. His batting eye is excellent and he can pilfer more bases in a given length of time than any prep in the business." With Ransom at the helm the Hyde Park team also beat Valparaiso College and even defeated the professional Chicago Union Giants, 8–3, in 1903.[9]

The Hyde Park track team also captured the state championship in 1902 with Eckersall competing in the sprints and Ransom scoring in the field events as a long jumper and shot-putter. A Chicago sportswriter recalled that "Ransom could play any game well and what a gentleman he was. I remember him at one indoor meet in which the opponents of his team were being hissed by his school. Ransom came out on the floor and held up his hand for silence. He got it. 'White people,' he said with a most appealing grin. 'Do you have to have a negro [sic] tell you to be fair to white folks?' They yelled the roof off and there was no more hissing."[10] In basketball too Hyde Park captured the 1903 county basketball championship with Ransom at the guard and forward positions. Football, however, captured the imagination of both college and high school sports fans, superseding the national game of baseball on campuses by the 1880s.[11]

The University of Chicago opened in 1892, and sports, especially football, served as a major means of marketing and revenue for the upstart institution. Youthful president William Rainey Harper hired his Yale acquaintance, Amos Alonzo Stagg, a football All-American and star baseball pitcher, to serve as athletic director and head of the Physical Education Department, with faculty rank and at a salary greater than that of other esteemed professors. Stagg and many other college coaches came under fire for proselytizing high school athletes. Stagg drew the particular ire of Edwin G. Cooley, superintendent of the Chicago schools, as he scheduled games or scrimmages against local high schools, allowed them to use the university facilities, and hosted interscholastic track meets and later a national high school basketball tournament. By so doing, Stagg could identify and evaluate the most promising talent, who might then be offered athletic scholarships to the university. By 1905 eight of the eleven players on his national championship football team came from local high schools.[12]

Stagg knew the nearby Hyde Park contingents well. In 1900 his University of Chicago football team barely beat Hyde Park, 5–0. As a freshman, Ransom starred as a halfback, distinguishing himself by long and elusive runs. The next year he scored on a 40-yard run against the Chicago Dental College team, but 1902 brought the greatest accolades to the school and its players. Hyde Park traveled to Madison, Wisconsin, to play the state university in football, a game the collegians took lightly. They particularly targeted Ransom for abuse, but the stalwart black blocked a kick that resulted in a score, and the game was tied at the half. Although the older, heavier collegians eventually triumphed, they had learned a lesson in respect. After Hyde Park steamrolled its rival, Englewood High, 57–0, and then claimed the county championship, both Walter Eckersall and Sammy Ransom were named to the *Chicago Tribune*'s all-city team. Hyde Park arranged a postseason game with the Manual Training School in Louisville, Kentucky, for November, but the southerners refused to let Ransom play. Hyde Park then offered to play Brooklyn Poly in what was billed as the national high school championship. The top eastern colleges declined to play the midwestern powers and safeguarded their top rankings by adhering to their traditional mass plays in internecine competitions. Midwestern colleges featured a more open strategy based on speed, end runs, and reverses. The contest served as a surrogate battle between different regional styles. The Brooklyn boys were coached by Harvard players (including their captain, Robert Kernan), who were alums of the high school. Stagg offered to coach the Hyde Park team for two weeks on his own field, where the game was to be played in a showdown of competing systems. The media promotion surpassed the game of football as rapidly growing Chicago challenged New York for cultural supremacy beyond the athletic field. The game proved to be anticlimactic. Hyde Park's speed overwhelmed Brooklyn, 105–0, as Ransom scored seven touchdowns.[13]

The *Chicago Tribune* asserted that "Ransom was the particular star of the game. It was Sammy who was always in evidence, running now around one end and now the other, gaining twenty, thirty, forty yards with ease, always on hand when a fumble was made[,] ready to fall on the ball. Ransom it was who made touchdown after touchdown, Ransom the irresistible."[14]

Walter Eckersall, the team quarterback, punter, and sprint champion was ardently courted by the college coaches, particularly Stagg at Chicago and Fielding Yost, Stagg's chief rival at the University of Michigan. Stagg won out by allegedly extracting him from a train bound for Michigan and managed to get Eckersall into the university despite his lack of credits for graduation at Hyde Park. He enrolled in the fall of 1903 and would become the mainstay of Stagg's teams as a quarterback over the next few years and a three-time All-American, but he was twice banished from school and left with unpaid debts and without a degree.[15]

With the departure of Eckersall from Hyde Park, Ransom's brilliance showed even more brightly in 1903. The yearbook referred to his leadership on the football team, noting that "Sam was every place," and the newspapers covered his performances weekly. Stagg allowed the Hyde Park team to practice at the university's field during the football season, and Eckersall was one of eight alumni who began coaching the team. Despite Hyde Park's falling one game short of the championship with a young team, Ransom was again elected to the *Daily News* all-star team, yet the top football schools seemed uninterested in his services. Seven of Ransom's white Hyde Park teammates went to Michigan, and five played on its football teams. When Coach Yost at Michigan was informed of Abner Powell, a black schoolboy sensation in Salt Lake City who weighed 180 pounds and ran one hundred yards in ten seconds, it proved to no avail. Coach Yost seemingly had an aversion to black players during his long tenure at the institution, never awarding a football letter to an African American athlete, and there is no evidence that he pursued Ransom.[16]

At Chicago President Harper sought greater credibility for his new institution by stipulating distinct social relationships. As early as 1895 he admonished Stagg because "we have had a series of [baseball] games with negroes etc. [*sic*] which has brought disgrace upon us."[17] Stagg apparently tried to recruit Ransom, "who considered entering Chicago, but dropped out at the last moment," according to the *Chicago Daily News*. The newspaper speculated that Ransom lacked the necessary academic preparation, but Stagg had managed to get Eckersall and other white athletes enrolled.[18] More than two decades after Harper's admonition, when Dan McGugin, the football coach at Vanderbilt in Tennessee, sought a game with Chicago, he wanted assurances that race would not be an issue. Stagg wrote that "we have no negroes [*sic*] on the University of Chicago football team, and there is no chance of there being any candidates for the team next fall. Up to date there has never been a negro on a University of Chicago team. In twenty-four years only three negroes have competed . . . in track athletics." Some coaches thus negated the promise of education and equal opportunity by limiting the complexion of their teams.[19]

Despite his acknowledged athletic abilities, leadership, and friendliness, Ransom led a marginalized existence even within the confines of the high school. All clubs and fraternities were reserved for whites. As was the case for his adult peers, sport provided one of the few means for a measure of acceptance, recognition, and self-worth. Despite the snubs by college coaches Ransom knew that he was not only the equal of but better than whites on the athletic fields. Even the white mainstream newspapers named him to a succession of all-city and all-county teams.[20]

Ransom took his athletic talents to tiny Beloit College in Wisconsin, where he quarterbacked the football team, captained the baseball team, and led the basketball team to winning records, going undefeated in 1908. He lettered in four sports against Western Conference (today's Big Ten) competition. Despite achieving all-league honors Ransom departed the school short of earning a degree after three years to seek his fortunes with black professional baseball and football teams in St. Paul, Minnesota, while his white high school teammates gained All-American accolades at major universities. (The yearbook lamented the loss of an athlete "as good as any the college has ever had.")[21] Ransom's venture proved short-lived, and he moved on to coach at Meharry College and Lane College, two black schools in Tennessee. There he led Meharry to championship football seasons in 1909, 1910, and 1911 and returned for one year at Lane in 1916.[22]

While Ransom may have followed an accommodationist path as a youth, he began to develop a greater racial consciousness as he grew older. Blacks began to realize that the opportunities of the North resulted in less than they promised. While the majority of the freedmen and their children remained shackled by institutionalized segregation in the South, progressive reformers struggled to assimilate the throngs of European migrants who overwhelmed the urban centers in the North. The small numbers of blacks who resided there before 1900 were relatively neglected. That brief time period allowed a historical window where black athletes, unfettered by the lack of a cohesive racial ideology, gained limited access to the white sporting culture. A few, such as Ransom, gained a toehold and prospered, albeit unequally and temporarily. As black baseball players, black jockeys, and Marshall "Major" Taylor, a world champion cyclist who trained in Chicago, began to threaten the tenets of Social Darwinism, the progressive ideology relative to people of color began to crystallize in a reactionary fashion. Whites chafed at losses to those of darker skin, whom they considered physically and intellectually inferior. Taylor had set seven world records between 1898 and 1900, but jealous white rivals conspired to block and obstruct his efforts during races. After 1901 he traveled to Europe and Australia to compete, winning as much as $10,000 annually. By 1904 President Theodore Roosevelt had proposed that "blacks would progress by subordinating themselves to white men of high character who would then protect them." Other people of color, such as the Chinese, who held no inherent birthright to American citizenship, faced complete exclusion by law after 1902.[23]

A Chicago Parks Commission report of 1907 indicated the white sentiments and the development of segregationist policies. The report stated that "it may be that those of the colored race have not been made to feel at home in the playgrounds by white children. . . . For the welfare of the colored children . . . give them a playground to themselves."[24]

A similar pattern of exclusion relative to blacks assumed greater proportions thereafter, exacerbated by the greatest black sporting icon of the early twentieth century. While successful black athletes like Ransom had operated within the established social system, Jack Johnson threatened to completely overturn it. Johnson traveled northward from his birthplace in Galveston, Texas, eventually settling in Chicago. Acknowledged as "the colored heavyweight champion" by 1903, Johnson chased the white champion, Tommy Burns, around the world to Australia, where a promoter offered the then astronomical sum of $30,000 if Burns would give Johnson a shot at the world title. George Dixon and Joe Gans, both black fighters, had previously won world championships at lighter weights, but the heavyweight title, from which all blacks since Peter Jackson had been systematically excluded, symbolized the ultimate prize in the individual combat that carried distinct connotations for the Social Darwinian belief in white superiority. Johnson toyed with, then battered, the overmatched Burns in a meeting that would never have taken place in the United States. Johnson not only reveled in his new celebrity, but he also defied white presumptions and the established racial and social etiquette by his very public liaisons and eventual marriages to white women. Moreover, Johnson established a cabaret in Chicago where the races might mingle and listen to the popular black ragtime music that transcended class and racial lines. Outraged whites embarked on a crusade to find a "Great White Hope" who might restore their honor by putting Johnson in his place and reclaiming the crown. When Johnson repeatedly defeated such adversaries, blacks regaled such successes, which reinforced their pride and fostered racial consciousness. Whites then prevailed upon the undefeated previous champion, Jim Jeffries, to come out of retirement to finally resolve the issue in whites' favor. A large crowd, estimated at eight thousand, gathered at Johnson's Chicago home amid rockets and foghorns for his sendoff, and the *Chicago Defender*, a black newspaper, gave front-page coverage to the upcoming event, stating that "the future welfare of his people forms a part of the stake."[25]

Johnson's own pronouncements clarified matters for other blacks, as he declared that they must stick together in the face of the opposition united against them. His most ardent followers responded by chartering a train to go and lend their support at the fight.[26]

The bout took place in Reno, Nevada, on July 4, 1910, and drew a global audience but much to the chagrin of most, Johnson prevailed easily, the first opponent to ever send Jeffries to the canvas. The result engendered race riots throughout the nation, and black boys and young men reasoned that they no longer needed to subject themselves to white oppression. Unable to conquer Johnson in the ring, the federal government prosecuted him under the Mann Act, which banned the transport of women across state lines for illicit purposes. Johnson became a fugitive and roamed the world, holding the title until 1915.[27]

As Johnson reigned over the heavyweight ranks, black intellectual heavyweights, including W. E. B. Du Bois, founded the National Association for the Advancement of Colored People (NAACP) in 1909 to seek greater civil rights for all blacks. In 1912 Ida Wells Barnett, a black civic leader in Chicago, complained that YMCAs, the Salvation Army, and the Mills hotels all excluded blacks. A separate black YMCA was established the following year, and the federal government also moved to segregate its personnel. When black encroachment on Chicago's parks reached sufficient proportions, a black park director was appointed with the implicit understanding that the park had become a "black" park, no longer suitable for whites. The segregation of schools and housing patterns followed in like manner, forcing blacks to develop parallel civic, social, and community institutions.[28]

Returning to St. Paul during his Tennessee sojourns, Ransom initiated such organizations in his adopted city. He became a trustee of the Pilgrim Baptist Church and a member of the NAACP, a grand master of the Masons, and a patron of the Eastern Star. When the United States considered entry into World War I, Ransom traveled back to Illinois to enlist in the army, one of the few African Americans to do so. His St. Paul clubmates honored him with a banquet that ended with all present signing a petition to President Woodrow Wilson and House and Senate committees protesting the recent race riot in East St. Louis, Illinois, which took place on July 2, 1917, cost the lives of forty blacks and eight whites and forced six thousand from their homes. The blacks had been employed in local factories with government contracts producing war materials.[29]

White laborers perceived a similar threat to their jobs in Chicago as up to a million southern blacks migrated northward in search of a better life between 1916 and 1919. Excluded from most labor unions, African Americans devised their own strategies for survival. The Urban League, established in 1910, negotiated jobs with employers, promising docile workers to replace those on strike or called to military service. By 1917 blacks constituted 25 percent of all workers in the Chicago stockyards. A labor issue quickly became a racial one in Chicago, and the tension transcended the workplace. Employers provided financial support for black churches in exchange for the clerics' anti-union stance. The alliance of the ministers and the industrialists led to the sponsorship of athletic teams in organizational structures segregated from the mainstream. The separate black YMCAS, endowed by corporate interests, intended to limit racial mixing and potential alliances between white and black workers in their leisure time. Such seclusion only exacerbated the strife and culminated in a race riot in 1919, when whites stoned a black youth who had crossed a line demarcating segregated sections of a beach. He consequently drowned, and the resultant riot lasted two weeks, cost thirty-eight lives, and required intercession by the national guard to end the hostilities. Militant black soldiers returning from the battlefields of France safeguarded their neighborhoods, no longer willing to submit to white domination.[30]

When the numbers of blacks in the North reached a tipping point around World War I, progressive reformers and some sociologists transferred their attention from the European immigrant hordes who had settled in the industrial centers to the rising tide of African Americans. As one of the primary sites of black settlement, Chicago drew an inordinate amount of attention, and the earliest studies of African American urban culture emanated from the University of Chicago Press in the 1920s. Robert Park, head of the university's sociology department, claimed that blacks emulated whites as they lost their African influences. E. Franklin Frazier, a black student of Park, differed with his mentor by stating that the lack of social intimacy between the races precluded any sense of identification with whites. Blacks acculturated to a degree, but segregation did not allow for full assimilation, and such practices led to a self-perception of black identity first and American identity second. Oscar Handlin, in his *Fire Bell in the Night*, later contended that the black situation had been self-imposed, while Allan Spear reasoned that such conditions were imposed by white hostility and racial oppression. Only Spear, in his *Black Chicago*, touched upon the role of sport in the process of alienation.[31] Sport might be used by its practitioners to include or exclude participants in the formation of a society or a nation (i.e., the symbolic importance of Joe Louis or Jackie Robinson for African Americans or Joe DiMaggio for Italian Americans).[32]

In the army Ransom gained promotion to the rank of lieutenant and trained recruits for initial assignment to border duty in the Southwest. In transit to Texas, members of his unit tore down Jim Crow signs in the train stations of the South and even looted a store that refused to serve them. The unit was later reassigned to duty in France. Sport proved a means of social control yet fostered an aggressive spirit during soldiers' leisure time. Ransom continued his own sport participation in the military by helping his division to athletic honors in baseball and track competitions in an era when military units were still segregated. Combat, however, curtailed such endeavors. Ransom's unit engaged in some of the most vicious fighting of the war, particularly in the Meuse-Argonne offensive of 1918, and the casualty lists numbered him among the severely wounded. When the Eighth Illinois Regiment returned to Chicago in early 1919, it was roundly feted with a jubilant parade and homecoming celebration. Ransom returned to St. Paul, where he initially resumed work in a businessman's club and then gained work as a mail clerk for the U.S. postal service. He became an active member of the workers' union and continued his service in the national guard, winning promotion to major. He married later in life but had no children.[33]

By that time sport had assumed more strained relationships between whites and blacks. Blacks faced a rash of lynchings in the South, and the Ku Klux Klan had spread its threats to the northern states in the aftermath of the war. Some of the ethnic immigrant groups displayed their claim to whiteness by participating in nativist raids on black neighborhoods and battling over the rights to swimming pools and ball fields in the parks. In Chicago violent beatings, fire bombings, arson, and murder assured the ghettoization of black residents. Most blacks realized that their hopes of full equality in America had proved to be no more than a pipe dream. Nearly half a million supported Marcus Garvey's "Back to Africa" movement and his call for blacks' self-sufficiency.[34]

Rube Foster, born in 1879 in Texas, where he started his baseball career, moved to Chicago to join the Leland Giants after the turn of the century, but he formed his own team and booked games for others. In the aftermath of the Chicago race riot and still faced with the black ban in the white major leagues, Foster organized the Negro National League, which allowed African American ballplayers a measure of independence and a means to display their talents and retain their pride. When barnstorming, however, even the black professionals sometimes had to resort to clowning, a style of play that had served their ancestors well by mixing sport with entertainment. Such practices permitted blacks to mask or express feelings behind the veil of acceptable behavior. The timeworn methods of coping provided a measure of solidarity and power to them as tricksters who might outwit presumably superior foes. Such a style enhanced the commercial possibilities for black teams, but it also demeaned their skills, relegating them to practices more acceptable to their white audiences. Only when they encountered overt racism did the players retaliate by running up the score. Black baseball teams often played only well enough to win and even occasionally lost on purpose so as not to jeopardize more lucrative return matches by humiliating their overmatched opponents. Players provided musical accompaniment and comic relief, particularly at postgame events or carnivals. Despite the whites' perceptions, Arthur Hardy, one of the barnstormers, claimed that it was at such affairs that the players really "got all the whites' money."[35]

Such "hustling" allowed black athletes to maintain a sense of independence, and at times, provided retribution for white oppression. They maintained, and still retain, a heroic stature in the African American community and served as a symbol of racial pride as they traveled in a relatively lavish style and earned salaries greater than most whites.[36]

The Harlem Globetrotters, a barnstorming Chicago basketball team initiated by high school students, soon followed the entrepreneurial lead of Rube Foster in the 1920s. The burgeoning pro football circuit also provided black athletes with opportunities to showcase their skills at the highest levels, unlike Major League Baseball. Fritz Pollard, another Chicago resident whose parents had moved northward from Missouri and one of eight children, exemplified the possibilities. His brother Leslie starred on the North Division High School football team, from which Amos Alonzo Stagg recruited Leo

De Tray and Walter Steffen. The latter replaced Eckersall as the quarterback and was twice named All-American. Leslie Pollard fared better than Sammy Ransom, for he attended Dartmouth in 1908, where he displayed his football talents for only a year before departing. His younger brother, Fritz, after a stellar athletic career of his own, landed at Brown University, another Ivy League school, where he attained All-American honors and then began professional play in 1919. He became the first black quarterback in the nascent National Football League and its first black coach before expanding his business interests to the music industry. His son, Fritz Jr., won a bronze medal as a hurdler in the 1936 Olympics.[37]

Pioneers such as Jack Johnson, Rube Foster, and Fritz Pollard refused to be subjugated and symbolized both pride and hope for other African Americans. By the 1920s, with the emergence of the "new Negro" and a heightened racial consciousness, Sam Ransom, too, came to realize that his early athletic successes belied the true fate of his people. He campaigned for civil rights, playing a key role in desegregating the Minnesota National Guard, and helped to establish and then serve on Minnesota's Interracial Commission (now the Department of Human Rights). The governor cited him for distinguished service to the state. He later scolded the United States for its racial policies, yet he retained his patriotism and remained "friendly, enthusiastic, kind and gentle, with a superb sense of humor."[38] Though less flamboyant than Johnson, Foster, or Pollard, Ransom was no less a hero in his quest for racial equality. He had entertained, even fascinated, whites with his athletic abilities. His former teammate, Walter Eckersall, who had become a prominent sportswriter of national status by 1918, rated Ransom with All-Americans Bob Marshall of Minnesota and Fritz Pollard as the best black players up to that time. Six years later he was still described as "the greatest high school colored athlete." Carl Cobelli, a Hyde Park gymnastics teacher and coach since 1893, declared Ransom to be the greatest Hyde Park athlete ever. Ransom had earned sixteen varsity letters in four years and greatly contributed to a multitude of city, county, state, western regional, and national championships. Hyde Park High School named him to its all-time football team. In 1973, three years after his death, Beloit

College informed his wife, Queen, that it had elected him to its Athletic Hall of Honor. But his athletic successes proved fleeting compared to his civil rights work, which endures. An obituary recognized Ransom as "a great man among the great."[39]

Sam Ransom had played at a time when great wasn't good enough. Blacks might be lauded for their physical abilities, especially if they won greater social capital for white communities, but few won full respect or the equality they sought and deserved. Perhaps Sam Ransom best summarized his own life when he wrote to a friend that "I might have been a greater athlete had I gone to Chicago, but by going to Beloit, I am a better man."[40]

## Notes

1. Maureen A. Flanagan, "Suffrage," in *Chicago Encyclopedia*, ed. James R. Grossman, Ann Durkin Keating, and Janice L. Rieff (Chicago: University of Chicago Press, 2004), 803; James R. Grossman, *Land of Hope: Chicago, Black Southerners, and the Great Migration* (Chicago: University of Chicago Press, 1989); William L. Katz, ed., *The Negro in Chicago* (Chicago: University of Chicago Press, 1968 [1922 reprint]), 89; Allan H. Spear, *Black Chicago: The Making of a Negro Ghetto* (Chicago: University of Chicago Press, 1967), 12.

2. David W. Zang, *Fleet Walker's Divided Heart: The Life of Baseball's First Black Major Leaguer* (Lincoln: University of Nebraska Press, 1995); Gerald R. Gems, Linda J. Borish, and Gertrud Pfister, *Sports in American History: From Colonization to Globalization* (Champaign IL: Human Kinetics, 2008), 144–45; Stephen Fox, *Big Leagues: Professional Baseball, Football, and Basketball in National Memory* (New York: William Morrow, 1994), 306–13; Leslie Heaphy, ed., *The 8th Annual Jerry Malloy Negro League Conference* (Chicago: SABR, 2005), 8–28, 33–47, 51–55. Anson later became a vice president of the American Bowling Congress and worked to ban blacks from participation in that organization.

3. *Chicago Tribune*, October 6, 1890, 3; Fox, *Big Leagues*, 317. Quote from Ralph Stone to T. Hawley Tapping, January 10, 1955, and Roger Sherman to T. Hawley Tapping, January 19, 1955, in Jewett file, Box 35, University of Michigan Archives. The Northwestern University Archives indicate that Jewett entered its medical school in 1893 and played football in 1893 and 1894.

4. Gerald R. Gems, *For Pride, Profit, and Patriarchy: Football and the Incorporation of American Cultural Values* (Lanham MD: Scarecrow Press, 2000), 114; Fox, *Big Leagues*, 319 (quote). See Jack Berryman, "Early Black Leadership in Collegiate Football," *Historical Journal of Massachusetts* 9 (June 1981): 17–28.

5. David K. Wiggins, "Good Times on the Old Plantation: Popular Recreations of the Black Slave in the Antebellum South, 1810–1860," *Journal of Sport History* 4 (1977): 260–84; Gems, Borish, and Pfister, *Sports in American History*, 207; Bob

Petersen, "Peter Jackson: Heavyweight Champion of Australia," in *The First Black Boxing Champions: Essays on Fighters of the 1890s to the 1920s*, ed. Colleen Aycock and Mark Scott (Jefferson NC: McFarland, 2011), 32–47.

6. W. E. B. Du Bois, *The Souls of Black Folk* (New York: Vintage Books, 1990).

7. Hyde Park High School, *The Libethrian* (Chicago: Windemere Press, 1904), n.p.; Walter Eckersall, "Sam Ransom Fearless in War or Sport," *Anaconda Standard*, July 21, 1918, 2.

8. Hyde Park High School, *Libethrian*, n.p.

9. Hyde Park High School, *Libethrian*, n.p.; *Chicago Inter Ocean* clipping, May 13, 1903, in Amos Alonzo Stagg Papers, Box 141, Football Scrapbook 29 (February–May 1903), University of Chicago Library, Special Collections; Archie Oboler, ed. *The Oski-Wow-Wow: A History of Hyde Park High School Athletics* (Chicago: Hyde Park High School, 1924), 16–17, 97.

10. Cited in Oboler, *Oski-Wow-Wow*, 99.

11. Hyde Park High School, *Libethrian*, n.p.; Oboler, *Oski-Wow-Wow*, 8–18; Gems, *For Pride, Profit, and Patriarchy: Football and the Incorporation of American Cultural Values* (Lanham MD: Scarecrow Press, 2000), 11–46.

12. *Chicago Daily News*, November 19, 1903, 6; Edward S. Jordan, "Buying Football Victories," *Collier's*, November 11, 1905, 19–20, 23; Robin Lester, *Stagg's University: The Rise, Decline, and Fall of Big-Time Football at Chicago* (Champaign: University of Illinois Press, 1995); Gerald R. Gems, *Windy City Wars: Labor, Leisure, and Sport in the Making of Chicago* (Lanham MD: Scarecrow Press, 1997), 96–102; Hal Lawson and Alan Ingham, "Conflicting Ideologies Concerning the University and Inter-Collegiate Athletics: Harper and Hutchins at Chicago, 1892–1940," *Journal of Sport History* 7 (Winter 1980): 37–63; *Chicago Daily News*, November 7, 1903, 2; November 12, 1902, 6; November 19, 1903, 6; November 21, 1903, 1. See the Stagg Papers, Box 13, Folder 19, on his guarded correspondence with athletes. See Robert Pruter, *The Rise of American High School Sports and the Search for Control, 1880–1930* (Syracuse NY: Syracuse University Press, 1913) for such developments on the national level.

13. Oboler, *Oski-Wow-Wow*, 1–17; Gems, *For Pride, Profit, and Patriarchy*, 115; *Chicago Tribune*, November 24, 1902, 6; *Chicago American*, clipping, December 2, 1902, in Stagg Papers, Box 141, Football Scrapbook 28.

14. *Chicago Tribune*, December 7, 1902, 9.

15. Jordan, "Buying Football Victories"; Amos Alonzo Stagg and Wesley W. Stout, *Touchdown!* (New York: Longmans, Green, 1927), 240; *Chicago Daily News*, November 19, 1903, 6; James A. Peterson, *Eckersall of Chicago* (Chicago: Hinckley and Schmitt, 1957). The last is a whitewash of Eckersall's career at the university.

16. Hyde Park High School, *Libethrian*, n.p.; Oboler, *Oski-Wow-Wow*, 19; *Chicago Daily News*, November 7, 1903, 4; November 9, 1903, 4; November 19, 1903, 6; November 21, 1903, 2; November 23, 1903, 4; November 30, 1903, 4; W. J. Davis to Keene Fitzpatrick, August 17, 1904, Box 1, Board in Control of Intercollegiate Athletics, University of Michigan Archives; Eckersall, "Sam Ransom Fearless in War or

Sport," 2. The Yost Papers at the University of Michigan contain no correspondence with Ransom; Karen Jania to Gerald R. Gems, email correspondence, August 1, 2013.

17. Cited in Lester, *Stagg's University*, 40.

18. *Chicago Daily News*, November 19, 1903, 6. Neither the Stagg Papers at the University of Chicago nor the Stagg Papers at the University of the Pacific have any correspondence between Stagg and Ransom; Nicole Grady to Gerald R. Gems, email correspondence, July 22, 2013.

19. The Stagg-McGugin correspondence is in Stagg Papers, Box 42, Folder 13, November 16, 1916; December 11, 1916; December 14, 1916 (quote). The University of Chicago Registrar's Office provided materials indicating that a few black students had taken degrees at the school during that time—in 1896, ca. 1900, and not again until 1917.

20. Hyde Park High School, *Libethrian*, n.p.

21. *Round Table*, 1905, 1909 (Beloit yearbooks on Codex in archives). Although Ransom played for three years on Beloit's athletic teams, he did not officially matriculate until 1906, and his academic records show only 2.5 credits over his first two years there. Apparently he engaged in remedial coursework at the adjacent secondary school, a program that allowed him to engage in athletic activities. High school teammates Walter Eckersall and Tom Hammond became All-Americans at Chicago and Michigan respectively. Hammond eventually became a brigadier general in the Illinois National Guard. Teammate Ralph Bard played football for Princeton and became assistant secretary of the navy.

22. Beloit Archives; "St. Paul Gophers Base Ball Club," *The Appeal*, April 31, 1907, 3.

23. Gems, Borish, and Pfister, *Sports in American History*, 207; letter of Theodore Roosevelt to Booker T. Washington, June 8, 1904, cited in Robert M. Crunden, *Ministers of Reform: The Progressive Achievement in American Civilization* (New York: Basic Books, 1982), 202. The Chinese Exclusion Act originated in 1882 and was renewed thereafter until the 1902 version established its permanency until 1943.

24. Special Parks Commission, *Annual Report, 1907* (Chicago, February 1908), 6; see Michael W. Homel, "Negroes in the Chicago Public Schools, 1910–1941," PhD diss., University of Chicago, 1972, on the development of segregation.

25. *Chicago Defender*, February 5, 1910, 1; April 23, 1910, 1.

26. *Chicago Tribune*, April 1, 1910, 14; April 24, 1910, pt. 3:1.

27. Among the numerous accounts of the Johnson saga, see Randy Roberts, *Papa Jack: Jack Johnson and the Era of White Hopes* (New York: Free Press, 1983); Theresa Runstedtler, *Jack Johnson: Rebel Sojourner, Boxing in the Shadow of the Global Color Line* (Berkeley: University of California Press, 2012); and Gerald R. Gems, "Jack Johnson and the Quest for Racial Respect," in *Out of the Shadows: A Biographical History of African American Athletes*, ed. David K. Wiggins (Fayetteville: University of Arkansas Press, 2006), 59–77.

28. Barnett letter to the *Record-Herald*, cited in Spear, *Black Chicago*, 46–47; see Special Parks Commission, *Annual Report 1910* (Chicago, 1911), 5, on separate parks; and Homel, "Negroes in the Chicago Public Schools," on school segregation.

29. *St. Paul Appeal*, July 21, 1917, 3. Byron Farwell, *Over There: The United States in the Great War, 1917–1918* (New York: W. W. Norton, 1999), 149–50, indicates that only 10 percent of the 367,710 blacks who served in the army during the war enlisted. All others were drafted, and many resented service for a country that did not fully include them.

30. John Bodnar, Roger Simon, and Michael P. Weber, *Lives of Their Own: Blacks, Italians, and Poles in Pittsburgh, 1900–1960* (Urbana: University of Illinois Press, 1982), 133, 188, estimates the 1916–19 migration figures at five hundred thousand to one million. James R. Barrett, *Work and Community in the Jungle* (Urbana: University of Illinois Press, 1987), 190–94, 210–18; Katz, *The Negro in Chicago*; Chicago Commission on Race Relations, *The Negro in Chicago: A Study of Race Relations and a Race Riot* (Chicago: University of Chicago Press, 1922); William M. Tuttle Jr., *Race Riot: Chicago in the Red Summer of 1919* (Urbana: University of Illinois Press, 1970).

31. Isabel Wilkerson, *The Warmth of Other Suns: The Epic Story of America's Great Migration* (New York: Random House, 2010), 556, estimates more than six million black migrants during the course of the twentieth century. Other estimates are much higher. The Chicago Commission on Race Relations, *The Negro in Chicago*, 106, registered 44,103 blacks in the city in 1910, a figure that had risen to 109,594 by 1920. See Stow Persons, *Ethnic Studies at Chicago, 1905–45* (Urbana: University of Illinois Press, 1987), 74, 105–31, on the influence of the Chicago School of Sociology, and Spear, *Black Chicago*, 110–17, 174, 205–6, 225–28, for a revisionist account.

32. See Quintin Hoare and Geoffrey N. Smith, *Selections from the Prison Notebooks of Antonio Gramsci* (New York: International Publishing, 1971) on Gramsci's concepts of hegemony and human agency relative to inclusion and exclusion. On the symbolic importance of sport in social, racial, ethnic, and political matters, see David Margolick, *Beyond Glory: Joe Louis vs. Max Schmeling, and the World on a Brink* (New York: Alfred A. Knopf, 2005); Lewis Erenberg, *The Greatest Fight of Our Generation: Louis vs. Schmeling* (New York: Oxford University Press, 2007); Randy Roberts, *Joe Louis: Hard Times Man* (New Haven CT: Yale University Press, 2010); Arnold Rampersad, *Jackie Robinson: A Biography* (New York: Random House, 1997); Gerald R. Gems, *Sport and the Shaping of Italian American Identity* (Syracuse NY: Syracuse University Press, 2013).

33. *Rockford Republic*, February 25, 1919, 12. See Farwell, *Over There*, 149–58, and Edward G. Lengel, *To Conquer Hell: The Meuse-Argonne, 1918* (New York: Henry Holt, 2008), 36–37, 120–22, 159–60, 194–95, 427–29, for the experiences of black soldiers in World War I, most of whom were used as laborers; others were loaned to the French Army and used as cannon fodder. The Eighth Illinois Regiment homecoming is detailed in Tuttle, *Race Riot*, 218–19. Its heroism can be discerned by the twenty-one Distinguished Service Crosses awarded by the U.S. government and the sixty-eight Croix de Guerre bestowed on its members by the French government.

34. Grossman, *Land of Hope*, 86, 118, 127, 247–54; Dempsey J. Travis, *An Autobiography of Black Chicago* (Chicago: Urban Research Institute, 1981), 15, 20, 25–26;

Tuttle, *Race Riot*, 235, 237–38; Chicago Commission on Race Relations, *The Negro in Chicago*, 11, 253–54, 266–86; Paul F. Cressey, "The Succession of Cultural Groups in Chicago," PhD diss., University of Chicago, 1930, 238–40; Leon Despres, "The Most Segregated City in the North—Chicago," *Chicago Scene*, February 15, 1962, 14–17; John M. Blum, Edmund S. Morgan, Willie Lee Rose, Arthur M. Schlesinger Jr., Kenneth M. Stampp, and C. Vann Woodward, *The National Experience: A History of the United States* (New York: Harcourt, Brace, Jovanovich, 1981), 616.

35. David K. Wiggins, "Sport and Popular Pastimes: Shadow of the Slavequarter," *Canadian Journal of the History of Sport* 11 (May 1980): 61–88; John Holway, *Blackball Stars* (Westport CT: Meckler Books, 1988), 92, 111, 192–93, 262; Donn Rogosin, *Invisible Men: Life in Baseball's Negro Leagues* (New York: Atheneum, 1983), 26, 36, 57, 119 (quote), 121, 262, 320–21; Kathleen Neils Conzen, "Ethnicity as Festive Culture," in *The Invention of Ethnicity*, ed. Werner Sollors (New York: Oxford University Press, 1989), 44–76; Gerald R. Gems, "The Athlete as Trickster," *Ethnic Studies Review* 24, nos. 1–3 (Winter 2001): 48–57.

36. Rogosin, *Invisible Men*, 8, 66–71.

37. John M. Carroll, *Fritz Pollard: Pioneer in Racial Advancement* (Urbana: University of Illinois Press, 1992).

38. Mary J. Kyle, "A Man to Remember," *Twin Cities Courier*, February 21, 1970 (clipping in the Beloit Archives); letter form Joseph P. Kobylka to the Ransom family, February 18, 1970, in Beloit Archives (quote).

39. Oboler, *Oski-Wow-Wow*, 17, 99, 102–3; Eckersall, "Sam Ransom Fearless in War or Sport"; Robert G. Nicholls to Mrs. Ransom, June 18, 1973, in Beloit Archives; Kyle, "A Man to Remember." Bob Marshall earned All-American honors in 1905 and 1906 and played in the NFL until 1927 at the age of forty-seven. No black players were signed to NFL contracts from 1934 to 1946.

40. Sam Ransom to Francis J. Platt, February 19, 1967, in Beloit Archives.

# FOUR

# A League of Their Own

## Rube Foster's "Pitfalls of Baseball" Revisited

MICHAEL E. LOMAX

By the early twentieth century black baseball had been transformed into a commercialized amusement by a generation of African American entrepreneurs who sought to advance their own economic interests. They operated their successful enterprises—black professional teams—within the fabric of a national economy—white semiprofessional baseball. They ran their teams on the strategy of going where the money was and creating a demand for their clubs in several locales. They scheduled games with white and black baseball clubs and at times with Cuban baseball teams.

Operating their segregated baseball teams within the context of white semiprofessional clubs did have its consequences. Racial prejudice among players and team owners led to the development of a color line. In other words, players of color were denied entry into the Major and Minor Leagues. It led to several black entrepreneurs' forming their own independent clubs. Black baseball did not have any leagues or associations where they could develop or revise rules, settle disputes, and control their own game. With no leagues or associations, black clubs did not play the game within the traditional sense of pursuing a pennant or sponsoring a season-ending championship. Within in this context Andrew "Rube" Foster forged the initial black baseball enterprise within the United States.

On July 2, 1910, the Chicago American Giants and Frank Leland's

Chicago Giants began the first of a series of games for midwestern supremacy. In the first series both clubs engaged in a best of four out of seven game series. In a hard fought series the American Giants took a 3–2 series lead. Controversy surrounded the sixth game, resulting in the Chicago Giants' walking off the diamond. Cooler heads prevailed, and both teams resumed the series. American Giants pitcher Pat Dougherty held the Giants to four hits in a 1–0 shutout victory and won the midwestern colored championship.[1]

A second series began on August 13, 1910, a three-game series scheduled at Schorling Park. The Chicago Giants were no match, as the American Giants swept them in three games. The American Giants series win over the Chicago Giants marked the start of Rube Foster's dominance as the booking power of the Midwest. Foster made two unsuccessful attempts during the pre–World War I era to encourage midwestern clubs to form a black professional league. When those endeavors failed, the Chicago American Giants embarked on a year-round barnstorming tour that was unprecedented to that time. Despite possessing one of the best African American teams as an owner and manager, Foster acknowledged the need for black baseball clubs to organize in some form of an association. He spent the entire 1919 winter season making his most passionate plea for black clubs to organize into a national organization. This chapter analyzes the entrepreneurial efforts that led to Rube Foster's becoming the booking power of the Midwest and traces the ways in which his series of articles—titled "Pitfalls of Baseball"—led to the formation of the Negro National League (NNL) in 1920. The following questions will serve to guide the narrative: What were the forces that led to Rube Foster's emerging as the booking power of the Midwest? How did his rise as booking power lead to the formation of the NNL?

Rube Foster exemplified the African American entrepreneur who was willing to operate within the parameters of a biracial institutional structure. In other words, he recognized that in order to do business he would have to negotiate with the white power structure. His successful black baseball club—the Chicago American Giants—worked within the parameters of a mainstream economy—white semiprofessional baseball. Yet at the same time Foster's business and administrative acumen was consistent with the cooperative business strategy so prevalent among early black baseball teams. Foster's partnership with John Schorling, a white tavern owner and baseball operator, enabled him to establish his booking control in the Midwest. This partnership also provided Foster with a considerable advantage over other midwestern black clubs because he operated out of the region's largest market, allowing him to establish a symbiotic business relationship with white semiprofessional teams and concurrently tap into the Windy City's growing black consumer market.

Beginning in late November 1919, Rube Foster wrote a series of articles titled "Pitfalls of Baseball" in several black newspapers, especially the *Chicago Defender*. Foster stressed the need for economic cooperation, an end to destructive business practices—most specifically player jumping—and a truce among the owners relative to past disputes. He also called for the eastern and western magnates to form an association patterned after the white Major Leagues. By organizing into two leagues, black club owners could, in Foster's view, reconstruct their business practices and form a national association. Eastern owners, however, rejected Foster's plan. Yet a group of midwestern owners formed the NNL.

Rube Foster was born in Calvert, Texas, on September 19, 1879. Devoutly religious, Foster never drank or allowed the consumption of spirits in his household, but he tolerated drinking from others. He exhibited his organizational skills at a young age, operating a baseball team while in grade school. He left school in the eighth grade to pursue a career in baseball. By 1897 Foster was pitching for the Waco Yellow Jackets, a traveling team that toured Texas and the bordering states.[2]

In the spring of 1902 Chicago Unions magnate William Peters invited Foster to join his team, but as he sent no travel money, the pitcher remained in Texas. Simultaneously Frank Leland invited Foster to join his newly formed Chicago Union Giants, initiating a stormy relationship between the two men. By mid-spring Foster had quit the Union Giants to join a white semiprofessional team in Ostego, Michigan. When its season ended, he headed east to play for the Cuban X Giants. It was with the X Giants that Foster emerged as the premier pitcher of black baseball. In 1903 he led the Cuban X Giants to a series victory over the Philadelphia Giants for the "colored championship of the world."[3]

From 1904 to 1906 Foster played for the Philadelphia Giants. In addition to Foster the Giants featured several legendary stars: Danny McClellan, John Henry Lloyd, and Grant "Home Run" Johnson. In 1904 the Giants turned the tables on the Cuban X Giants and defeated them for the colored championship. The Giants' success on the field prompted club owner H. Walter Schlichter to challenge John McGraw's National League champion New York Giants to a postseason series. The challenge went unanswered.[4]

Despite the Philadelphia Giants' success on the field, the players were upset with their inadequate compensation. In the fall of 1906 Foster and several of the Giants left the club and traveled to Chicago. The player revolt Foster led coincided with Frank Leland's efforts to persuade him to manage the Leland Giants. Foster accepted, and his first move was to release the players of the previous season despite Leland's opposition. Next Foster assumed the responsibilities of booking the team's games, marking the start of his emergence as the top booking agent in the Midwest.

On August 6, 1907, the Leland Giants began the first of two three-game series with Mike Donlin's All-Stars. Donlin was a former Major League player who composed an All-Star team of former Major Leaguers that included Jimmy Callahan, Jake Stahl, and Jimmy Ryan. Both series turned out to be the Rube Foster show. The Lelands defeated Donlin's All-Stars four games to two, and Foster won all four games.[5]

The black press applauded the Leland Giants' spectacular performance against Donlin's All-Stars. Understandably the spotlight shined bright on Rube Foster. The *Broad Ax* proclaimed Foster "one of the greatest [baseball] players in this country." Under the pseudonym "Frederick North Shorey," a black sportswriter for the *Indianapolis Freeman* stated, "As for Rube Foster, well, if it were in the power of the colored people to honor politically or to raise him to the station to which they believe he is entitled, Booker T. Washington would have to be content with second place." The accolades Foster received were warranted. He pitched four complete games, giving up only seven runs in thirty-six innings. Foster struck out eighteen batters and compiled a 1.75 earned run average.[6]

From 1907 to 1910 Foster perfected the barnstorming pattern that would be his trademark for the next decade. On February 20, 1907, the *Indianapolis Freeman* reported that the Leland Giants would embark on a spring training tour. It marked the first time that a semiprofessional club that was black-owned and -operated had accomplished this feat. Two years later the *Freeman* reported that the Giants had traveled 4,465 miles, playing black and white teams in Memphis, Birmingham, Fort Worth, Austin, San Antonio, Prairie View State, and Houston. The Leland Giants traveled in their own Pullman car to illustrate their reputation as an elite black independent club. In October 1910, after winning twenty straight games in the East and West, the Giants made their first trip to Cuba. Along with the American League Detroit Tigers, the Lelands played the top Cuban clubs, including the Havanas—an aggregate of black stars that included John Henry Lloyd and Grant "Home Run" Johnson—and the Almendares. While the Lelands won the majority of their games, they lost a tough series to the Almendares.[7]

In 1911 Foster left the Leland Giants and formed the Chicago American Giants. His leaving the Leland Giants goes beyond the scope of this chapter. What is important here is that his departure marked the beginning of his rise as the booking power in the Midwest. In the following years he would make a series of moves that resulted in his accomplishing this task.

Foster's first move was to enter into a partnership with John M. Schorling. Schorling had operated a sandlot club in Chicago for several years. He leased the grounds of the old White Sox Park on Thirty-Ninth and Shields Avenue after the American League team moved into its new stadium. The White Sox had torn down the old grandstand, and Schorling built a new one with a seating capacity of nine thousand. He approached Foster with an offer of a partnership. Foster now had a ballpark in which to operate, and Schorling had the best booking agent and field manager in the Midwest.[8]

Foster's partnership with Schorling accomplished several goals.

First, it provided the American Giants with a home ballpark where they could develop and maintain a fan base. Second, as noted above, it allowed Foster to maintain a symbiotic business relationship with white semiprofessional teams and simultaneously tap into Chicago's growing black market. Foster's partnership with Schorling coincided with the early black migration to northern cities in the early twentieth century. Migration would not expand the black consumer market significantly until the war years. Yet in Chicago migration had expanded the Windy City's black consumer market to the point that baseball magnates could no longer ignore it. Chicago's black population grew continuously between 1900 (30,150) and 1920 (109,455). The ball park's location was on the Windy City's South Side, with better access to the black consumer market. More important, Foster's primary objective was to present the best product available to Chicago's black community, a goal that meant securing the best talent available and developing a winning reputation.[9]

In 1911 Foster made his first call for African American clubs to organize. He also called for a new way for African American clubs to conduct business. According to Foster, "The reckless scramble under the guise of baseball is keeping [blacks] down, and we will always be the underdog until we successfully employ the methods that have brought success to the great powers that be in baseball of the present era." It was evident the "great powers" to which Foster referred were the white Major Leagues. The American Giants magnate called for a black professional league patterned after the Major Leagues, limiting one team per city to control consumer markets and gaining a hegemony over the player force. Foster proposed a league of six teams in St. Louis, Kansas City, Louisville, Indianapolis, Chicago, and Detroit. The formation of a black league would legitimize black baseball as a profession that, in Foster's view, "could force, by public sentiment, the same as Jack Johnson forced [Jim] Jeffries, the winners of the white league to meet us for the championship." Foster's clarion call, however, went unanswered.[10]

A second move Foster made was to establish a barnstorming tour on the West Coast in 1912 during the winter months. The American Giants played in the California Winter League (CWL), a compilation of former and current Major and Minor League players and teams from the Pacific Coast, Southern, and Northwest Leagues. The American Giants' performance in the CWL, however, was subpar. According to William McNeil, the Giants won six games and lost seven, although the league standings were incomplete. More impressive was the American Giants' extended tour on the West Coast once the CWL season was over. They reportedly amassed an 85-10 won-lost record during the winter. In any event, on July 5, 1913, the *Chicago Defender* reported that the American Giants celebrated winning the winter league championship with a parade, by unfurling a banner, and by displaying their new uniforms. Such success served to heighten Foster's and his American Giants' prestige in the Windy City.[11]

An effort to revive the East-West Colored Championship placed Foster in an even more visible light. On July 5, 1913, the *Chicago Defender* reported an upcoming championship series between the Chicago American Giants and the Lincoln Giants of New York. A thirteen-game series was scheduled in Chicago and New York. After nine games the series was tied at four victories apiece and one tie. The Lincoln Giants won the final four games in New York, earning the right to be crowned "World's Colored Champion." Although Foster's American Giants lost the series, he had won the hearts and minds of Chicago's black community. More important, the colored championship marked the first time in thirteen years an African American promoter had lured a prominent black club from New York to Chicago. Such an accomplishment further heightened Foster's prestige in the Midwest.[12]

Toward the end of the 1913 season Rube Foster made his second call for black baseball teams to organize. His argument for organization was similar to the one he had made previously. "We have the players," Foster added, "and it could not be a failure, as the same territory is traveled now by all clubs with no organization or money." Organization was black baseball's means for legitimacy. It was also vital for black baseball's salvation. For a second time Rube Foster's call for black clubs to organize went unanswered.[13]

Developing good press and community relations represented Foster's final move to establish his booking control in the Midwest.

In the prewar years Foster and Schorling had established a precedent that became a constant throughout the war years. Schorling had donated the use of the ballpark for local community activities, such as the Chicago Church League championship game. Foster had developed good press relations by granting an interview with the *Chicago Defender*, providing readers with insights about his early career in baseball. Throughout the war years he had granted many interviews and written articles to promote himself and the American Giants, and he had become a local patron as well. Clearly Rube Foster acknowledged the importance of the print media to sway public opinion in his favor.[14]

Foster's attempts to develop good press relations occurred simultaneously with the *Chicago Defender*'s having become the largest selling black newspaper in the United States by World War I. As historian James Grossman states, "Fearless, sensationalist, and militant, the *Defender* advertised the glories of Chicago so effectively that even migrants headed for other northern cities drew their general image of the urban North from its pages." Two-thirds of the "World's Greatest Weekly's" circulation was outside the Windy City. Robert Abbott, editor of the *Defender*, built his wide circulation essentially through his cultivation of black railroad men during the newspaper's struggling years. The *Defender*'s railroad column noted who worked on which lines and routes and shared anecdotes about the individual workers. The *Defender*'s circulation was astounding, reaching 33,000 by 1916 and skyrocketing along with black migration. By the early 1920s approximately 160,000–250,000 customers read the Windy City rag. The *Defender* was instrumental in providing invaluable publicity for Foster and his American Giants throughout the Midwest and South. In the following years it would be pivotal in aiding Foster to maintain his booking control, first in Chicago and then through several cities in the Midwest.[15]

### A Midwestern Alliance

It should be noted that at no time was the Chicago American Giants team reliant upon the black community for its economic and operational existence. Prior to 1915 northern black communities were not large enough to maintain a fan base, nor did they possess the disposable income to support a commercialized amusement. As a result, black baseball entrepreneurs developed a strategy of going where the money was. Consequently black baseball clubs developed rivalries and championships with white semipros that became the lifeblood of independent clubs. As black clubs like the American Giants exhibited their ability to generate revenue, white semipros recognized that it was good business to schedule them. At the same time, Foster sought to maintain a symbiotic business relationship with white semiprofessional teams in Chicago and throughout the Midwest.[16]

Concurrently the widening discrimination occurring in northern cities and the continuing black migration resulted in an increase in entrepreneurship among African Americans. Vishnu V. Oak's careful analysis of black businesses reveals a gradual progression in the growth of black business firms: in 1900, nationally there were 40,445 firms; in 1910, 56,592; and in 1920, 74,424. In the opening decades of the twentieth century a virtual black baseball explosion occurred. Throughout the United States several black independent clubs were at least operating at a traveling status. In the East nine black clubs emerged, including the Philadelphia Giants, Cuban X Giants, Genuine Cuban Giants, Brooklyn Royal Giants, Quaker Giants of New York, Wilmington Giants, New York Giants, Baltimore Giants of Newark, and Keystone Giants of Philadelphia. From the South clubs like the Louisville Giants, Birmingham Giants, and New Orleans Black Pelicans began making Chicago, St. Louis, and Milwaukee their annual stops on their barnstorming tours. In the Midwest the Indianapolis ABCs, St. Louis Giants, Chicago Giants, and the All Nations Team—later the Kansas City Monarchs—were but a handful of black clubs that emerged. Consequently Foster had the opportunity to develop rivalries with these clubs, as well as maintain his symbiotic business relationship with white semipros.[17]

Foster's business strategy expanded his booking control in the Midwest in several ways. First, he had a considerable advantage operating in Chicago—the Midwest's largest market. As early as the 1870s Chicago had provided an environment that fostered the growth and development of semiprofessional baseball. Political and business support led to the development of leagues and associations—like the Chicago City League—and amateur baseball associations—like the Chicago Amateur Baseball Association and the Park Owners Association. In the 1890s black and white semipros attempted to schedule Sunday games in the Windy City on a regular basis. Sunday was a big payday for independent clubs, and teams with their own ballparks benefited the most. Combined with the American Giants' ability to generate gate receipts, black and white semipros sought to schedule games with Foster's club when they were at home. The American Giants averaged approximately seven to nine thousand fans for Sunday games. Second, Foster had the foresight to book as many as three games on a single Sunday when the American Giants were at home and kept Schorling Park busy when his club was on the road. Scheduling the Havanas of Cuba—and at times Joe Green's Chicago Giants—Foster created an additional revenue source whereby he collected a 10 percent fee for booking their games. He also booked two white clubs under the same agreement, the Logan Squares and the Duffy Florals.[18]

Finally, Foster's winter barnstorming tours elevated his prestige among Chicago's blacks, provided a sense of race pride due to the American Giants' phenomenal success, and bestowed upon the Windy City's black community some invaluable publicity. The 1915–16 barnstorming tour exemplified the American Giants' heightened celebrity. It was undoubtedly their greatest tour. They won the California Winter League, and when the winter league season ended, the American Giants traveled to Cuba, playing in the Cuban Winter League, winning seven and losing eight games. They barnstormed the West and Southwest, winning fifty-seven and losing fifteen. When the local season began in May, the American Giants had traveled over twenty thousand miles. It was during this tour that sportswriter Frank Young made the somewhat exaggerated claim that "the Rube" had brought Chicago more promotion than all other city enterprises combined.[19]

The American Giants' popularity was not lost upon local politicians who sought to create a political machine to address the black community's needs. Beginning in the 1916 local season, a ritual emerged that remained a constant at American Giants home openers: a battery consisting of Windy City's black politicians or businessmen would throw out the first ball. The first battery consisted of black alderman Oscar DePriest (pitcher), who was later elected to the House of Representatives, and former Leland Giants secretary Beauregard Moseley, the mayor of Idlewood, a local satellite community. Such gestures illustrated Foster's recognition of the importance of middle-class support, in conjunction with Schorling Park's becoming a platform where local politicians could be seen as well as heard. Foster continued to merge politics and sport in the following years to maintain his influence on black community development.[20]

Foster made other concessions to black politicians, at the same time exhibiting his ability to promote the black game in the Windy City. In 1917 Foster reserved a special box for Chicago's black elite. At the opening of this local season, Alderman Louie Anderson and *Chicago Defender* editor Robert Abbott served as the ceremonial battery. Along with Abbott and Anderson, Alderman Edward H. Wright and local businessmen George Holt and Harry Basken watched Foster's American Giants defeat Jake Stahl's Chicago City League club, 5–3. Prior to the game a New Orleans jazz band also enthralled the Chicago faithful, a burgeoning link between sport and entertainment that was employed by early black basketball teams as well.[21]

Whereas the winter league championship and middle-class support solidified Foster's position in the black community, the American Giants magnate began making steps to expand his booking control throughout the Midwest. He established a business arrangement with Major League owners in Cincinnati and Detroit to rent their ballparks. On August 18, 1917, the *Chicago Defender* announced that a series of games was scheduled between the Havanas and the American Giants at Redland Field in Cincinnati. Two weeks later Foster booked games with the Indianapolis ABCs at Navin Field in Detroit. Establishing business agreements with these Major League owners, in addition to scheduling games at Schorling Park during the American Giants' absence, served to consolidate Foster's booking control in the Midwest.[22]

The formation of the Detroit Stars, in which Foster was instrumental, also contributed to stabilizing Foster's autonomy in the Midwest. The Stars, in which Foster had a controlling interest, played at

Mack Park, located at Mack and Fairview Avenues in the middle of a white working-class neighborhood about four miles from downtown. Foster installed John "Tenny" Blount as the Stars' business manager. (Blount was involved in gambling enterprises in Detroit and was one of several vice leaders who began to emerge in the promotion of black baseball.) In addition to Blount, former American Giants outfielder Pete Hill was selected to manage the Stars on the field, and Foster transferred several of his American Giants to the club. To maintain controlling interest in the Stars, Foster held the ballplayers' contracts and the lease to Mack Park.[23]

By 1919 Rube Foster had become the booking power in the Midwest. His alliances with leading black politicians ensured his place as a prominent member of Chicago's black middle class. His business arrangements with Major League owners, booking games at Schorling Park, and organizing the Detroit Stars placed him in an advantageous position. Even more important was the American Giants' ability to turn a profit. By July 1918 Foster expressed to a friend that the American Giants were "drawing double of any year here; even adding 2300 Boxes cannot accommodate the people." By the end of the season Foster had reportedly amassed a profit of nearly $15,000, a far cry from his $1,000 earnings in 1907. It was during this time that Foster used the power of the pen in an effort to create a national enterprise.[24]

Foster's endeavor to make his case for a black professional league reflected the overall changes occurring in the black baseball world. On January 1, 1919, Sol White outlined the formation of a black league in the *Cleveland Advocate*. White had been black baseball's premier player and co-owner in the late nineteenth and early twentieth centuries. His *History of Colored Baseball* served as a black baseball guidebook to spread the black game to a popular audience. White argued for a league consisting of six clubs—three would have ballparks, and three would operate as traveling teams or "floaters." Two of the three traveling teams would play league games in the ballparks of the home teams while the parent club was on the road. The remaining road club could play a home team. There are no indications that such a league came to fruition. Yet White's call for league formation marked a turning point: several sportswriters and club owners began advocating the need to organize into either a league or an association.[25]

On October 4, 1919, *Chicago Defender* sportswriter Carey B. Lewis predicted a circuit of western clubs for the 1920 season. Lewis asserted that the 1919 season had been so prosperous "and [the] fans so loyal [and the] attendance so great in most of the western cities that the circuit [would] become a reality." Rube Foster would be the man responsible for such a proposed western circuit. The league would be owned and controlled by "Race men" and consist of eight teams. Lewis envisioned the western pennant winner traveling east to play the best team there. The league would create more opportunities among African Americans. It would "give a number of our men work and confine a lot of money to the pockets of men of the Race that is now going daily into the pockets of the other fellows." It was within this context that Rube Foster skipped his winter barnstorming tour and called for the formation of a black professional league.[26]

### Pitfalls of Baseball

From November 1919 to January 1920 Foster made his third—and most passionate—plea for black baseball clubs to organize into professional leagues. Using organized baseball's institutional structure as a model, Foster called for a national organization of eastern and western clubs to form into two leagues. He called for the club owners to meet to resolve their past differences and to eliminate destructive business practices—like player jumping—to sustain black baseball's future. Foster laid out his vision to place the black game on a sound economic footing that included strong leadership and able lieutenants to carry out the organization's policies. Eastern club owners, like Nat Strong and Ed Bolden, rejected Foster's call for a national meeting. As president of the Intercity Association and club owner of the Brooklyn Royal Giants, Nat Strong reigned as the booking power in New York. In Philadelphia Ed Bolden transformed the Hilldale Athletic Club from a group of upstart youths playing sandlot baseball" into the leading independent club in the City of Brotherly Love.[27] Nonetheless, in February 1920 midwestern club owners met and formed the NNL.

Foster's opening article in his series on the pitfalls of baseball exemplified a presidential state of the union address. With the exception of one club—the American Giants—black baseball had evolved into a weekend enterprise. Scheduling issues and an increase in overhead expenses were the root causes for this predicament. Among other fractional issues, some teams refused to play each other. During the independent era scheduling was haphazard at best. While top black independent clubs had little trouble scheduling games (e.g., the American Giants), this was not always the case for independents, who either were not considered top-notch or did not possess the economic residuals to engage in extended barnstorming tours. New York's semipro scene was dominated by booking agent Nat Strong, who could keep a black club very busy or idle. There was not one club that could show a profit of $1,000 per season, and not one team knew that it would play ten games the next season. Even with the recent increase in attendance, profits were diminished by the high cost of materials, parks, and "everything connected with baseball." Using his American Giants as an example, Foster noted that the cost of maintaining Schorling Park was $945 a week when the park was idle and $1,346 when it was utilized three days a week. After the visiting team had been paid its share of the gate receipts, attendance would have to double in order for the American Giants to break even. Moreover, should a team experience three rainouts on a Sunday during the season, the club owner would operate at a loss. Based on these circumstances, Foster urged club owners to "reconstruct" their business practices to make black baseball a profitable enterprise.[28]

To remedy black baseball's plight Foster advocated the need for strong leadership, and he used an abridged history of the leading black clubs of the past to validate his claim. In order for such leaders to be successful, they would need able lieutenants who had the confidence of the public. Moral respectability was vital to ensure the support and patronage of middle-class spectators, those who had a measure of expendable income. The past salaries of the leading black clubs were used to illustrate this point. The Philadelphia Giants, for example, paid $850 a month in salaries, but the club "had to disband [because it] could not even get the money for such high prices." In other words, the Giants did not generate enough revenue to cover salaries and turn a profit. Player salaries would only increase in the upcoming years. The American Giants' monthly salary figures had never been lower than $1,500 a month. The current promoters were blind to many facts. "They do not realize," Foster stated, that "to have the best ball club in the world and no one able to compete with it will lose [more] money on the season than [if teams] are evenly matched."[29]

Foster's call for black clubs to organize embodied the economic cooperation philosophy that had been true of black baseball clubs in the early twentieth century. The strategy had its roots in the black community in the late eighteenth century. Early black entrepreneurs recognized that if they were to attain any success in developing black businesses to an appreciable level in the black community, it would come only through such cooperation. It was evident to them that no concrete help in obtaining credit could be expected from white America.

Foster's rhetoric was consistent with the ideology of economic Black Nationalism advocated by Booker T. Washington. Black businessmen were not to isolate themselves from the larger society, selling only to blacks, nor were black fans to patronize black baseball games only because they were black. African Americans were to advance themselves by free competition on the open market. Foster's economic philosophy was essentially a laissez-faire formula for black advancement through commitment by individual blacks to the gospel of work and wealth. Much like that of Washington, Foster's ultimate goal was not to build a black counterculture. Even in the nineteenth century Frederick Douglass had recognized that "a nation within a nation is an anomaly." The purpose of self-help and racial solidarity was to encourage black unity and self-assertion on a political level while encouraging cultural and economic assimilation. Such a strategy would, theoretically, result in the integration of blacks into the mainstream of American society.[30]

Foster's economic philosophy was also pluralistic in scope. He recognized that black baseball clubs were composed of black and white owners, all of whom were competing for players and gate receipts.

Such an arrangement was fine as long as each owner respected the others' player contracts. An amicable coexistence would allow each club to remain intact. Equal access to power that was continually strengthened and renewed through cooperation would lead to leagues and associations in which each component supported and enriched all others. Such an ideal, however, would remain a sticking point throughout the history of the Negro Leagues.[31]

Rube Foster was willing to operate within the framework of a biracial institutional structure. His partnership with Schorling provided him with a ballpark to maintain a fan base in Chicago that gave him a considerable advantage over the majority of black clubs in the Midwest. More important, black clubs were not expected to play each other exclusively. They were also expected to maintain their symbiotic business relationship with white semipros. In this way black clubs could tap into the white semiprofessional market and concurrently exploit the growing black consumer market.[32]

In his third article Foster highlighted the poor business judgment of past black baseball club owners. To assemble the best team possible, club owners—particularly in the East—would offer a player a higher salary to leave his current club. Players jumping their contracts proved catastrophic to the teams losing the players. This destructive practice could also work in reverse when a talented team failed to generate the revenue necessary to cover salaries and other expenses and, most important, turn a profit. Therefore club owners must cooperate to eliminate the destructive practice of player jumping to ensure the black game's profitability.

Foster continued to focus on the destructive practice of player jumping in his next article and simultaneously urged eastern and western club owners to meet to resolve their differences. He began by indicting club owners who advanced players money prior to the start of a season, only to watch them move to another club when the season began. This practice had resulted in cutthroat competition among the magnates. "When a player gets money from [an owner]," Foster claimed, "he jumps." He added, "Then the owner writes and tells you, 'Don't play against so and so, he owes me money.'" As a result of this practice, a lot of good businessman would leave the black game. Bacharach Giants owner John Connor, for example, was "very ambitious, wanting nothing but the best." "He should not be lost to baseball. His only failure," Foster concluded, was that he had "not been steered right."[33]

In an effort "to let bygones be bygones," Foster proposed that the eastern and western magnates meet in either New York or Chicago. The owners would "pick an arbitration board from experienced men of business" and draw up an agreement by which the owners would abide. Each club owner would make a $500 deposit in good faith that would ensure he would adhere to the agreement. Foster was quick to point out that this suggested meeting was not "a proposition to exchange players." Rather the meeting would mark the start of a partnership "in working for the organized good of baseball." The American Giants president concluded with a glimpse of his vision of organized black baseball: "This [meeting would] pave the way for such [a] champion team eventually to play the winner among the whites. This is more than possible. Only in uniform strength is the permanent success [plausible]. I invite all owners to write for information on this proposition. It is open to all."[34]

In his fifth article Foster continued to stress the need to eliminate player jumping, and he highlighted the necessity for ball clubs to have access to playing facilities. The elimination of player jumping was vital for the reconstruction of black baseball's business practices in Foster's view because the practice led to disreputable behavior among the players and owners, and both sides understandably mistrusted each other. It was problematic for players to be honest when the owners did not respond in kind. Foster stated, "When someone persuades the same man to leave him, disgusted, he will wire you, 'If you play such a club, I will not play you.'" A national organization would ensure that club owners would respect each other's players under contract, thus eliminating player jumping altogether. Rube Foster urged black club owners to used organized baseball as their pattern to place the black game on a sound economic footing.[35]

Playing facilities were crucial to the success of a black national organization. Without them there would be no incentive for either players or owners to choose black baseball as a profession. Essentially Foster continued to stress the need for club owners to organize because the money for parks would "naturally come from whites." Foster recognized that black baseball did not rely solely on a separate black economy for its economic and operational viability. By the same token, however, his analysis suggested that like with more conventional black enterprises, a separate black economy was being impose on the black game. African American club owners did not enjoy the advantages Major League owners had in regard to building or remodeling ballparks during the Progressive Era. They did not have the direct and indirect connections with urban politicians that allowed MLB owners to obtain valuable information on matters like transportation plans and real estate developments. For this reason black club owners negotiated with whites in the first place—to gain access to suitable playing facilities. Foster acknowledged that modern playing facilities had to adhere to building codes that increased the overhead expenses. With the expected increase in park rentals and the high cost of real estate, Foster illustrated the monumental task black club owners faced in the pursuit of owning their own parks. Therefore the remedy to the ballpark dilemma was to focus on the issues over which magnates had the most control—reconstructing the black game's business practices through the creation of a national organization. This was a practical and understandable solution to the Achilles' heel that had hindered black baseball's business and economic development.

On January 20, 1920, Rube Foster outlined his plan to organize a national organization. At the same time, he stated that the attempt to get the eastern and western owners together had ended in failure. The association Foster proposed would be composed of two circuits: the West, to include Chicago, Cincinnati, Detroit, Indianapolis, and Kansas City, and the East, to include Pittsburgh, Cleveland, Washington, Baltimore, Philadelphia, and New York. The winners of each league would meet in a world championship series. Such an organization "[would] have been the salvation of baseball." However, only one eastern owner (from Washington) wrote to Foster to express interest in forming a national association. Foster reiterated the fact that the substantial investment in building a park, the general maintenance to ensure that the facility adhered to building code specifications, and the expenses in the day-to-day operations of a club could be addressed only through the creation of a national organization. Organization was also vital to black baseball's future. For the first time Foster hinted at the possibility that whites could control the ownership and management of black teams: "I have fought delivering Colored baseball into the control of whites, thinking that with a show of patronage from the fans we would get together. The get together effort has been a failure."[36]

In his final article Foster highlighted his efforts to get the eastern and western owners together and sought to answer the question of why they did not want to organize into a national organization. He wrote to Brooklyn Royal Giants owner Nat Strong in an attempt to get the owners together to reach an agreement. Strong wrote back and supposedly stated that he wanted something done. Yet there were men "who at present identified with eastern clubs [that] are [an] *impossibility* [his emphasis]." In other words, they would refuse to play each other. To Foster the "player question [was] the root of all the trouble," resulting in the mistrust between players and owners. Given the past negotiations between the two sides, the mistrust was understandable. Foster indicted the eastern owners for blocking the efforts to create a national organization. "Had the eastern owners accepted the proposal," he concluded, "the bitter feelings that exist would have been eliminated, a working agreement respecting each other's rights, a chance to see all the clubs meet, the securing of places fit to play, then [the] launching of a league."[37]

While much of Rube Foster's analysis was self-serving, it did reveal that he, and others like him, recognized the need for black baseball to be placed on a sound economic footing. The black game experienced the same kinds of growing pains organized baseball had undergone in the late nineteenth century. Player salaries constituted a large percentage of team costs. The free market for players led to the destructive practice of player jumping, resulting in even higher salaries as teams tried to maintain their competitiveness. Although the eastern owners balked at Foster's call for a national organization, midwestern owners would meet to form a Negro baseball league.

## Rube's League

On February 13–14, 1920, Rube Foster made his initial steps to form a western circuit when the midwestern owners met at the YMCA at Street's Hotel in Kansas City to form the NNL. The following clubs were represented: the Detroit Stars, St. Louis Giants, Dayton Marcos, Chicago Giants, Indianapolis ABCs, Kansas City Monarchs, Cuban Stars, and Chicago American Giants. Foster stated that he had a charter incorporated for a Negro national league, a move that stunned the owners. The American Giants mogul was clearly sending a message that the NNL would be his league. Foster then announced that he would leave it to the newspapermen to decide all questions, select players for the various teams, and write the bylaws and constitution for the circuit.[38]

The constitution committee consisted of sportswriters Dave Wyatt of the *Indianapolis Ledger* and Carey B. Lewis of the *Chicago Defender*, *Indianapolis Freeman* editor Elwood C. Knox, and attorney Elisha Scott of Topeka, Kansas. After making several corrections, league owners agreed to pay a $500 deposit, respect each other's players under contract, and play a schedule of games to determine a league champion each season. In an effort to achieve competitive balance, several players were transferred throughout the whole circuit. League play was not scheduled to begin until April 1, 1921, or until each club owned or leased a park. However, the NNL opened in May 1920, despite the presence of two traveling teams, the Cuban Stars and the Chicago Giants. With Foster running league affairs, the NNL had a successful opening season, the American Giants capturing the first pennant.[39]

## Conclusion

Rube Foster's "Pitfalls of Baseball" revealed the challenges black professional baseball confronted in the early twentieth century. According to Foster, the most destructive business practice—player jumping—significantly hampered a black club's profitability. It also led to teams' boycotting each other and competent African American businessmen's leaving the game. Playing facilities remained black baseball's

Achilles' heel in regard to business and economic development. It would remain a monumental challenge, given the building codes and high real estate costs.

Foster's remedy to these predicaments was to reconstruct black baseball's business practices through the creation of a national organization. His rhetoric was consistent with the economic cooperation philosophy so prevalent among black clubs during the Progressive Era. Organization was the key to place the black game on a sound economic footing. Moreover, organizing black baseball teams into a national league would, theoretically, achieve Foster's ultimate goal: the winner of the black organization would play the white Major Leagues in a "*real* World Series" (my emphasis).

Clearly, as noted, most of Foster's rhetoric was self-serving, and eastern owners balked at his proposal. Yet a group of midwestern owners did form the NNL. It was a testament to Foster's emergence as the booking power in the Midwest, along with his organizational skills to elicit the vision necessary for the formation of the Negro Leagues.

Rube Foster represented a generation of African American entrepreneurs who sought to professionalize the black game and place it on a sound economic footing. Along with other African American club owners like C. I. Taylor, Frank Leland, and Ed Bolden, Foster embodied the continued efforts of African American entrepreneurs to advance their own economic interests. They recognized that in order to conduct business in the United States, they had to negotiate with the white power structure. This meant transacting business with white semiprofessional club owners and park managers and in some cases establishing partnerships with white entrepreneurs. Foster used the business practices established by successful black baseball clubs of the late 1880s and 1890s, going where the money was and creating a demand for such clubs in several locales. He kept a talented player force intact, secured a suitable playing facility to generate gate receipts, and mastered the barnstorming schedule to elevate his Chicago American Giants to an elite touring team.

The remarkable accomplishments of African American ballplayers who followed Jackie Robinson in crossing the color line clearly reveals the Negro leagues' influence specifically and in general the

NNL's lasting imprint on American baseball culture. Willie Mays, Henry Aaron, Larry Doby, Ernie Banks, and Monte Irvin had phenomenal careers in the Major Leagues, made possible by black club owners like Rube Foster. He operated by any means necessary to transform black baseball into a commercial enterprise that would be inherited by a new generation of African American entrepreneurs. Much like the black baseball entrepreneurs of the late nineteenth and early twentieth century, Rube Foster endeavored to form black baseball as a business enterprise in his own image.

## Notes

1. The midwestern colored championship was a synopsis of my book on black professional baseball. See Michael E. Lomax, *Black Baseball Entrepreneurs 1902–1931: The Negro National and Eastern Colored Leagues* (Syracuse NY: Syracuse University Press, 2014).

2. For secondary accounts on Andrew "Rube" Foster's career as a ballplayer, see Larry Lester, *Rube Foster in His Time* (Jefferson NC: McFarland, 2012); Robert Charles Cottrell, *The Best Pitcher in Baseball: The Life of Rube Foster, Negro League Giant* (New York: New York University Press, 2001); John Holway, *Blackball Stars: Negro League Pioneers* (New York: Carroll and Graff Publishers, 1992); Charles E. Whitehead, *A Man and His Diamonds* (New York: Vantage Press, 1980); Robert Peterson, *Only the Ball Was White: A History of Legendary Black Players and All-Black Professional Teams* (New York: Oxford University Press, 1970). For an account on his early days as a booking agent, see Michael E. Lomax, "Black Entrepreneurship in the National Pastime: The Rise of Semiprofessional Baseball in Black Chicago, 1890–1915," *Journal of Sport History* 25 (Spring 1998): 43–64.

3. *Evening Item* (Philadelphia), September 6, 12, 13, 14, 19, 26, 1903.

4. *Evening Item*, September 2, 3, 6, 1904.

5. *Chicago Tribune*, August 7, 8, 9, 28, 29, 31, 1907; *Chicago Inter Ocean*, August 28, 1907; *Indianapolis Freeman*, September 7, 1907.

6. *Broad Ax*, August 17, 1907; *Indianapolis Freeman*, September 7, 1907.

7. *Indianapolis Freeman*, February 20, 1907, and May 15, 1909; *Broad Ax*, October 8, 1910; *Chicago Defender*, October 8, 1910; *New York Age*, December 8, 1910.

8. Peterson, *Only the Ball Was White*, 108.

9. *Indianapolis Freeman*, September 21, 1907; Chicago's black population in *Fifteenth Census of the United States: 1930* (Washington DC, 1933), 67.

10. *Indianapolis Freeman*, December 23, 1911.

11. *Indianapolis Freeman*, December 28, 1912; *Chicago Defender*, March 22, 1913, and July 5, 1913. For the American Giants' performance in the CWL, see William F. McNeil, *The California Winter League: America's First Integrated Professional Baseball League* (Jefferson NC: McFarland, 2002), 42. See also *Seattle Post-Intelligencer*,

April 5, 6, 7, 1913. Coverage of the American Giants' winter tour by the black press includes *Chicago Defender*, April 12, 19, 26, 1913; *Indianapolis Freeman*, April 19, 26, 1913; and *New York Age*, April 3, 1913.

12. *Chicago Defender*, July 5, 1913, and August 9, 1913; *New York Age*, July 10, 24, 1913.

13. *Indianapolis Freeman*, December 23, 1913.

14. *Chicago Defender*, August 16, 1913. For the Foster interview, see *Chicago Defender*, February 20, 1915.

15. James R. Grossman, *Land of Hope: Chicago, Black Southerners, and the Great Migration* (Chicago: University of Chicago Press, 1989), 74.

16. For an account on the early business strategy of early black baseball clubs, see Michael E. Lomax, *Black Baseball Entrepreneurs, 1860–1901: Operating by Any Means Necessary* (Syracuse NY: Syracuse University Press, 2003).

17. Vishnu V. Oak, *The Negro's Adventure in General Business* (Yellow Springs OH: Antioch Press, 1949), 48. For an account on the proliferation of black teams, see Peterson, *Only the Ball Was White*, 59–72; Phil Dixon and Patrick J. Hannigan, *The Negro Baseball Leagues 1867–1955* (Mattituck NY: Ameron House, 1992), 31–56.

18. For secondary accounts on the evolution of white semiprofessional baseball in Chicago, see Stephen Freeman, "The Baseball Fad in Chicago, 1865–1870: An Exploration of the Role of Sport in the Nineteenth Century," *Journal of Sport History* 5 (Summer 1978): 42–64; Robert Pruter, "Youth Baseball in Chicago, 1868–1890," *Journal of Sport History* 26 (Spring 1999): 1–28; Raymond Schmidt, "The Golden Age of Chicago Baseball," *Chicago History* 29 (Winter 2000): 38–59. For Foster's booking of black and white clubs in Schorling Park, see Peterson, *Only the Ball Was White*, 82; *Chicago Defender*, March 29, 1917.

19. Frank Young's observation in Whitehead, *A Man and His Diamonds*, 49. *Chicago Defender*, November 6, 27, 1915; December 4, 11, 25, 1915; January 1, 8, 22, 1916; March 11, 1916; April 29, 1916; *Indianapolis Freeman*, February 12, 1916, and March 25, 1916.

20. *Chicago Defender*, September 16, 1916.

21. *Chicago Defender*, April 21, 28, 1917.

22. *Chicago Defender*, August 18, 1917, and September 1, 1917.

23. Richard Bak, *Turkey Stearnes and the Detroit Stars: The Negro Leagues in Detroit, 1919–1933* (Detroit: Wayne State University Press, 1994), 55–58; *Chicago Defender*, April 19, 1919, and February 19, 1920.

24. *Chicago Defender*, November 2, 1918, and August 30, 1919. Foster letter to W. T. Smith on July 9, 1919, in Neil Lanctot, *Fair Dealing and Clean Playing: The Hilldale Club and the Development of Black Professional Baseball, 1910–1932* (Jefferson NC: McFarland, 1994), 84.

25. Sol White, *History of Colored Baseball: With Other Documents on the Early Black Game, 1886–1936* (Lincoln: University of Nebraska Press, 1995); *Cleveland Advocate*, January 1, 1919.

26. *Chicago Defender*, October 4, 1919.

27. See any issue of the *Philadelphia Tribune* in the prewar era (roughly 1914–17).

28. *Chicago Defender*, November 29, 1919; December 13, 20, 27, 1919; January 3, 17, 19, 1920.

29. *Chicago Defender*, December 13, 1919.

30. For an interpretation of Booker T. Washington's economic philosophy, see Oak, *The Negro's Adventure in General Business*, 9–25. Wilson Jeremiah Moses, *The Golden Age of Black Nationalism 1850–1925* (Hamden CT: Archon Books, 1978), 83–102.

31. William L. Van Deburg, *New Day in Babylon: The Black Power Movement and American Culture, 1965–75* (Chicago: University of Chicago Press, 1992), 25–26. See also Solomon P. Gethers, "Black Nationalism and Human Liberation," *Black Scholar* 1 (May 1970): 43–50.

32. Juliet E. K. Walker, *The History of Black Business in America: Capitalism, Race, Entrepreneurship* (New York: Macmillan Library Reference USA, 1998); Earl Ofari, *The Myth of Black Capitalism* (New York: Monthly Review Press, 1998); Allan H. Spear, *Black Chicago: The Making of a Negro Ghetto* (Chicago: University of Chicago Press, 1967); August Meier, *Negro Thought in America, 1880–1915* (Ann Arbor: University of Michigan Press, 1963).

33. *Chicago Defender*, December 20, 1919.

34. *Chicago Defender*, December 27, 1919.

35. *Chicago Defender*, January 3, 1920.

36. *Chicago Defender*, January 10, 1920.

37. *Chicago Defender*, January 17, 1920.

38. *Chicago Defender*, February 14, 1920.

39. *Chicago Defender*, February 21, 1920, and March 20, 1920; *Indianapolis Freeman*, February 21, 1920.

# FIVE

# Bessie Coleman

## *"The Only Race Aviatrix in the World"*

BIEKE GILS

The 1920s have often been referred to as an era of change in North America as well as in many European countries. While World War I had left both continents wounded in many respects, there was also, as Sara Jane Deutsch noted, "a pervasive sense of newness," especially where gender roles were concerned.[1] During the war many women had shown themselves capable of taking care of jobs formerly executed by men and had started to demand greater autonomy and independence over their lives and bodies. Women's demand for the vote in the United States (among other countries) was finally heard, contributing to this sense of newness and to the so-called "New Woman." Emblematic of this era was also the female "flapper," who blended typical feminine and masculine categories by bobbing her hair, smoking cigars, dancing in short skirts, and thus breaking with conventional norms that stipulated appropriate behavior for women.[2]

The 1920s was also an era in which entertainment industries in the United States boomed. Large numbers of men and women from a wide range of socioeconomic backgrounds frequented the casinos, theaters, cinemas, and other entertainment venues that proliferated all over the country.[3] The amusement industry was not only attractive to various audiences, but it also opened up employment opportunities for adventure-seeking women and men who aspired to rather "unusual" careers. One of the industries in the 1920s that especially flourished and in which a considerable number of women found employment was that of aviation. It was a "golden age," as Susan Ware pointed out, for women who aspired to become pilots and, like their male counterparts, entice hundreds of spectators with their stunt flying, including the making of loops and figure eights, walking on wings, and jumping out of planes with parachutes.[4]

Flying at the time was an extreme sport. Altitude and speed records were set and shattered on a frequent basis, often at the cost of airplane crashes and deadly accidents. It is not surprising that there was a belief that women's supposedly frail and nervous nature made them more prone to accidents than men, and it made it often difficult for them to gain a foothold in this white- and male-dominated field. Moreover, for women and men of color, such as African Americans, becoming a pilot in the United States was nearly impossible. Indeed while the interwar period witnessed a gradual shift in gender roles and white women made their way into domains that were typically considered male (such as flying airplanes), racial barriers in the United States remained to be broken.

One pioneer who pushed the envelope by becoming the first African American woman to gain a pilot's license, organizing her own aerial exhibitions, and inviting both black and white audiences to attend her shows was Bessie Coleman. Coleman would become an ardent advocate of civil rights who saw aviation as a means for African Americans to enter mainstream society and counteract stereotypes that had inhibited their progress in the professional sphere. Her entrepreneurial spirit, her networking skills, and her ability to turn her aviation shows into a form of popular entertainment for all audiences made her desire to fly possible. She built a remarkable career as a stunt pilot, and her early death in 1926 was, like that of her contemporary Amelia Earhart, both tragic and surrounded by controversy.

### Behind Clouds of Smoke and Vapor

Over the past two decades Coleman's groundbreaking activities as the first African American female aviator have started to receive considerable attention from scholars and aviation institutions. Doris L. Rich produced Coleman's first extensive biography, *Queen Bess*

*Daredevil Aviator*, in 1993, soon to be followed by Elizabeth Amelia Hadley Freydberg's biography, *Bessie Coleman: The Brownskin Lady Bird*, in 1994.[5] More recently and in honor of the centennial of flight (1903–2003), the National Aeronautics and Space Administration of Washington DC published a collection of historical aviation essays, including a chapter by Amy Sue Bix on the gender and racial issues Coleman faced in her pursuit of flying.[6] Around the same time Dominick A. Pisano published *The Airplane in American Culture*, also a collection of aviation essays, in which he encouraged researchers to take aviation history out of isolation and increasingly connect it to a broader cultural context.[7] Jill D. Snider's chapter in that volume addressed the discourses and meanings associated with the roles and participation of African Americans, and Coleman especially, in the largely white field of aviation in the 1920s.[8]

While interest in Coleman's life has started to grow in recent years, among both scholars and the larger public, her accomplishments have long remained underrecognized. This is not at all surprising because aviation schools and institutions in the United States were generally hostile to African American women and men who wanted to learn to fly or find employment in the growing aviation industry. Although several African American inventors experimented with designing, building, and flying airplanes prior to World War I, their efforts were not part of the dominant discourse on aviation at the time and remain largely unknown even today.[9]

Illustrative, for example, is the recent discovery that Emory Malick was probably the first African American who, in 1912, gained a pilot's license in the United States. He learned to fly at the Curtiss Aviation School on North Island, San Diego. Malick reportedly built and flew his own gliders before 1910 and had bought his own biplane by 1914. Later in his career he moved to Philadelphia, where he was an aerial photographer and worked for the Flying Dutchman Air Service, which offered flight instruction, aerial photography, and passenger flights. Whether Malick was an anomaly or part of a larger group of "minority" pilots at the time is not known.[10] What is remarkable, however, is that unlike Bessie Coleman and the first African American military pilot, Eugene Bullard, Malick was able to obtain a pilot's license in the United States and find employment as an aviator there as well. Both Bullard and Coleman obtained their licenses in France, where flying schools were less reluctant to hire African American students than were schools in the United States.

Bullard was a boxer in England and France before he joined the French Foreign Legion in 1915 and won the Croix de Guerre, the highest French military honor, while serving as an infantry soldier during World War I. The following year he transferred to the French Flying Service and flew combat missions as a member of the French-American air squadron, the Lafayette Escadrille. Although Bullard was an incredibly skilled fighter pilot and was credited with the destruction of two German aircraft, for reasons of discrimination he was forced to leave the squadron when the United States entered the war in 1917 and the Lafayette Escadrille became part of the U.S. Army Service.[11] His career as a fighter pilot thus came to an abrupt end, and there would not be another certified African American pilot until Bessie Coleman gained her license in France in 1921.[12]

Unlike her contemporary aviator Amelia Earhart, whose accomplishments received reports in almost every white newspaper and whose aviation columns appeared in popular magazines in the 1920s, Bessie Coleman did not "grace the pages of aviation record books" and for a long time was "conspicuously absent from aviation histories."[13] Coleman did not seem to have written about her life, nor were her feats remarked upon by the white, mainstream newspapers. What we know about Coleman, and from which I draw in this chapter, are a large number of reports in black newspapers, including the *Chicago Defender*, whose editor, Robert Abbott, sponsored some of Coleman's exploits, as well as the Baltimore *Afro-American* and the *Pittsburgh Courier*. Nevertheless, and as her biographers have also noted, tracing details about Coleman's past and personality remains a complex task.[14]

### In Pursuit of Flying

Bessie Coleman was born in 1892 in Atlanta, Texas, to a large family of sharecroppers.[15] When Coleman was two years old, her family moved to Waxahachie, Texas, in the hope that there would be more job opportunities in the cotton industry than there had been in the small town of Atlanta. Later on Coleman's father, George, who had Cherokee heritage and had become tired of the racial discrimination he and his family faced in the South, tried to convince his wife, Susan, to move to Oklahoma in 1901. Susan did not want to move away, so George left his family.[16] In 1915 Bessie Coleman, like several of her siblings and eventually her mother, also fled from the racist and increasingly violent climate in the segregated South to the urban North. She settled in Chicago, a city that attracted large numbers of African Americans in the 1910s and 1920s because it offered freedom from legally sanctioned racial discrimination. Work was hard to come by, however, as stereotypical beliefs about African Americans' incompetence as disciplined workers made employers reluctant to hire them.[17]

At the same time, Chicago was a vibrant city, and like the popular city of New York, its increasing urbanization went hand in hand with a developing entertainment industry. It was here that many African Americans found employment, if not a space that seemed more welcoming to them. While popular entertainment remained for the most part segregated, as Jayna Brown has noted, spaces such as cafes and theaters became key sites for the expression of black female and male identities, the circulation of expressive forms, and the intermingling of individuals from different racial backgrounds.[18] In other words, notions of race became unstable—sometimes broken down, sometimes reinforced. Many African American jazz musicians in Chicago, for example, felt compelled to choose between continuing to play the original "hot" New Orleans style of jazz or adopting the so called "sweet" jazz that was more popular among white performers and audiences. Many black musicians modified their repertoires to fit in with the musical tastes of white performers and audiences in an attempt to cater to mainstream expectations.[19]

Coleman often adopted similar strategies to accommodate both black and white audiences and managers, while navigating her need to make a living and following her passion of flying. As I will further illustrate, it was a combination of Coleman's excellent networking and entrepreneurial skills, the increasingly open attitude toward racial intermingling in the urban North, and the opportunities provided by the French aviation industry that made possible her career as a black woman in a male and white field.

Shortly after Coleman had moved to Chicago, she started work as a manicurist at a barbershop. Already then her entrepreneurial skills were remarked upon by a *Chicago Defender* reporter, winning her the prize of best and fastest manicurist in black Chicago.[20] Coleman was "an example of what a progressive up-to-date young woman should be," and she "should be an inspiration to other young women who contemplate following the same line of endeavor," the reporter wrote.[21] In reference to her successes as a manicurist, Coleman's name would appear several more times in the *Defender*, although she soon left the barbershop scene for pursuits that were perhaps more exciting and exclusive, such as flying an airplane. This was not a surprising development, given her desire for entrepreneurial opportunities, her energy, and her zest for life.

Like many other Americans, Bessie Coleman was enthralled by the burgeoning aviation industry. Not only did the stories about aviators in World War I that she heard from her male clientele in the barbershop arouse her interest, but her two older brothers, John and Walter, who had both served in France as soldiers, also told her about their fascination with airplanes and flying. They also mentioned that several French women had learned to fly, not thinking that this would ever be a possibility for their sister.[22]

Coleman had a strong personality and was determined to pursue her goals regardless of other people's advice. She clearly did not follow the usual path dictated for a woman of her age and background. When she married Claude Glenn in 1917, a man who was fourteen years her senior, she did not inform any of her close family members, and it is not clear whether Coleman and Glenn ever actually lived together. According to her niece Marion, Coleman was an attractive woman who had various relationships with both black and white men. Because she was relatively light-skinned, she was able to "make herself up to look like different nationalities," the wife of one of Coleman's brothers noted.[23]

Undoubtedly Coleman's business acumen and her good looks facilitated her aviation career. In her article on the history of manicurists, Julie Willett takes it one step further by suggesting that in the 1910s and 1920s many male patrons saw little difference between a female manicurist and a saloon girl or prostitute, and she suggests that Coleman developed relationships with Chicago's most powerful and influential men while working in the barbershop. No doubt, she writes, many men "found her an object of titillation."[24] Although there is no evidence as to how exactly Coleman was able to secure funds, it is clear that she was able to establish various connections with influential businessmen who encouraged her to become involved in aviation and financially supported her plans to fly.

One of these businessmen was Robert Abbott, the wealthy editor of the *Chicago Defender* and an ardent promoter of the advancement of African Americans. He shared a vision with Coleman that African Americans should be encouraged to take an interest in aviation. He also wanted to promote his newspaper, and in Coleman he saw the perfect candidate for boosting the public's interest in the *Defender*. Whether Abbott genuinely believed in Coleman's abilities or whether he simply saw the unusual story of an attractive young woman attempting to fly as an opportunity to increase his revenues is not clear. It was Abbott and, presumably, African American philanthropist Jesse Binga, founder of the Binga State Bank, who provided Coleman with the initial funds necessary to pursue her ambitious plans. According to Freydberg, Binga and Abbott were the benefactors behind the practical business pursuits of many prominent African Americans during the early 1920s.[25]

### On a Mission to France

At the time Coleman wanted to learn to fly almost all flying schools in the United States were operated by white men. None of them seemed to accept black candidates, and only a small number of schools accepted women. As a black woman it was thus impossible for Coleman to find an aviation teacher in the United States. Therefore Abbott encouraged Coleman to try to find a flying school in France, the country that had offered Eugene Bullard his flight training in 1917.

In France, and in Paris especially, an African American community had formed after the end of World War I. Many of the large numbers of black soldiers who had been sent to serve in France had remained there after the war because of violent racism in their home country. Instead of the greater acceptance they had hoped for upon returning home, given their contributions to the military, tensions between blacks and whites escalated in 1919 and gave way to what was called "the Red Summer," a period of massive riots in many cities in the United States. The worst of the riots occurred in Chicago and lasted more than a week, resulting in thirty-eight deaths and more than five hundred injured. According to Tyler Stovall, these postwar riots, as well as an upsurge in lynching, were mostly instigated by white vigilantes who feared the presumably newly assertive black population. These and other incidents reinforced the belief of many black Americans in the contrast between a tolerant France and a racist United States and contributed to the rise of a black expatriate community in interwar Paris.[26]

Paris in the 1920s, like Chicago, was a lively city known for its art and entertainment scene, and it was attractive to a host of African American musicians, singers, dancers, athletes, and other performers who had started to migrate there after 1900.[27] Coleman was not the first among her fellow country(wo)men to go to Paris in the hope of finding opportunities in this supposedly "color-blind land of tolerance."[28] Like Bullard, who went to Paris to box on the European circuit, Texan boxer Jack Johnson tried his luck as a boxer and vaudeville performer in Europe between 1908 and 1915.[29] Another of Coleman's contemporaries, Josephine Baker, started her career in 1921 as a member of the infamous Broadway musical *Shuffle Along* before opening her own cabaret in France in 1925, revolutionizing the Parisian entertainment scenery with her erotic, almost nude, dance performances.[30]

France at the time was not only a popular site for staged entertainment, but it was also a hub for barnstormers and other aviation enthusiasts in the 1920s.[31] The country had been the first to host an international air meet in 1909 in Reims, and it was well known for its numerous aviation pioneers and the good reputation of its aircraft manufacturers.[32] Coleman's career thus took off at the crossroads of aviation's popularity as a form of entertainment in both

France and the United States and France's more welcoming attitude toward African Americans.

In November 1920 Coleman sailed for France.[33] She visited several flying schools near Paris, though flight instructors there tried to discourage her from taking up flying because two other women had recently died in a crash during practice.[34] Coleman was still determined to earn her license and finally found the Caudron School of Aviation, which was willing to accept her. René and Gaston Caudron had opened their flying school in 1912 in Le Crotoy, near the bay of the Somme, where long stretches of sandy beach offered an excellent base for takeoffs and landings.[35] The school had been closed during the war and reopened in 1919. The brothers wanted to attract students to their flying school, so they kept the tariffs for lessons low and they also welcomed women.[36] Coleman completed the ten-month course requirements, and on June 15, 1921, after passing the strict Fédération Aéronautique Internationale (FAI) examination, she earned the first international pilot's license ever awarded to an African American woman.[37]

### The Tulsa Race Riot

While Coleman was abroad, another violent riot that would greatly affect and shape the meaning of airplanes and aviation for African Americans took place in Tulsa, Oklahoma, in June 1921. An unresolved lynching incident gave rise to a violent aerial attack. Six white pilots in airplanes dispatched from the nearby Curtiss flying field set the Greenwood District on fire and thereby killed seventy-five Tulsans, two-thirds of whom were black. It was the first time in history that airplanes were used to attack a black community, and the incident generated much debate about the dangers for African Americans in the coming aviation age. There was much fear that the airplane, in white men's hands, could result in the extermination of the African American race.[38]

According to Jill Snider, two main philosophies emerged in the riot's aftermath. The Garvey Movement, established by the Black Nationalist leader Marcus Garvey, focused primarily on the airplane as a menace and a tool of the white man for controlling the African

American race. Anticipating a great race war, Garvey encouraged African Americans to become involved in aviation and to secure as many airplanes as possible. Adopting an apocalyptic undertone, he was convinced that the Tulsa incident was just the beginning and that if African Americans did not take action immediately, it would lead to their elimination. On the other hand, the *Chicago Defender,* the *Pittsburgh Courier,* and the *Afro-American* all entertained a more constructive and positive perspective, promoting aviation as industry that held opportunities for African Americans rather than viewing it as a menace. By learning how to fly, African Americans would not only be able to become part of the "winged gospel" of mainstream society but would also dispel stereotypes about their lesser intelligence, incompetence, and lack of ambition.[39] It was Bessie Coleman who would become the promoter and, indeed, the personification of this view.

Approximately four months after the atrocities in Tulsa, Coleman arrived back in Chicago. Much hope now lay with her, as she was the only black pilot in the United States and was already perceived as a successful woman by the black community. The Shuffle Along musical company welcomed her with a cup "as a token of their appreciation of her achievement in aviation."[40] Coleman had become the African American winged gospel's missionary—almost literally an angel from the sky—who held together the belief that there was a future for African Americans in aviation. Playing up her own courage and the perceived urge for African Americans to enter aviation and catch up with white pilots, Coleman told a *Chicago Defender* reporter, "Well, . . . I knew we had no aviators, neither men nor women, and I knew the Race needed to be represented among this most important line, so I thought it my duty to risk my life to learn aviating and to encourage flying among men and women of the Race who are so far behind the white men in this special line."[41]

Despite her enthusiasm and the black community's confidence in her abilities, Coleman's plans did not run smoothly. In order to locate an airplane and a flying field for her shows in the United States, she had to rely on the white aviation community. Yet few white newspapers picked up her remarkable story. White aviators and owners of airfields either did not know her or simply chose to ignore her because of their lack of confidence in the flying abilities of a black woman, and thus her aspirations for a flying show did not materialize.[42] On February 22, 1922, Coleman sailed back to France in the hope of finding a solution there.[43] It is not clear how she was able to fund this second trip, but "in circumstances different from her first departure," Rich pointed out, "Bessie now had not only chic Paris gowns and attractive leather flying apparel but much favorable newspaper exposure, especially from hometown supporter Robert Abbott's *Chicago Defender.*"[44]

### Missionary, Entrepreneur, Entertainer

Upon her arrival in New York on August 14, 1922, having spent approximately six months abroad, Coleman was not only welcomed by African American reporters but also by those from the *New York Times* and the *Chicago Tribune.*[45] The news about her success in Europe must have reached the United States before her arrival, as it certainly sparked the curiosity of the white newspapers. The *New York Times* announced that the "Negro aviatrix" had arrived and enthusiastically reported on Coleman's accomplishments abroad:

> Termed by leading French and Dutch aviators one of the best flyers they had seen, Miss Bessie Coleman, said to be the only negro [*sic*] aviatrix in the world, returned from Europe yesterday to give a series of exhibitions in this country, particularly among her own people. At Staaken, the flying field outside Berlin, Miss Coleman, without any instruction, flew a 220-horsepower Benz motored LFG plane, winning for herself, according to documents she brought back, the distinction of having piloted the largest plane ever flown by a woman. German newspapers spoke in high terms of her ability. Miss Coleman visited Amsterdam, where she flew planes manufactured by Anthony G. H. Fokker, and at Friedrichshafen she gave a series of flights in a Dornier flying boat.[46]

The favorable acknowledgements of her accomplishments by both black and white newspapers now enabled the organization of her long-planned flying shows. It would not prove an easy task, however, to balance expectations from black audiences, white audiences, managers, and other individuals who tried to capitalize on her success while simultaneously finding enough financial support to rent or buy airplanes and organize air shows.

In an attempt to pursue her goals in aviation, Coleman had to play several roles. Not only did she have to be an aviation missionary or crusader, as Snider points out, but she also had to be an entrepreneur and an entertainer.[47] These roles frequently conflicted, and they made Coleman's motivations often seem controversial. Such controversy occurred mostly when companies tried to lure her into some kind of lucrative project that would offer her financial support but was at the same time disrespectful of her personal ambitions and background. The manner in which Coleman negotiated opportunities that also imposed restrictions on her ambitions is best illustrated in the ways she organized her shows, entertained both black and white audiences, and interacted with her managers.

By the end of August 1922, with Abbott as her sponsor and publicity manager, Coleman had established headquarters at the *Chicago Defender*'s offices in New York to book her barnstorming exhibitions.[48] For her first exhibition, on September 3, 1922, at the Curtiss airfield in Garden City, Long Island, New York, the Glenn Curtiss Company, the largest aircraft manufacturer in the United States, lent her one of its airplanes.[49] "Beyond question, this event will be the greatest attraction ever staged in America," the *Chicago Defender* asserted, guaranteeing that the "wonderful little woman, the only aviatrix of the Race, will do heart-thrilling stunts that will be astounding."[50] The newspaper also promised "eight other sensational flights by American aces," as well as "giant passenger planes holding 16 or more passengers in which sightseeing flights by the public will be made."[51]

Revealing her talent as a brilliant entertainer, Coleman did not disappoint her audience. She arranged a show that appealed to both white and black audiences by playing on America's patriotism in general and on the promotion of African Americans in particular. She staged the show in honor of the Fifteenth New York Infantry, the first African American regiment sent to France during World War I, which was comprised primarily of jazz musicians and theater practitioners. Although the regiment no longer existed, the Fifteenth's regimental band, known for introducing Europe to brass-band jazz, was still operational.[52] After the band played "The Star Spangled Banner," Coleman, dressed in breeches and a French officer's jacket with a Sam Brown belt, went up twice "to the delight of the hundreds of enthusiasts of both races."[53] Although stunt flying was not allowed on the Curtiss field and Coleman could not perform the aerial tricks she had learned in Europe, her show proved a spectacular success. In addition, while the eight promised American aces did not make an appearance,[54] Hubert Fauntleroy Julian, a black aviation enthusiast and parachute jumper from Trinidad, "thrilled the spectators with a parachute drop from a Curtiss plane from over 2,000 feet in the air and landed without injury."[55] This jump would be the beginning of Julian's own aviation career.[56]

In September 1922 Coleman returned to Chicago, where she began preparations for her second airshow, which was to be held at the Checkerboard Aerodrome a month later. The *Chicago Defender* announced that "an elaborate program of special flights has been arranged for 'Queen Bess,' whose daredevil flying amazed continental Europe and was applauded in Paris, Berlin and Munich."[57] This time Coleman performed stunts, including figure eights, in honor of the African American Eighth Illinois Infantry regiment.[58] While the regiment band entertained the audience with jazz music, Coleman executed several stunts named after famous flying aces. She took off, for example, with a "French Nungesser start," referring to France's third-ranking World War I fighter pilot, Charles Nungesser. According to Freydberg, this stunt consisted of staying low to the ground during takeoff and dipping the plane close to the audience before ascending into the air.[59] In this same flight, the *Defender* wrote, "the Spansih [sic] Bertha Costa Climb was made[,] and the American Curtis McMullen turn, the Eddie Rickenbacker straighten-up, the Richtofen-German glide and the Ralph C. Diggins landing were featured."[60] The "Bertha Costa Climb" referred to American (not Spanish) pilot Bertrand B. Costa.[61] American Eddie Rickenbacker, German Manfred von Richthofen, and American (Chicagoan) Ralph Diggins were all World War I flying aces, credited with several air combat victories.[62] In addition to Coleman's stunts, the *Defender* had also announced a "drop of death," or parachute jump, by Coleman's sister Georgia.[63] According to Freydberg, Bessie had not instructed her sister about how to perform a parachute jump until the actual moment she was supposed to jump out of the plane, so Georgia refused.[64] According to Rich, however, Bessie had discussed the jump with Georgia the night before, and it was then that she refused.[65] Regardless of what actually happened, the fact that Coleman seemed to trust that her sister would be able to perform a parachute jump without prior instruction illustrates her adventure-seeking, daredevil personality. It did not seem to occur to her that not everyone shared her delight in such risky stunts.

Coleman's shows were successful in that she was able to provide entertainment for both black and white audiences. Whereas white audiences may have perceived Coleman as an attraction per se, seeing a black woman performing aerial stunts was a spectacular novelty. For the black community her shows symbolized courage and hope for African Americans' increased involvement in aviation. Her public displays of courage, intelligence, and bravado challenged whites' notions of black debility and female fragility. To foster courage and to inspire African Americans to take aviation seriously, Coleman presented herself as a strong-minded, fearless woman. The military outfits she wore for her exhibitions not only symbolized her deep respect for both the black and white individuals who had fought in the war but also emphasized the seriousness with which she undertook the role of aviation's advocate.

Unquestionably the media played a major part in the construction of Coleman's persona as a brave and intrepid African American woman. The femininity of white female pilots was emphasized in the media by references to them as "lady fliers," "angels," "sweethearts of the air," or "flying flappers";[66] references to Coleman in white newspapers were less playful, often impersonal, and usually pointed to her racialized identity.[67] Headlines such as "First Colored Aviatrix," "Negress an Air Pilot," or "Negro Aviatrix Arrives" were frequently used.[68] As Evelyn Brooks Higginbotham has noted, "Ladies [as white female aviators were often termed] were not merely women; they represented a class, a differentiated status within the generic category of "women. . . . But no black woman, regardless of income, education, refinement, or character enjoyed the status of lady."[69] Also, as Susan Cahn has pointed out, "womanliness" in the 1920s was rooted in the privileged position of the "lady," in contrast to the view of black women as "robust, unruly, insensitive to pain or exhaustion, and rough in manners."[70] At the same time, black newspapers referred to Coleman as "Queen Bess," "Queen of the Air," "Bird Woman," and "pioneer air bird of the race," titles that perhaps also deemphasized Coleman's femininity but showed respect for her position as a leading figure and an advocate for African Americans in aviation.[71] Higginbotham explains that to be called a "race leader," "race woman," or in Coleman's case "race aviatrix" by the black community "was not a sign of insult or disapproval." It was a way for blacks to fashion "race into a cultural identity that resisted white hegemonic discourses."[72]

A few days after Coleman's show in Chicago, the *Afro-American* announced that she had agreed to star in the film *Shadow and Sunshine*, to be produced by the African American–owned Seminole Film Company.[73] "Bessie Coleman, the only colored woman aviatrix, will be the featured artist. Supporting her will be about twelve carefully selected and experienced movie performers," the newspaper reported in October 1922.[74] Although Coleman had indeed signed the contract, to the great frustration of the Seminole filmmakers, she did not show up for the filming. The production of the film had been delayed, the *Afro-American* wrote in early December 1922,

> because of the temperament of that young lady [Bessie Coleman], who after coming to New York at the expense of the company, changed her mind and abruptly left New York without notice to the director. Six autos filled with a cast of thirty people, two photographers and the directors waited in vain for two hours on the lady. . . . The Seminole is fortunate in that they have obtained the services of Miss Bessie Allison, a pretty little girl with both personality and theatrical experience, to say nothing of an unmistakable culture and a social status that will be an asset to the company.[75]

The reason Coleman did not show up for the filming remains obscure. According to Rich, Coleman was told she would have to dress in ragged clothing and carry a walking stick and a pack on her back to portray an ignorant girl who had just arrived in New York.[76] Coleman clearly decided that such an "Uncle Tom" depiction would not further her cause and would not only diminish both her personal efforts and remarkable accomplishments but would also reinforce stereotypes about African Americans.[77] Although her withdrawal set her back financially and put her reputation at risk, by the end of January 1923 she had taken a job of flying to advertise rubber tires for the Californian Coast Tire and Rubber Company of Oakland.[78]

With the money Coleman made advertising for the tire company (by dropping leaflets out of an airplane, for example), she was able to gather enough funds to buy a Curtiss JN-4, or "Jenny," one of the most commonly used and cheapest airplanes at the time. During an exhibition in Santa Monica, California, in February 1923 her motor stalled, and the plane dove into a crash. Coleman was injured, sustaining a broken leg, fractured ribs, cuts, and possibly internal injuries.[79] Fearful that her accident would discourage African Americans from taking up flying and concerned that the general public and her sponsors might lose trust in her abilities, Coleman claimed that the fact she was still living proved that "flying in the air is no more dangerous than riding an automobile on the surface."[80] Moreover, despite the reality that she had not only lost her plane but also had to recover from severe injuries, Coleman urged the *Chicago Defender* to inform her fans that she would come back.[81] To support her the *Defender* insinuated that perhaps "some mechanics had tampered with the steering apparatus in an effort to keep her from gaining the recognition due to her."[82] It is uncertain whether Coleman's plane was indeed sabotaged. The accident may well have resulted from the poor state of her airplane. As Edward DeV. Bunn Jr. points out, unlike Earhart, who "flew top notch technologically advanced planes, Coleman was forced by her meager financial means to fly second rate, broken down, and falling-apart aircraft."[83]

Between the time of Coleman's accident in 1923 and May 1925, newspaper coverage of her aviation career dwindled significantly.

Not only had the accident cost her possible sponsors, but Coleman had also gained a reputation for being unreliable. The *Afro-American*, for example, wrote in May 1924 that "Bessie Coleman, the colored girl who has been presenting herself as an aviatrix for the past two seasons . . . has in that time accumulated a long list of incomplete contracts, and an almost as lengthy list of managers and agents."[84] Around the same time an article in the *Chicago Defender* warned managers not to book Coleman because "a large number of complaints against Miss Coleman from reliable showmen and noted citizens" had been made.[85]

It was not until May 1925 that Coleman finally succeeded in arranging a series of lectures and exhibition flights in her home state of Texas.[86] P. DeWalt, owner of one of the most successful black playhouses in the South, Houston's Lincoln Theater, supported the cause of "lifting up" African Americans through aviation and agreed to manage Coleman's shows.[87] Aside from Coleman's stunts, the Texas shows also featured established white stunt flyer Captain R. W. Mackie, who probably provided Coleman with an airplane, and one of his troop members, parachute jumper Ulysses Stallings.[88] Coleman's initial shows in Houston proved so successful that she was invited to perform in Austin, San Antonio, Wharton, and Waxahachie, Texas. In Waxahachie the organizers initially arranged separate admission gates for black and white spectators, but Coleman opposed this plan and refused to perform unless the city provided a single entrance. Although her demand was accommodated, the fact that the audience was segregated again as soon as it had entered the venue must have infuriated Coleman.[89] Asked to perform a parachute jump at the annual flower show of the Orlando Chamber of Commerce in Florida for a white-only audience, she refused until the organizers, despite strictly enforced segregation laws in Florida, finally gave in and opened the event to both black and white spectators.[90]

## The Sky Is the Limit for Queen Bess

In 1926 the Negro Welfare League in Jacksonville, Florida, asked Coleman to perform at its annual First of May Field Day. Honored, Coleman accepted this invitation, hoping to be able to raise the necessary funds for the flying school she had dreamed of for some time. In Florida she had trouble locating an airplane because dealers were reluctant to sell planes to African Americans. Instead she contacted her (white) mechanic, William D. Wills, in Dallas, Texas, and asked him to fly a plane to Florida for her performance. The plane, again a Jenny, was not very well maintained, and Wills had to make two forced landings on his way to Jacksonville.[91] Nevertheless, that was the plane Coleman could afford and the one she was to use for her show.[92]

The day before the exhibition Wills test-piloted the plane with Coleman as his passenger. When the plane unexpectedly went into a nosedive, Coleman, who was peering over the edge of the cockpit without her seatbelt attached, was catapulted out of the plane and fell to her death. Wills, still in the plane thanks to his seatbelt, righted the aircraft but then hit the top of a tree and plunged to the ground. It was reported that John T. Betsch, Coleman's Florida publicity manager and a member of the Jacksonville Negro Welfare League, rushed to the plane and, to calm his nerves, struck a match to light a cigarette, thereby igniting the gasoline fumes surrounding the plane. Wills died inside the burning aircraft.[93]

Inevitably Coleman's death spurred a number of speculations. According to Freydberg, some African Americans believed that Wills or "white people" had sabotaged Coleman's plane. It seemed to make sense, given that Wills had succeeded in regaining control over the plane after Coleman had fallen out.[94] The *Chicago Defender*, however, silenced most suspicions by reporting that the "expert aviators" who had examined the wreckage believed that a wrench had slid between the control gears and jammed them, causing the accident. According to the experts, the plane was an "old-fashioned army type," and they concluded that the accident would not have happened in a modern plane with protected gears.[95] Coleman's death was mourned by many, and both black and white admirers attended her three memorial services. The first was held on May 2, 1926, in Jacksonville, Florida, followed shortly by a service in Orlando, Florida, and a last one in Chicago. Coleman was buried in the Lincoln Cemetery in Blue Island, Illinois, where several famous African Americans, such as Robert Abbott (1870–1940), blues musician Big Bill Broonzy (1898–

1958), and jazz pianist and singer Lil Harding Armstrong (1898–1971), were laid to rest as well.

Although Coleman's career was short, her tragic death made her an inspiring symbol—even a martyr, some would argue—of African American pursuits in the field of aviation. In the first decades after her death the *Chicago Defender*'s readers were frequently reminded of Coleman's courageous exploits and encouraged to follow her example. Although Coleman had begun to pave the way for the acceptance of African Americans in aviation, those who tried to gain a foothold continued to be discouraged because of the discrimination they faced from the white aviation industry. "Disaster seems to attend all our efforts in this field," a reporter in the *Chicago Defender* noted, "partly because of a lack of interest on our part, and partly because of insufficient preparation on the part of those who are trying. We are barred from schools of aviation; the government shuts the doors in our faces, and lack of funds makes it impossible for us to procure first class equipment for our efforts in aviation."[96]

It soon became clear that Coleman's accomplishments were exceptional and not something many black Americans at the time would be able to repeat. The rallying notion of "racial uplift," as promoted by Coleman, "illustrates the problematic aspect of identifying a standpoint that encompasses all black women" or all black Americans, Higginbotham explained. Also, the notions that black Americans had to catch up with the white and learn how to fly to enter white mainstream society equated normality with conformity to white middle-class standards and values. Racial uplift certainly stood in sharp contrast "with daily practices and aesthetic tastes of many poor, uneducated, and 'unassimilated' black men and women dispersed throughout the rural South or newly huddled in urban centers."[97]

William Powell (1897–1942) was among the first African Americans to earn a pilot license following Coleman's death. After being turned away from flight schools in Chicago, he earned his permit at Warren College of Aeronautics in Los Angeles in 1928. Powell, inspired by Coleman, went on to establish a Bessie Coleman Aero Club and the first aviation school for African Americans.[98] The first African American woman to follow in Coleman's footsteps was Willa

Brown (1906–92), who earned her pilot license in 1937 and would in later years become an advocate for the advancement of aviation for African Americans.[99] Brown was able to set up a flying school in Chicago, but as flight training remained a segregated activity, the school's flying field had to be created outside the city limits. In the military African Americans continued to face discrimination and prejudice; they were barred from flight training in the United States until World War II, when the first black air corps, the Tuskegee Airmen, was established, with Coleman as their inspirational muse.[100] Today the Bessie Coleman Foundation in Washington DC encourages African American women to take up flying and provides a strong base of support for both female and male African American aviators.[101]

While the percentage of African American male, and especially female, airline pilots in the United States today is still very small as they continue to face discrimination, Bessie Coleman remains an important source of courage and inspiration.[102] Unlike Earhart, who was backed in most of her endeavors by her manager and husband George Palmer Putnam, Coleman was a self-made woman who boldly confronted and surmounted the racial and gender barriers of her era, making her a lasting symbol of black progress in aviation.

### Notes

The title reflects the words of the *Chicago Defender*. See "Bessie Coleman Makes Initial Aerial Flight," *Chicago Defender*, October 21, 1922. On several other occasions the *Chicago Defender* refers to Bessie Coleman as "the only Race aviatrix" (in "World's Greatest Event," August 26, 1922) or "the only aviatrix of the Race" (in "Rain Halts the Initial Flight of Miss Bessie," September 2, 1922).

1. Sara Jane Deutsch, "From Ballots to Breadlines 1920–1940," in *No Small Courage: A History of Women in the United States*, ed. Nancy F. Cott (New York: Oxford University Press, 2000), 413.

2. See, for example, Carroll Smith-Rosenberg, *Disorderly Conduct: Visions of Gender in Victorian America* (New York: Alfred A. Knopf, 1985).

3. See Kathy Peiss, *Cheap Amusements: Working Women and Leisure in Turn-of-the-Century New York* (Philadelphia: Temple University Press, 1986).

4. Susan Ware, *Still Missing: Amelia Earhart and the Search for Modern Feminism* (New York: W. W. Norton, 1993), 61. Many women would exchange their daring jobs as stunt pilots for more secure jobs as airplane demonstrators, airplane salespersons, flight instructors, or aerial photographers later on. See Joseph

J. Corn, "Making Flying 'Thinkable': Women Pilots and the Selling of Aviation, 1927–1940," *American Quarterly* 31, no. 4 (1979): 556–57.

5. Doris L. Rich, *Queen Bess Daredevil Aviator* (Washington DC: Smithsonian Institution Press, 1993); Elizabeth Amelia Hadley Freydberg, *Bessie Coleman: The Brownskin Lady Bird* (New York: Garland, 1994).

6. Amy Sue Bix, "Bessie Coleman Race and Gender Realities behind Aviation Dreams," in *Realizing the Dream of Flight*, ed. Virginia P. Dawson and Mark D. Bowles (Washington DC: National Aeronautics and Space Administration, NASA History Division, 2005), 1–27.

7. Dominick A. Pisano, "New Directions in the History of Aviation," in *The Airplane in American Culture*, ed. Dominick A. Pisano (Ann Arbor: University of Michigan Press, 2006), 10.

8. Jill D. Snider, "'Great Shadow in the Sky': The Airplane in the Tulsa Riot of 1921 and the Development of African American Visions of Aviation, 1921–1926," in *The Airplane in American Culture*, ed. Dominick A. Pisano (Ann Arbor: University of Michigan Press, 2006), 105–47.

9. Robert Jakeman, "America's Black Air Pioneers," unpublished dissertation, Maxwell Air Force Base, Alabama, 1988, 3–5. See also Von Hardesty, *Black Wings: Courageous Stories of African Americans in Aviation and Space History* (New York: HarperCollins, 2008), and Samuel Broadnax, *Blue Skies, Black Wings* (Westport CT: Praeger, 2007).

10. Rebecca Maksel, "The Unrecognized Firsts," *Smithsonian Air and Space Magazine*, March 2011, http://www.airspacemag.com/history-of-flight/the-unrecognized-first-79496373/?no-ist (accessed August 25, 2014).

11. Jakeman, "America's Black Air Pioneers," 4; Jill D. Snider, "Flying to Freedom: African-American Visions of Aviation, 1910–1927," PhD diss., University of North Carolina, 1995, 35–36.

12. The U.S. military services remained segregated throughout World War II, but the African American "Tuskegee Airmen," known as the "Red Tails," earned fame as combat aviators.

13. Freydberg, *Bessie Coleman*, 18.

14. One of the few known accounts of Coleman's life story is by her sister, Elois Coleman Patterson, *Memoirs of the Late Bessie Coleman Aviatrix: Pioneer of the Negro People in Aviation* (Washington DC: Bessie Coleman Foundation [BCF], 1969).

15. Controversy exists around Coleman's date of birth. Although Elois Patterson writes in *Memoirs of the Late Bessie Coleman Aviatrix* that Coleman was born in 1893 and her pilot license indicates 1896, most sources refer to 1892 as the correct year.

16. For a brief but good overview of Coleman's history, see the official Bessie Coleman website: http://www.bessiecoleman.com/Other%20pages/universal.html (accessed August 16, 2014).

17. James Grossman, "Great Migration," entry in *Encyclopedia of Chicago*, http://www.encyclopedia.chicagohistory.org/pages/545.html (accessed August 8, 2014).

18. Jayna Brown, *Babylon Girls: Black Women Performers and the Shaping of*

*the Modern* (Durham NC: Duke University Press, 2008). See also Freydberg, *Bessie Coleman*, 5, 25, 30.

19. Lynne Seago, "From Potent to Popular: The Effects of Racism on Chicago Jazz 1920–1930," *Constructing the Past* 1, no. 1 (2000): 43–51.

20. Rich, *Queen Bess Daredevil Aviator*, 14, 19–20. See also K. Creasman, "Black Birds in the Sky: The Legacies of Bessie Coleman and Dr. Mae Jemison," *Journal of Negro History* 82, no. 1 (1997): 158–68.

21. "Miss Bessie Coleman among the First to Clamp on 'Flu' Lid," *Chicago Defender*, November 2, 1918, 12.

22. Freydberg, *Bessie Coleman*, 179; Rich, *Queen Bess Daredevil Aviator*, 26–27.

23. Rich, *Queen Bess Daredevil Aviator*, 3, 23, 31, 80.

24. Julie Willett, "'Hands across the Table': A Short History of the Manicurist in the Twentieth Century," *Journal of Women's History* 17, no. 3 (2005): 63.

25. Freydberg, *Bessie Coleman*, 72–74; Rich, *Queen Bess Daredevil Aviator*, 29–30.

26. William M. Tuttle Jr., *Race Riot Chicago in the Red Summer of 1919* (Urbana: University of Illinois Press, 1970); Tyler Stovall, "Gender, Race, and Miscegenation: African Americans in Jazz Age Paris," in *The Modern Woman Revisited: Paris between the Wars*, ed. Whitney Chadwick and Tirza True Latimer (New Brunswick NJ: Rutgers University Press, 2003), 21–23 (quote, 23).

27. David McCullough, *The Greater Journey: Americans in Paris* (New York: Simon and Schuster, 2011); Gerald R. Gems, *Boxing: A Concise History of the Sweet Science* (Lanham MD: Rowman and Littlefield, 2014), 30–33, 35, 76–77, 91, 95.

28. Karen C. C. Dalton and Henry L. Gates Jr., "Josephine Baker and Paul Colin: African American Dance Seen through Parisian Eyes," *Critical Inquiry* 24, no. 4 (1998): 904.

29. Theresa Runstedtler, *Jack Johnson: Rebel Sojourner Boxing in the Shadow of the Global Color Line* (Berkeley: University of California Press, 2012).

30. Dalton and Gates, "Josephine Baker and Paul Colin." See also Elisabeth Ezra, "A Colonial Princess: Josephine Baker's French Films," in *The Colonial Unconscious: Race and Culture in Interwar France* (Ithaca NY: Cornell University Press, 2000), 97–128.

31. Freydberg explains: "Barnstorming was a term initially associated with theatre, and it referred to actors who traveled from city to city and town to town. Because in most cases there was nowhere for them to board, or lodge temporarily while on the performing circuit, they found the nearest barn to sleep in for the night, and by day they moved on to the next town to perform. By the early 1920s aeronautical barnstorming had become synonymous with adventurous people, primarily unemployed former World War I fighter pilots, who flew surplus army aircraft for entertainment. These pilots would 'buzz' a town in their aircraft—fly low to get the townspeople's attention and then fly off towards the nearest open field. There they would exhibit stunts of parachute jumping, wing walking, low dives and dangerously daring maneuvers in the air. The performance usually culminated in taking an eager passenger up for a brief ride in the plane for a fee of

$1 to $5, depending on the reputation and the skill of the pilot. At day's end, the pilots would locate a barn in which to board themselves and the plane for the night" (Freydberg, *Bessie Coleman*, 85).

32. See Luc Robène, Dominique Bodin, and Stéphane Héas, "Pau et l'invention de l'aviation 'sportive' (1908–1910). Des enjeux technologiques aux plaisirs mondains: Naissance d'un loisir et nouveaux pouvoirs du corps," *Revue Internationale des Sciences du Sport et de l'Éducation Physique* 87 (2010); James M. Laux, "The Rise and Fall of Armand Deperdussin," *French Historical Studies* 8, no. 1 (1973): 95–104; Thomas Ameye, Bieke Gils, and Pascal Delheye, "Belgian Pioneers in Rally Racing and Aerial Sports during the Belle Époque," *International Journal for the History of Sport* 28, no. 2 (2011): 205–39.

33. Freydberg, *Bessie Coleman*, 72–74; Rich, *Queen Bess Daredevil Aviator*, 29–30.

34. "Aviatrix Must Sign away Life to Learn Trade," *Chicago Defender*, October 8, 1921.

35. Jacques Béal, *Bessie Coleman, l'ange noir* (Paris: Éditions Michalon, 2008), 73–74.

36. Béal, *Bessie Coleman*, 75.

37. "Chicago Girl Is Full-Fledged Aviator Now," *Chicago Defender*, October 1, 1921; "Aviatrix Must Sign Away Life to Learn Trade," *Chicago Defender*, October 8, 1921; Freydberg, *Bessie Coleman*, 82. The FAI, established in France in 1905, was the official organization that mandated the first air safety guidelines in 1910 for France, the United States, and sixteen member nations. It still exists today and governs the eligibility guidelines for the acquisition of an international license and validates flying records. See Freydberg, *Bessie Coleman*, 82.

38. Snider, "Great Shadow in the Sky," 105, 112. See also Tim Madigan, *The Burning: Massacre, Destruction, and the Tulsa Race Riot of 1921* (New York: St Martin's Press, 2001).

39. Snider, "Great Shadow in the Sky," 115.

40. "'Shuffle Along' Company Gives Fair Flyer Cup," *Chicago Defender*, October 8, 1921.

41. "Aviatrix Must Sign Away Life to Learn Trade," *Chicago Defender*, October 8, 1921.

42. Freydberg, *Bessie Coleman*, 83.

43. "Bessie Coleman Leaves New York for France," *Chicago Defender*, February 25, 1922; Rich, *Queen Bess Daredevil Aviator*, 39.

44. Rich, *Queen Bess Daredevil Aviator*, 39. It needs to be stated that information on Coleman's time abroad is hard to find; also her biographers—of whom one, Jacques Béal, is French—remain rather unspecific on this particular time in Coleman's life. The information that is available is largely based on the accounts of the *Chicago Defender*.

45. Freydberg, *Bessie Coleman*, 83–85.

46. "Negro Aviatrix Arrives," *New York Times*, August 14, 1922.

47. Snider, "Flying to Freedom," 135, 138.

48. "Bessie to Fly over Gotham," *Chicago Defender*, August 26, 1922; Freydberg, *Bessie Coleman*, 86; Rich, *Queen Bess Daredevil Aviator*, 48.

49. For more information on Glenn Curtiss, one of the most influential airplane manufacturers at the time, see C. R. Roseberry, *Glenn Curtiss, Pioneer of Flight* (New York: Doubleday, 1999).

50. "Rain Halts the Initial Flight of Miss Bessie," *Chicago Defender*, September 2, 1922.

51. "Rain Halts the Initial Flight of Miss Bessie," *Chicago Defender*, September 2, 1922.

52. Elizabeth Amelia Hadley Freydberg, "Bessie Coleman: Original Fierce Flying Sistah," *Abafazi: The Simmons College Journal of Women of African Descent* 7, no. 1 (1996): 10; "Rain Halts the Initial Flight of Miss Bessie," *Chicago Defender*, September 2, 1922.

53. Freydberg, "Bessie Coleman," 10; "Bessie Gets Away; Does Her Stuff," *Chicago Defender*, September 9, 1922, 3.

54. Rich, *Queen Bess Daredevil Aviator*, 49.

55. "Bessie Gets Away; Does Her Stuff," *Chicago Defender*, September 9, 1922. According to Freydberg, "Hubert Fauntleroy Julian, an officer of Garvey's United Negro Improvement Association of New York, dressed in a bright red outfit, joined her in the cockpit. Julian was a flamboyant, wealthy, adventuresome young man born in Port of Spain, Trinidad, a year after Coleman's birth. He had arrived in Harlem in July 1921, by way of Canada, with the intent of becoming a pilot. Julian had not yet earned the title of 'Black Eagle.' His aviation career was launched when he parachuted from the wing of Coleman's airplane at approximately 1,500–2,000 feet in the air during this event" (Freydberg, "Bessie Coleman," 10, 11).

56. Freyberg, "Bessie Coleman," 11.

57. "'Queen Bess' to Try Air October 15," *Chicago Defender*, October 7, 1922.

58. "'Queen Bess' to Try Air October 15," *Chicago Defender*, October 7, 1922.

59. "Bessie Coleman Makes Initial Aerial Flight," *Chicago Defender*, October 21, 1922; Freydberg, "Bessie Coleman," 11.

60. "Bessie Coleman Makes Initial Aerial Flight," *Chicago Defender*, October 21, 1922.

61. Rich, *Queen Bess Daredevil Aviator*, 49.

62. Freydberg, "Bessie Coleman," 11.

63. "'Queen Bess' to Try Air October 15," *Chicago Defender*, October 7, 1922.

64. Freydberg, "Bessie Coleman," 11; Freydberg, *Bessie Coleman*, 88.

65. Rich, *Queen Bess Daredevil Aviator*, 54–55.

66. Frances Drewry McMullen, "The First Women's Air Derby, An Interview with Amelia Earhart," *Woman's Journal*, October 1929, 38.

67. Bix, "Bessie Coleman Race and Gender Realities behind Aviation Dreams," 11.

68. "First Colored Aviatrix," *Philadelphia Tribune*, October 1, 1921; "Negress an Air Pilot," *Washington Post*, July 4, 1922; "Negro Aviatrix Arrives," *New York Times*, August 14, 1922.

# SIX

# Sol Butler

*The Fleeting Fame of a World-Class Black Athlete*

JAMES E. ODENKIRK

J im Crowism, exacerbated by the famous or infamous *Plessy v. Ferguson* Supreme Court decision of 1896, sounded a half-century death knell for integration in America's sports. This virtual exclusion of African Americans from collegiate and professional competition coincided with the advent of the modern Olympic Games in 1896. There were a few African Americans who excelled on the sporting scene in spite of Jim Crowism, notably Moses Fleetwood Walker (baseball), Marshall "Major" Taylor (bicycle racing), Jack Johnson (boxing), Fritz Pollard (football and track and field), and the multi-talented Paul Robeson. In the five Olympic Games held prior to 1920, only one African American won medals. George C. Poage from the University of Wisconsin won bronze medals in the 400-meter hurdles and 200-meter low hurdles in St. Louis in 1904. Only 496 athletes from eleven countries participated in the games that year. Howard Porter Drew (from Virginia) likely would have won the 100-meter race in Stockholm in 1912. Unfortunately this speedster pulled up lame after qualifying in his heat and was scratched from the finals.[1] The Olympic Games would not be played again until 1920 due to the ongoing conflict of World War I, which ravaged much of Europe.

In the aftermath of the war during the spring of 1925, Harold Ross, founder of the *New Yorker*, was determined to provide a publication that would be attractive to intellectuals in American society. He wished to distinguish his magazine from Henry Luce's *Time*, which had debuted two years earlier and featured aspects of the popular culture. Ross remarked, "In Dubuque, Iowa, there lives, doubtless, an old lady." Ross was convinced his magazine had to strive for excellence that would appeal to "the little old lady in Dubuque" and others interested in more meaningful aspects of American culture.[2] Meanwhile, "the little old lady" was not the only individual to bring notoriety to this small Iowa city on the west side of the Mississippi River. A black athlete by the name of Solomon "Sol" Butler had already commanded headlines in the Dubuque *Telegraph Herald* and national newspapers.[3]

Butler's is a little-known name in the annals of American track and field history. He was born on March 3, 1895, one of four children (with one brother and two sisters), near Kingfisher, Oklahoma. In 1905 his father, Benjamin, reputedly an emancipated slave, migrated to Kansas (a non-slave state) and worked as a laborer; Sol's mother, Mary, took care of domestic duties at home. Sol's younger brother, Benny, was an integral part of his brother's athletic career for several years. Eventually the Butler family managed a soft drink stand in Wichita, and Solomon began to display his athletic prowess.[4]

After Sol finished grade school, the Butler family moved to Hutchinson, Kansas. Butler had won the grade school marbles championship, and in junior high school he competed in football and track and field. By the time he reached high school, the squatty, barrel-chested young athlete, saddled with the sobriquet of the "Dark Ghost," excelled in football, where his speed and elusiveness made him literally a one-man backfield. In the state track and field competition at Lawrence, Kansas, in 1913, the talented youth won six events (permitted in those days)—namely, three dashes, the high hurdles, the shot put, and the running long jump.[5]

While the Butler boys were in college, they published a small book depicting Solomon's high school athletic exploits. The title page contained the quote "Labor Conquers All Things," and the young men stated their purpose in life: "We hope someday to take our stand as leaders of our race. To do things we must have a liberal education. We have written this book as a means to this end."[6] This narrative contained many interesting side stories about Butler's achievements. In his 1913–14 school year Butler had encountered overt racial prejudice when Pratt and Wichita High Schools refused to play Butler's Hutchinson High in football because they had "drawn the color line." It is likely no coincidence that these two reticent high schools were competing for championship honors.[7] Butler's Hutchinson team won all but one game during that season.

In 1914 Herbert N. Row, Butler's coach and friend at Hutchinson High School, moved to Rock Island High School on the Illinois side of the Mississippi River. Sol and his family moved to Rock Island also and participated in several track and field meets in the Chicago area. It was believed that the more intense athletic competition in Illinois offered a better opportunity for a youngster to gain national recognition and collegiate athletic offers. This river town was noted for its athletic prowess, and Butler gained the attention of collegiate recruiters during his senior year. His acclaim grew when in 1914 the young phenomenon broke the national interscholastic record for the sixty-yard dash. One year later Butler won the national Amateur Athletic Union (AAU) junior championship in what was then called the running broad jump.[8]

Recruiters from the University of Illinois were thought to have successfully garnered Butler's athletic talents; however, fate intervened in the guise of the Reverend Benjamin Lindamen, pastor of the First Presbyterian Church in the nearby Iowa town of Bettendorf. Lindamen, a graduate of Dubuque German Theological Seminary, noticed Butler shining shoes in Rock Island one Saturday afternoon. The minister approached Butler with the idea of his attending Dubuque German Theological Seminary (later known as the University of Dubuque), some one hundred miles north of Rock Island on the Iowa side of the Mississippi River.[9]

Lindamen's selling job was so good that Sol and his brother Benny both enrolled in classes at the beginning of the fall semester in 1915. Though not an outstanding athlete, Benny stayed close to the athletic program as team manager, ran the 440-yard dash, and was a member of the mile relay team. These two freshmen were the only African American students seen on the small Presbyterian liberal arts campus. Sol soon distinguished himself as arguably the greatest athlete ever to compete at the University of Dubuque. A four-sport letterman, the young phenom competed in football, basketball, track and field, and (to a lesser extent) baseball in the spring to keep active between track meets. Butler's all around athletic prowess might be gauged by the twelve letters he won while at Dubuque.[10]

One pundit described the speedster as the "fastest man who ever set foot on Hawkeye soil."[11] An example of his athletic prowess in football occurred on November 16, 1917, when Dubuque played conference opponent Buena Vista College from Storm Lake, Iowa. Dubuque had a weight advantage of twenty to thirty pounds per man, and the great Sol Butler was now reputed to be the "fastest man in the Midwest." Clifford M. Drury, the center for Buena Vista, vividly recalled the game: "We couldn't catch Sol Butler. On the average they [Dubuque] got a touchdown every four minutes. I remember the crowd yelling: 'We want a hundred.' They got it and the cry was 'We want another hundred.' The game was my idea of hell when you have lived a bad life. [I] was unconscious three quarters of an hour after having touched the ball once. Also touched the nigger once."[12]

Drury, who was knocked unconscious during the last five minutes of play, regretted that "he had not been knocked out the first five minutes."[13] When the game finally ended, Dubuque had won 125–0. The ethnic slur in Drury's comments above indicated that black athletes such as Butler might be subjected to both verbal and physical abuse whenever they stepped onto an athletic field. Butler answered such disparagement with his physical prowess.

In the early 1900s collegiate competitors in track and field were not restricted to four events. In one dual meet Butler won the 100- and 220-yard dashes, both the low and high hurdles, and the running long jump. He took second in the high jump and third in the pole vault and ran anchor leg on the winning 440-yard relay team. A teammate recalled that on the following Monday morning in chapel after this Saturday track meet, Coach John Chalmers presented his men with their medals. After presenting the medals to all the team except Butler, the coach made a pile of Sol's medals and commented, "There is only one Sol Butler," and gave him his numerous medals. The track and field star set seven school records, of which the running long jump still stands. Butler was a modest individual who never volunteered to show his awards. Best estimates indicate that by the end of his athletic career he had garnered 186 medals, 25 cups, 8 gold shields, and 4 watches.[14]

Although more widely known for his track and field exploits, Butler was nicknamed "Blue Kaiser" (the college colors were blue and white), as he was adept at both line play and in the backfield. The all-around athlete was a key factor in Dubuque's gridiron victory in 1915 over archrival Loras College, a Jesuit institution located only one mile from Dubuque's German Theological Seminary. Gus Dorais, former teammate of Knute Rockne at Notre Dame, was coaching at Loras. Noted sports journalist Arch Ward of the *Chicago Tribune* wrote of the epic battle:

> Both schools loaded up with players of dubious academic background and even stranger athletic eligibility for the climatic meeting. . . . One of the University of Dubuque's hirelings was Butler. . . . Loras was headed by an Indian from Chippewa Falls, Wisconsin named Porlier. . . . There was the usual pre-game talk of scalpings, knifings, and other lugubrious forecasts. . . . Naturally, nothing like that occurred. . . . It was a well played game won by Butler's Dubuque team 13–7 before 6,000 spectators, the largest crowd that ever had seen a [football] game in the Mississippi Valley community. Butler was the toast of Dubuque that night.[15]

Butler also excelled in basketball, where he played center. He was known for his defense and speed and was heralded as a great leaper. One sportswriter wrote that he was the shortest player on the court but was always the tallest in jumping and getting the ball with a tremendous spring in his legs.[16]

Through all of Butler's athletic exploits, track and field won for him national and international acclaim. He competed in several events wherever and whenever available during his collegiate career. National collegiate championships did not yet exist, and there was little indoor competition. The nearby Drake Relays in Des Moines, in their formative years, did not include the running broad jump.

In 1916 Butler represented the blue and white colors at the Penn Relays. He took first place in the running long jump and finished third in the 100-yard dash. He repeated these victories in the 1917 Penn Relays. America's entry into World War I in April 1917 restricted athletic competition at all levels in 1917 and 1918. On April 4, 1919, the Dubuque speedster competed in the pentathlon at the Penn Relays. He broke the Pennsylvania pentathlon running long jump record with a leap of 22 feet, 4½ inches. The young competitor finished fourth overall in this event. By this time Butler had been twice selected to the All-American track and field team as the nation's best running long jumper.[17]

Immediately after graduation in 1919 Butler joined the U.S. Army, most of which was still in France awaiting the finalization of the Treaty of Versailles. He was soon recruited to be a member of the American team for the Inter-Allied meet in Paris, a precursor to the 1920 Olympic Games. These "Military Olympics," as the event was popularly known, foreshadowed one way in which the 1920 Olympic team would be used to advertise American culture and athletic prowess. American military units erected a stadium in Paris and named the facility after General John J. "Black Jack" Pershing, leader of America's Expeditionary Forces during World War I. Intense competition took place in these games to help determine the Olympic qualifiers.

The Americans, including Butler, dominated the games. World-class sprinter Charles Paddock (from the University of Southern California), who became a media darling during the 1920s, was the star of the competition.[18] Sol Butler was not far behind. On June 28, 1919, Butler won the running long jump with a distance of 24 feet, 9½ inches, and stepped upon the world stage. He had broken the American record and missed eclipsing the world record by 2¼ inches, competing against athletes from eighteen nations. The young man smiled shyly when King Nicholas of Montenegro, the reigning dignitary at the Pershing Games, bestowed upon him a medal of the Fourth Class of the Order of Danilo. Three U.S. bands blared patriotic music, and thirty thousand spectators cheered. Butler wept unashamedly. This young African American who was shining shoes in Rock Island in 1915 had come a long way in four years.[19] While still in Europe, Butler competed in the Tuileries Games. Amazingly he defeated Charles Paddock in a 90-yard dash. Paddock was the 100-meter Inter-Allied champion.[20] At one time Paddock held every important sprint record. At the Antwerp Olympics in 1920 he won the gold medal in the 100-meter dash; four years later he came away with a silver medal in the same event.[21]

Butler's showing in France encouraged the Kansas native to try out for the 1920 Olympic team in the long jump. At the trials in Harvard Stadium in July 1920 Butler set a new American record for U.S. Olympic trials, leaping 24 feet, 8 inches, on his fifth and final attempt. The world record of 24 feet, 11¾ inches, had been set by Patrick O'Connor of England in 1901. Butler now had his sights set on becoming only the second African American to win a medal in modern Olympic Games.[22]

The U.S. Army transport *Princess Motoika* sailed from New York on July 26, 1920, for the Seventh Olympic Games in Antwerp, Belgium. The ship carried 124 U.S. track and field members, including 2 African Americans—R. Earl Johnson, competing in the 10,000-meter run, and Sol Butler. On August 14 three thousand athletes representing twenty-seven nations passed in review before Belgium's King Albert and Queen Elizabeth.

On August 17 one day after Ray Chapman, shortstop for the Cleveland Indians, became Major League Baseball's first and only onfield fatality, tragedy struck Butler as well. Heavily favored to win the running long jump, Butler strained a tendon in his right leg on his first jump. In much the same way that the injured Howard Porter Drew had tried to compete in the 100 meters in the 1912 Olympics, Butler tried mightily to force his injured body to perform, but he had to retire. His great opportunity had "gone by the boards."[23] He stood aside, a lonely and dejected figure, with tears drenching his face. The *New York Tribune* reported, "The disaster which overtook Sol Butler . . . when he was eliminated . . . had a dampening effect upon the Yankee team, but their spirits raised quickly when two Americans placed easily in the shot put trials."[24] William Petersson of Sweden eventually won the running long jump, leaping 23 feet, 5½ inches, well below Butler's best efforts. Butler's one jump placed him seventh in the final results.

There is little doubt that a healthy Butler would easily have won the gold medal and established himself as the world's premier long jumper. Such a feat might have addressed, to some degree, whites' continued belief in black inferiority. Before 1930 there were a scant number of nationally recognized black track and field athletes. Only one African American had won medals in the Olympic Games prior to 1924. Butler was one of three black tracksters who competed in the 1920 Antwerp Games, but all came home empty-handed. Butler so wanted to become the first black athlete to win a gold medal in the Olympic Games, but he was not destined to achieve this feat. Four years later that honor went to William DeHart Hubbard from the University of Michigan. He became the first black athlete to win an individual Olympic gold medal in the Paris Olympics of 1924, leaping 24 feet, 5 inches, in the running long jump. Not a single black athlete made the Olympic team in 1928, when dashman Eddie Tolan failed to qualify for the final trials.[25]

Another African American, Jesse Owens, would shatter the world record at the Western Athletic Conference (Big Ten) meet in 1935 at Ann Arbor, Michigan, and then break the Olympic record in the 1936 Berlin games.[26] It was twenty-four years later, in 1960, before Owens's running long jump record would fall, but by that time athletes had the advantage of performing on composition tracks. Ralph Boston of Tennessee A&I (now known as Tennessee State University) broke Owens's record with a leap of 26 feet, ¾ inches.[27] Eight years later Bob Beamon of North Carolina A&I broke Boston's record with an unbelievable jump of 29 feet, 2½ inches, at the 1968 Olympic Games in Mexico City. The cap was put on the running long jump for the time being when Michael Powell from UCLA jumped 29 feet, 4½ inches, at the 1991 World Championships in Tokyo, Japan.

The disappointed Butler returned to Chicago after the 1920 Olympic Games and worked at a local YMCA. He kept in shape playing baseball, football, basketball, and tennis. The twenty-five-year-old still had his sights set on competing in the 1924 Olympics. Butler continued to compete in the running long jump at AAU meets. On June 3, 1922, he won his event with a jump of 23 feet, 3 inches. Three weeks later in Bridgeport, Connecticut, he jumped 23 feet, 2½ inches. By now the twenty-seven-year old realized he likely could not contend for a medal in the 1924 Olympic Games. He also desired to exploit his talent playing professional football and basketball. Late in the summer of 1922 Butler walked into AAU headquarters in New York City and handed in his AAU card to Frederick W. Rubien, president of the Metropolitan Association. Butler's illustrious track and field career had come to an end. Meanwhile, Butler and his brother Benny were busy representing several automobile companies as public relations agents in Gotham City.[28]

Unfortunately, much like Jim Thorpe, Butler became entangled in the legality of competing with so-called amateur football and basketball teams who played against semipro or professional teams. The talented athlete played on an amateur football team called the Lincoln Athletic Club, coached by Fritz Pollard, a former collegiate star at Brown University during the war years and the first black to quarterback and coach a team in the fledgling National Football League. In 1922 Butler played on Pollard's All-Stars, consisting of all black players, some of whom played in the nascent NFL, notably Paul Robeson, John Shelbourne, and Fred "Duke" Slater, in a season-ending game against a white All-Star team in Chicago. Pollard's All-Stars won 6–0 on a 20-yard touchdown pass from Pollard to Robeson.[29] The *Chicago Defender* reported the African American victory, which indicated that blacks were capable of playing at the highest levels, but the game got little coverage in the white media.

Following the football season Butler joined the eastern branch of the *Chicago Defender*'s (a black newspaper) basketball team, playing out of New York City. He was working for the Chicago paper at this time. A charge of professionalism was leveled at Butler by the Amateur Athletic Union. He was accused of playing in a basketball game in Pittsburgh in 1921 and receiving pay for his services. He pleaded ignorance of any wrongdoing. He also maintained that he had served a sixty-day suspension for this alleged infraction. These so-called amateur restrictions placed upon Olympic competitors in the early twentieth century now seem ludicrous. Present-day Olympic competitors are often multi-million-dollar athletes, and these same Olympic victors have even been awarded significant prize money at various track and field events; but in those days middle-class administrators dictated and ardently enforced a code of amateurism that forbid not only playing for money but also competing with anyone who did.

Butler's athletic career was not finished, but he continued to feel the sting of racism in his athletic endeavors. In 1921 he had joined the Forty Club basketball team, sponsored by black socialites in Chicago. The team embarked on an eastern tour and played in an AAU tournament, where it defeated a white team from the American Legion, which had expected an easy victory. The referees tried to aid the Legion team in the second half by calling an "orgy of fouls" on the Forty Club, but the whites could not overcome their big deficit. In the next game against another white team, the *Chicago Defender* charged that "all fairness and clean sportsmanship were thrown to the wind" as the referees assured a white win by calling fouls repeatedly on the black players in the closing minutes.[30]

Butler then played professional basketball for the Zenia, Ohio, American Legion team during the winter of 1923. Prior to playing basketball that year, he signed with the Rock Island Independents football team, and the *Chicago Defender* reported that Butler had then been sold to the Hammond, Indiana, NFL franchise for $10,000. For the next three years Butler played sporadically for the Hammond Pros and the Akron Pros and briefly as a quarterback with thirty-nine-year-old Jim Thorpe and the Canton Bulldogs. Hammond could be a particularly difficult location for African Americans, as Indiana experienced a resurgence of Ku Klux Klan activity during the 1920s.[31]

Despite any misgivings, several teams such as Hammond and Canton, which disbanded in 1926, were more willing to sign African American players than other teams. Alva Young, the white owner of the Hammond team and an ardent gambler, simply signed the best athletes regardless of color in his desire to win. Racial tensions became more prevalent in the NFL in the mid-1920s. Butler was one of only four blacks who played in the American Football League or National Football League in 1922, 1923, and 1926. The other black players were Fritz Pollard, Paul Robeson, and Jay "Ink" Williams.

Shortly after Fritz Pollard's retirement in 1926, the New York Giants players refused to take the field against the Canton Bulldogs at the Polo Grounds. Giants' management maintained that the large crowd might object to the presence of Sol Butler on the field. The *Chicago Defender* linked the protest to a number of southern players on the New York team including Steve Owen, Harry "Cowboy" Hill, and Cecil "Tex" Grigg. After a ten-minute delay, Butler withdrew voluntarily, advising his teammates to play and not disappoint the crowd.[32]

Aside from this prevailing racial climate, a number of other factors made it difficult for African Americans to find employment in the NFL. The most obvious was the small number of blacks who played football at white colleges, which were the recruiting grounds for professional teams. In 1915, when Pollard and Butler attended college, fewer than two thousand African Americans attended black colleges, and fewer than fifty blacks were enrolled in predominately white institutions.[33] Most African Americans had to achieve All-American status just to be considered for the professional teams. "Only occasionally did any number of black fans turn out to see professional games, such as the eight hundred (out of three thousand) who watched Jay "Ink" Williams and Sol Butler perform for Hammond against the Chicago Cardinals in 1924. There was little incentive for pro football owners to hire black players unless they were clearly superior and could assure victories."[34]

For a brief time Butler wrote for the *Chicago Defender* and played on the newspaper's basketball team. In the late 1920s Golden Gloves competition was the rage in boxing, particularly in Chicago. Butler became enthusiastic over Altus Allen, a young Golden Gloves champion. He served as the boxer's manager, but Allen's talents proved to be of less than championship caliber.

Butler supplemented his income as a coach in Chicago, working with athletes in the growing black community known as Bronzeville, on the city's South Side. Beginning in 1921 he managed the Chicago Roamers women's basketball team, affiliated with the Grace Presbyterian Church Sunday School. The team featured Isadore Channels and Lulu Porter, both of whom would win the national black tennis championship. Butler also served as the sports editor for the *Chicago Bee*, a black newspaper.[35] In such roles Butler served as an intermediary for the flood of southern migrants who traveled to Chicago after World War I. As a college student he had played on white teams, and his familiarity with white culture enabled him to negotiate the changing social mores of northern urban society.

By 1925 the Roamers had become members of the Chicago City League, a position that would have been an impossibility in the South. In 1928 the team members split to form new teams, including the Savoy Colts, the female counterpart to the Savoy Five men's team, which would evolve into the Harlem Globetrotters. Black women's teams would gain even greater celebrity in the 1930s as the Club Store Coeds team featured Helen Smith, a six-foot-seven center, and Olympian track star Tidye Pickett. The team barnstormed the West, playing both men's and women's teams until 1950. While Butler cannot claim all the accolades for the burgeoning of black women's basketball in Chicago, the legacy started with him.[36]

Like for other job seekers of the Depression era, jobs proved even more scarce for black applicants, and Butler relied on his diminishing athletic celebrity and the contacts that it brought to secure a living. As late as 1931 Butler still competed in football exhibition games. A member of the Fritz Pollard Stars semipro team, which again included Fred "Duke" Slater, Butler scored a touchdown, and the Stars defeated the Duffield Coast Stars on December 27, 1931, in Los Angeles before eight thousand fans.[37] While in Los Angeles, the former Dubuque star became intrigued with show business and the movie industry. Earl Dancer, the former manager of singer Ethel Waters, recommended him for several parts. At this time the movie industry was overrun with athletes, and Butler played only bit parts in Tarzan movies. He packed his bags and returned to Chicago.

(An aside: from 1959 to 1962, I served as athletic director and head basketball and baseball coach at the University of Dubuque, a member of the Iowa Conference. All of the NAIA members of this conference were small, private, church-related colleges with the exception of Upper Iowa University, and racial attitudes were still changing slowly. None of these colleges at that time recruited black athletes.

Large Division I universities were just beginning to recruit African American players in a serious manner. This trend was motivated by the integration of Major League Baseball, Martin Luther King's civil rights movement, federal legislation requiring racial equality, and the fact that black recruits began to help bring winning teams to campuses and professional franchises. This dramatic change on the American sporting scene took nearly forty years after Sol Butler had displayed his athletic skills.)

How Butler survived financially after his athletic career remains somewhat of a mystery. This world-class athlete held many and varied jobs. Joe Duke, a former classmate at the University of Dubuque, wrote the following:

Sol left the [Chicago Defender] and along with Benny, opened a haberdashery shop in south Chicago. This was a mistake since he couldn't possibly have known much about the retail store business. . . . Benny was not too careful about the till. Then I learned of a real tragedy. It seems the haberdashery business was failing and . . . bankruptcy was staring at Sol. . . . Benny took all of Sol's cups, medals, and watches to a gold and silver rendering place, had them all melted down, took the money and skipped. As far as I know, Sol never saw Benny afterwards.[38]

Sol took a job as a clerk in a south Chicago liquor store for several months. Later in the 1930s and 1940s Butler found his niche as director of a South Side park for the Chicago Parks and Recreation Department. The park was located in a heavily populated black neighborhood. He was proud of his effort to improve the athletic skills of participants and wrote a former classmate, who noted that he "was developing several youngsters [whom] he hoped to send to Dubuque. [Butler] felt he owed a debt [to] Dubuque and wanted to repay it in this way."[39]

In the early 1950s Butler, who was a widower, managed Pappy's Lounge on the South Side of Chicago (4700 South Cottage Grove Avenue). He was on duty on December 1, 1954, as bartender, when fifty-two-year-old Jimmy Hill, an African American, came into the lounge and molested a female patron. After a scuffle Butler escorted

Hill out of the bar. A short time later Hill returned with a pistol, and Butler grabbed a gun from behind the bar. In an exchange of bullets both men were struck in the chest and abdomen. Both Butler and his attacker died a few hours later. Butler's sisters, Anna R. Gardner and Josephine Butler, accompanied the fifty-nine-year-old Butler back to Wichita for burial in Maple Grove Cemetery.[40]

Solomon Butler, the first African American to matriculate from the University of Dubuque, won twelve letters and was posthumously inducted into the University of Dubuque Hall of Fame and Iowa Sports Hall of Fame. From the time Butler entered this small liberal arts college, his name was synonymous with the University of Dubuque. He was an unselfish messenger of goodwill throughout Iowa, the Midwest, and the world. Sol was an athletic trailblazer in the mode of other early black athletes whose pioneering feats have been all but forgotten as the pace of the civil rights movement accelerated in the 1950s and 1960s. Butler's accomplishments stand as a testimony to the courageous struggle of black Americans in the twentieth century to gain full dignity and citizenship under the law. Sol Butler had done everything right. He had obtained an education. He had served his country in the military and as an Olympian. He had brought a sense of moral uplift to the community in his role as a coach. Yet his fame proved fleeting and he labored in obscurity, lacking economic and social capital despite his efforts.

In retrospect if Butler had been white, his name would have been well known throughout the sporting world. If there had been professional acceptance of African Americans in his day, this outstanding athlete would have commanded a large salary. But material wealth was not Butler's dream. He wanted to work with youth, wanted to achieve the highest athletic goals, and wanted to make a mark for the black people he was chosen to represent. That is the kind of personality he possessed. It is likely that had not Butler experienced a career-ending injury in the Inter-Allied meet in 1919, his name would be heralded in the record books alongside the later exploits of Jesse Owens. Arch Ward of the *Chicago Tribune* said it best: "You won't find [Butler's] name emblazoned in sport page headlines of metropolitan newspapers, but they'll never forget him on the hills of Dubuque that overlook Iowa, Illinois, and Wisconsin."[41]

## Notes

1. One noted sports historian, commenting about black athletes, erroneously wrote that "not until 1920 did any black athletes make the U.S. Olympic team"; in Arthur R. Ashe Jr., *A Hard Road to Glory*, vol. 1: *1619–1918* (New York: Amisted Press, 1988), 8.

2. Jill Lepore, "A Critic at Large: Henry Luce vs. Harold Ross," *New Yorker*, April 19, 2010, 111.

3. *Dubuque Telegraph-Herald*, August 31, 1958, 16; also see *Des Moines Register*, *Chicago Tribune*, and *Chicago Defender* for similar references.

4. *Wichita Morning Eagle*, December 5, 1954; Beccy Tanner, "Sol Butler Was First Black Kansan to Compete in Olympics, in 1920," http://www.kansas.com /news/local/news-columns-blogs/the-story-of-kansas/article1097167.html (accessed August 12, 2012).

5. http://www.kansas.com/news/local/news-columns-blogs/the-story-of-kansas /article1097167.html (accessed August 12, 2012).

6. Cited in Roger Crimins, "Olympic Trials," *River/Land* 2, no. 2 (August 1984): 19.

7. *Dubuque Telegraph-Herald*, August 31, 1958.

8. *Dubuque Telegraph-Herald*, August 31, 1958.

9. Bert McGrane, "Success and Misfortune Followed Hall of Famer," *Des Moines Register*, March 30, 1958, 21.

10. Bert McGrane, "Sol Butler, Dubuque, 1958," *Des Moines Register*, June 24, 2005 (online).

11. McGrane, "Success and Misfortune Followed Hall of Famer."

12. Cited in William H. Cumberland, *The History of Buena Vista College* (Ames: Iowa State University Press, 1966).

13. Cumberland, *The History of Buena Vista College*.

14. Letter from Henry J. Reemstema, former Sol Butler teammate, to Ocania Chalk, author of *Black College Sport* (New York: Dodd Mead, 1976), October 22, 1975.

15. Arch Ward, "In the Wake of the News," *Chicago Tribune*, December 6, 1954.

16. McGrane, "Sol Butler, Dubuque, 1958."

17. Mark Dyreson, "Selling American Civilization: The Olympic Games of 1920 and American Culture," *Olympika: The International Journal of Olympic Studies* 8 (1999): 8.

18. Dyreson, "Selling American Civilization."

19. Dyreson, "Selling American Civilization."

20. David K. Wiggins, ed., *African-Americans in Sports* (Armonk NY: M. E. Sharpe, 2004), 161.

21. William J. Baker, *Jesse Owens: An American Life* (New York: Free Press, 1986), 24.

22. Crimins, "Olympic Trials," 19; Chalk, *Black College Sport*, 315, 349–50.

23. Chalk, *Black College Sport*, 315, 349–50.

24. Cited in Chalk, *Black College Sport*, 315.

25. Baker, *Jesse Owens*, 24.

26. Baker, *Jesse Owens*, 50.

27. Wiggins, *African-Americans in Sports*, 24, 41.

28. Chalk, *Black College Sports*, 350.

29. John M. Carroll, *Fritz Pollard, Pioneer in Racial Advancement* (Urbana: University of Illinois Press, 1992), 154–55.

30. *Chicago Defender*, April 2, 1921, 10.

31. Carroll, *Fritz Pollard*, 155.

32. Carroll, *Fritz Pollard*, 155, 179 (quote); Frank Young, "A Few Words to the Sporting Editor of the *Chicago American*," *Chicago Defender*, February 9, 1924.

33. Chalk, *Black College Sports*, 315; Wiggins, *African Americans in Sports*, 55.

34. Chalk, *Black College Sports*, 316; Carroll, *Fritz Pollard*, 179.

35. Gerald R. Gems, "Blocked Shot: The Development of Basketball in the African-American Community of Chicago," *Journal of Sport History* 22, no. 2 (Summer 1995): 135–48.

36. www.blackfives.org/chicago-roamers-girls-were-pretty-magnificent (accessed January 4, 2016); www.blackfives.org/death-by-chocolate-coeds/ (accessed January 4, 2016).

37. Gems, "Blocked Shot."

38. Letter from Joe Duke, former teammate of Sol Butler, to Ocania Chalk, August 1, 1975.

39. Letter from Henry J. Reemstema, former Sol Butler teammate, to Ocania Chalk, August 1, 1975.

40. Letter from Henry J. Reemstema, former Sol Butler teammate, to Ocania Chalk, August 1, 1975.

41. Ward, "In the Wake of the News."

# SEVEN

# Robert L. "Bob" Douglas

*"Aristocracy on the Court, an Architect of Men"*

SUSAN J. RAYL

It was 1971, nearly forty-eight years after the New York Renaissance professional black basketball team had first taken the floor and eight years after the team had gained entrance into the Basketball Hall of Fame. Now it was time for Renaissance owner/manager Robert L. "Bob" Douglas to gain the recognition he so justly deserved. Nominated by Richard Montgomery, a lifetime member of the Basketball Hall of Fame, Douglas broke the color barrier as the first African American to gain enshrinement into the Basketball Hall of Fame. "He is a man of poise and dignity," wrote Montgomery. "In his quiet way he developed great players, and instilled confidence in players, fans, and officials. Each game his team played was a masterpiece of skill and ability."[1] Douglas never set out to make a name for himself. He simply wanted the team he organized and managed to be the best and to be recognized as such. Bob Douglas was a remarkable man. What he achieved in his lifetime against many challenges is noteworthy: creating a superb professional basketball team and developing good citizens in the process.

Born on November 4, 1882, in Basseterre on the island of St. Kitts in the British West Indies, Douglas emigrated to New York City in 1902. Though nothing is known about Douglas's birth mother, his father, Robert Gould Douglas, worked as a commercial ship purser, the first man of color to do so on the ship *Madrianna*. Douglas had two sisters, Rosetta and Georgiana, from his father's first marriage. Five half siblings (James, Robert III, Helen, Minnie, and Jane) resulted from a marriage between Robert Gould Douglas and Sarah Frazier Douglas.[2]

As a new immigrant with little money to his name, Douglas first obtained a job as a doorman, where he earned four dollars a week, and then as a messenger for the Musical Courier, a job he held for twenty-three years. "He was ideally suited for his role as an impresario because he was a notably handsome and elegant man—and he was smart," noted Bruce Newman in 1979. Douglas found a roommate, and the two split the three-dollar-a-week rent on a small apartment. Earning seventy-five cents in tips each week, Douglas thought he was living large.[3] As the son of an accountant and financial manager, Douglas seemed destined to follow his father and many other Caribbean immigrants into the business world.

Douglas was one of the approximately five thousand foreign-born blacks in New York City in the early 1900s, most of whom had come from the British West Indies. Unlike the American blacks who had migrated north, most black immigrants viewed class distinctions as more significant than the color line. Not accustomed to racial slurs, they refused to accept name calling without a challenge. They also viewed menial labor as undesirable. West Indian immigrants owned a large number of small businesses in Harlem. For example, Dr. P. M. H. Savory owned and published the *New York Amsterdam News*.[4]

Church affiliations also differed, with American-born blacks attending Baptist and Methodist churches and black immigrants attending Episcopal and Catholic churches. St. Martin's Episcopal Church was founded in Harlem in 1928 to serve West Indian immigrants.[5] The rector of St. Martin's, Reverend John H. Johnson, who had played basketball at Columbia University and served as its first black team captain, became close friends with Bob Douglas. A religious man, Douglas spent much time at St. Martin's, and the church held many of its social functions at the Renaissance Ballroom, where Douglas's teams also played.[6] The traits that Douglas developed and mirrored as a child on St. Kitts and as a young adult in New York City would affect the way he conducted his life and his business.

Sometime in 1905 a colleague took Bob Douglas to an upstairs gymnasium on Fifty-Second Street and Tenth Avenue, and Douglas discovered the game that would eventually consume his life: basketball. "I thought it was the greatest thing in the world," Douglas recalled later in life. While growing up in St. Kitts, Douglas had played two of the island's main sports, soccer and cricket, though he admitted he was a mediocre player of both sports at best. Instead Douglas excelled at swimming as a youth. But after witnessing basketball for the first time, Douglas fell in love with the game and soon became an avid player.[7]

In 1908 Bob Douglas, George Abbott, and J. Foster Phillips organized the Spartan Field Club. This club offered black youth opportunities for participation in amateur cricket, soccer, track, and basketball. Because of its success, the basketball team came to be emphasized, with Douglas playing regularly for the Spartan Braves, as the team was called, from 1910 to 1918. In 1918 Douglas retired from active participation with the Braves and became the general manager of the Spartan Field Club.[8] As a member of the Metropolitan Basketball Association (MBA) in 1921, the Spartan Braves team agreed to follow specific rules and regulations, including those for amateur play.[9]

Questions surrounding professionalism and what constituted a professional player emerged in late 1921. At a mid-December meeting the MBA barred Frank "Strangler" Forbes of the Spartan club and Leon Monde of the Borough club. Both had been given tryouts by several professional baseball teams during the previous summer, and in the eyes of the MBA a baseball tryout constituted professionalism in basketball.[10] Because of the clubs' refusals to suspend their players, the MBA declared the Spartan and Borough clubs to be professional basketball teams. Over the next month players from several clubs were suspended from the MBA.[11] Douglas attempted to appease the MBA at times in not playing barred players, but he also began to schedule games with many teams outside the MBA, such as one from the Defender Athletic Club of Chicago. The removal of key players from the Spartan Braves lineup negatively affected the team on the court, though, as the Braves suffered losses to MBA teams they would ordinarily have defeated.[12]

In the fall of 1922 the McMahon brothers, popular white Harlem boxing promoters, organized a professional black basketball team, the Commonwealth Five. Frank Forbes, formerly of the Spartan Braves, served as the captain/manager, and five of the other six players had played for MBA teams the previous season.[13] In the "amateur" realm Bob Douglas's Spartan Braves and other MBA teams opened the 1922–23 season. Almost immediately, however, Douglas ran into problems with scheduling and a lack of support from MBA officials.[14] He attempted to work through the differences, but when dissension continued, he withdrew his Spartan Braves from the MBA, substituting them with the Spartan Field Club's "B" team, the Hornets.[15]

Two months later Bob Douglas placed his Spartan Braves on the floor for the team's last game of the season against the professional New York Defenders at the newly built Renaissance Ballroom Casino. Completed in late 1922 on 138th Street in Harlem, the multipurpose facility was black-owned and designated specifically for use by Harlem blacks.[16] It wasn't long before Bob Douglas approached William Roach, the Renaissance Ballroom owner, with a proposal. In exchange for practice and play space, Douglas would change his team name from the Spartan Braves to the Renaissance Five or "Rens." With the ultimate goal that the Rens would become the top professional black team in New York City, Douglas found support from friends such as Romeo Dougherty, theater and sportswriter for the *New York Amsterdam News*.[17]

The New York Renaissance Five played and won its first game, 28–22, against the Collegiate Five, a white team, on Saturday, November 3, 1923, at the Renaissance Casino. Douglas's inaugural Rens team included Leon Monde, Hilton "Kid" Slocum, Frank Forbes, Zack Anderson, Hy Monte, and Harold Jenkins. Monde, Slocum, and Forbes had played for Douglas's Spartan Braves. Little did the large crowd that attended the game that night know it was witnessing a team that would break many barriers in its twenty-six-year history, all the while managed by Bob Douglas.[18]

Early on, despite many other worthy opponents, Douglas viewed the Original Celtics, a superb white team, as the true challenge for his Rens. The two teams developed an intense rivalry on the court, equaled only to the close lifelong friendships developed among the players off the court. Meeting the Celtics for the first time in January 1925, the Rens lost four games to them over the next eleven months. But in their fifth matchup in December 1925, the Rens finally defeated the Original Celtics, 37–30, at Manhattan Casino before a capacity crowd of three thousand. Termed "the battle of the gods," by Romeo Dougherty, the victory was a symbolic one for the black population, demonstrating that a black team could be at the top. "All Negroes have asked is a fair chance, and when given that chance, they have more than made good," wrote Dougherty.[19]

With the Harlem Renaissance and expression of the "New Negro" in full swing, Douglas mirrored Marcus Garvey as an example of black entrepreneurship, negating the stereotype that blacks lacked intelligence or the motivation to achieve. Black basketball served as a symbol for Harlem blacks in the 1920s. By defeating white teams, blacks could dispel the notion of their athletic inferiority and attain equality with their white counterparts—at least on the basketball court. Challenging the supremacy of the Original Celtics not only drew respect from fans, players, and coaches but also demonstrated that blacks could compete successfully against the best team whites could offer. Renaissance players proved so good, however, that Original Celtic management showed more interest in them than in a game in the late 1920s.

Douglas must have been surprised when during the summer of 1929 four of his players—Eyre Saitch, Clarence "Fats" Jenkins, Charles "Tarzan" Cooper, and possibly Bill Yancey—signed contracts to play for the Original Celtic organization during the 1929–30 season. Jim Furey, manager of the Original Celtics, made the players financial offers that were more lucrative than the pay they received from Douglas. In mid-October the Central Opera House, owner of the Original Celtics, attempted to secure an injunction to prevent the players in question from playing for the Renaissance team. But Douglas had rights to the players because they had previously signed contracts with him, and he carried an option on his players from season to season. "I am simply trying to protect that which I have developed," Douglas stated, "the same as they would try to protect themselves if I tried to secure men from the Celtics, or any other outstanding white team."

The application for an injunction against the Renaissance players by the Original Celtics was ultimately denied because the players had signed contracts without the knowledge of Douglas or his release.[20] Douglas knew the law, and he possessed a keen sense for business that allowed him to maintain his team when the Depression of the 1930s caused a decline in attendance at the Renaissance Ballroom.[21]

Throughout the 1930s the Rens remained in business by barnstorming in the Northeast, Midwest, and South, despite facing discriminatory treatment from restaurants and hotels. For example, following a game in Indiana, the team went into a restaurant, and when the owner came out from behind the counter, he reached for his shotgun and told the players, "You niggers get out of here."[22] While they played most of their games on the road, they usually opened the season at home on election day and played annual Thanksgiving and Christmas Day games at the Renaissance Ballroom. From 1932 to 1936 the core traveling team of seven men remained virtually intact. The team included Captain Clarence "Fats" Jenkins, Eyre Saitch, Charles "Tarzan" Cooper, John Holt, Bill Yancey, and Willie Smith. In the 1935–36 season Jackie Bethards replaced Pappy Ricks. Despite financial problems caused by both the Depression and poor weather, the team enjoyed success. Decades later, with a record of 497-59 and a winning percentage of 89, this group of players would be called "the Magnificent Seven."[23]

In early 1933 the owners of the Renaissance Ballroom named Bob Douglas as their manager, a position he would hold for nearly thirty-nine years. With Eric Illidge, appointed by Douglas as the new road secretary, and Clarence "Fats" Jenkins in charge as a player/coach on the road, the Rens thrived. Remaining unbeaten during their southern and midwestern tours in January 1933, they returned home to a large illuminated sign outside the casino, erected by Douglas, that read, "Welcome Rens," for his champs.[24] But the winning wasn't over. By late February the Rens had sixty consecutive wins, and despite an accident during a snowstorm outside of Albany, New York, resulting in the loss of John Holt for the rest of the season, they defeated the Original Celtics the following night, 25–17, before "a banner crowd" at the Renaissance Ballroom.[25]

A second midwestern tour added more wins, and after defeating the Union City Reds in late March, the Rens held an eighty-eight-game win streak for the season. The streak ended the following night in Philadelphia, however, when the Rens lost to their rivals, the Original Celtics.[26]

The Rens grew accustomed to long hours on the road while traveling by bus in the Midwest and South, never knowing what hotels or restaurants would be open to them because of the accepted discrimination and legalized segregation of the era. Typically the Rens centralized their operation. "If we were in Chicago, we went up to Oshkosh, Milwaukee, or Sheboygan, for the game and returned to our home base in Chicago afterward," recalled John Isaacs, who joined the team in late 1936. Often driving two to four hundred miles one way to night games was difficult on the players. "We didn't mind the games every night—it was the traveling that was hard," explained Isaacs.[27]

In January 1937 the Rens defeated the Original Celtics, 40–31, in Louisville, Kentucky. The game against the Celtics was the first ever for the Rens in Louisville and the first time a professional black team had played a white team there. White teams rarely played black teams in the South because of segregation laws. During their southern tours the Rens usually played black college teams before small crowds and roomed on black college campuses or with private families. It is interesting that white coaches and teams attended the Rens' games and diagrammed their plays.[28] Both socially and strategically the Rens proved to be trailblazers.

Hard work on the road paid off in 1939, when the Rens were one of twelve teams invited by white co-promoters Harry Hannin and Harry Wilson to the first "World Professional Tournament," held in Chicago at the Madison Street Armory on March 26–28. The twelve teams included ten white teams and two black teams, the Rens and the Harlem Globetrotters.[29] Bob Douglas traveled from New York to see his Rens play. In a semifinal game the Rens defeated the Harlem Globetrotters, 27–23, before a crowd of seven to eight thousand. Experience, height, and defense favored the Rens, who won in the last fifteen seconds with a basket by Tarzan Cooper. The black press questioned why the Rens and the Globetrotters were placed in the same bracket.

"If they hadn't paired [the Globetrotters] in the same bracket with the flawless Rens, we might have two sepia teams playing for the title," wrote Wendell Smith of the *Pittsburgh Courier*. Nonetheless, both teams received several ovations from the crowd for their stellar play.[30]

Three thousand fans, mostly Oshkosh All-Star fans, witnessed the Rens defeat Oshkosh, a white team, 34–25, to win the first World Professional Tournament. The Rens led for the entire game and won $1,000 for their efforts.[31] After the championship game Bob Douglas hosted a banquet for his team at the Hotel Grand, where the team had roomed during the tournament. The Rens' win fulfilled Douglas's lifetime dream to see his team officially declared world champions. At the end of the 1938–39 season the Rens' sixteen-year record stood at 1,583-239.[32]

Douglas successfully maintained his Rens throughout World War II, despite limits placed on travel and the formation of several black and integrated teams that successfully lured his Ren players with higher pay. With the Colored Intercollegiate Athletic Association banning play against professional teams in 1941, the Rens no longer traveled south to play the black college teams. Many Ren players worked in the war industries, while Douglas served on a local draft board. Because of the uncertainty of player availability, Douglas did not hold his players to contracts during the war. As a result, Ren players revolved from team to team to earn money. Many Rens had played for both the Rens and the Lichtman Bears of Washington DC since the fall of 1941, and while Douglas expected these players to remain loyal to the Rens, they let him down in March 1943. Looking forward to a Renaissance win in the World Professional Tournament, Douglas entered his team. Just before the tournament, however, several Ren players quit the team in order to make more money playing for the Washington (formerly Lichtman) Bears. Believing that promoter Harry Hannin had encouraged Washington to "steal" the Rens club, Douglas withdrew his Rens from the tournament.[33] The Bears lineup included Dolly King, Pop Gates, Zach Clayton, John Isaacs, Sonny Woods, Charlie Isles, Tarzan Cooper, and Puggy Bell—all former Rens. In the final game the Washington Bears defeated Oshkosh, 43–31, before twelve thousand spectators, thereby winning the fifth World Professional Tournament and earning $1,500 in prize money.[34]

Several of the players who had suited up for the Washington Bears in the World Professional Tournament in Chicago requested that Douglas allow them to represent the Rens in another tournament in Cleveland, but Douglas turned them down. "I'm through with those men that left me for a few more dollars than I could afford to pay them for the Chicago Tournament," explained Douglas. The Rens team that Douglas put on the floor won the Cleveland Tournament.[35] Nine months later Douglas released Dolly King and Pop Gates from the Rens when they refused to play in a Thanksgiving game against the SPHAS, a Jewish team from Philadelphia, without an increase in pay. Douglas believed the two players had also influenced younger players to play for the Bears when the games conflicted with those of the Rens. The *People's Voice* gave its "Weekly Slam" to King and Gates for their actions against Douglas at the SPHA game, noting it was "a crummy thing to do to a decent man like Douglas."[36] But both King and Gates would reconcile with and play for Douglas and the Rens in coming years.

In January 1945 Rochester management recognized the talent of black players after a loss to an all-black team led by Dolly King and Pop Gates, and it gave King and Gates contracts to play for their team. These two players then starred for Rochester in its defeat of Fort Wayne—the first time blacks had played for Rochester. It was also a foreshadowing of things to come, as in October 1946 Dolly King signed to play with the Rochester Royals, the 1946 National Basketball League (NBL) champions, and Pop Gates signed with the Buffalo Bisons, which soon became the Tri-Cities Blackhawks, both for the 1946–47 season. While Gates's salary was unknown, King's contract paid $7,000 and $2,000 in bonuses. Douglas, an advocate of integration, supported his former players in their new endeavors despite his personal loss. The signing of the two former Rens by a major professional league, like the signing of Jackie Robinson in base-ball, validated the high level of play exhibited by black professional players. In fact King and his new Royals team met and defeated the Rens by seven points in November.[37]

Though the newly organized Basketball Association of America (BAA) banned black players or teams in its league in 1946, it recognized the obvious financial benefit to having them play in preliminary games. Douglas accepted an offer from Les Scott of Madison Square Garden to play his Rens in the first game of a doubleheader in Madison Square Garden on March 13, 1947. The Rens had last played in Madison Square Garden in 1933 against the Visitations in an unemployment benefit game. The Rens had already demonstrated their ability to draw a large crowd in a BAA preliminary game against the SPHAS in Philadelphia. Without the Rens/SPHAS game, the Philadelphia Warriors averaged two thousand spectators per game, but seven thousand attended when the Rens played. Following the game, more offers came to Douglas for the Rens' participation in preliminary games to BAA games.[38] Wendell Smith of the *Pittsburgh Courier* made his sentiments known through his weekly column. Stated Smith, "The two Negro quintets, most colorful in professional basketball, have been signed to the twin bills, because teams in this so-called major-league of cagedom can't draw flies and are reportedly losing money."[39] Not only did the BAA deny admittance to black players and teams, but it also exploited them for the purposes of financial stability and greater profits. Yet Bob Douglas believed the BAA would eventually open its doors to his Rens, and he remained optimistic.

But in the fall of 1947, just after Jackie Robinson's debut season with the Brooklyn Dodgers, Bob Douglas's dream remained deferred. According to Richard Lapchick, son of Joe Lapchick, a pioneer in professional basketball, "It was a year of great hope for Douglas and the Rens." Douglas felt sure that the new league would integrate, as Ned Irish of Madison Square Garden had hired Joe Lapchick to coach the New York Knickerbockers. Douglas drove to Philadelphia and sat in on a discussion among the owners about the potential admission of the Rens as a BAA team, while Joe Lapchick, Douglas's (white) friend, supported the admission of the Rens into the league. When a majority of the owners voted no, their decision affected Douglas tremendously, and while Lapchick considered resigning his position with the Knickerbockers, Douglas encouraged him to remain with the BAA and eventually break through the color barrier.[40]

Though disappointed, Bob Douglas persevered and prepared his Rens for another season on the road. Both Dolly King and Pop Gates returned to play for the Rens. Evidently neither player agreed to the cuts in salary from their NBL teams. With an excellent 110-10 season record going into the tenth World Professional Tournament in Chicago, the Rens faced the Minneapolis Lakers in the final game. The Lakers featured 6-foot-10 George Mikan and were the pre-tournament favorites. Despite Sweetwater Clifton's twenty-four points, George Mikan scored forty points to lead his Lakers in defeating the Rens, 75-71, in a hard-fought and close contest.[41]

After managing the Renaissance team for twenty-five years, Bob Douglas turned his Rens over to Eric Illidge for the 1948–49 season. Though Douglas maintained ownership, Illidge leased the team and ran it on his own. Under Illidge the Rens began their twenty-sixth season with a 75–67 defeat of the SPHAs before six hundred fans in early November on election night.[42] On Friday, December 17, however, history was made when the New York Rens accepted a franchise in the NBL. With 2,078 career wins as the New York Rens, they would now represent Dayton, Ohio, replacing the Detroit Vagabond Kings, who withdrew from the league because of poor attendance and with $11,000 in debt.[43] The Rens not only adopted Detroit's schedule but also its abysmal 2-17 record. In addition to league play, the Dayton Rens continued an extensive traveling schedule to play teams with which they had agreements as the New York Rens.[44]

The Dayton Rens tried valiantly to fulfill both the NBL and New York Ren schedules. And while they recorded wins against Tri-Cities and Sheboygan, they also lost to the Waterloo Hawks, Anderson Packers, and Sheboygan. Unable to obtain a gymnasium when needed in Dayton, the Dayton Rens played their home games in various locations.[45] Final standings for the season put the Dayton Rens in last place with a 16-43 record (14-26 without the Detroit record), the worst ever for a Renaissance team. To make matters worse, the Dayton Rens players never received their final month of pay. Within two months the NBL revoked the Rens' contract.[46]

Competition in the NBL had proven much tougher for the Rens than Douglas had expected. With an increasing number of black players signing with mostly white professional teams, Douglas realized he could no longer compete financially. So a month after the dissolution of the Dayton Rens team sixty-six-year-old Bob Douglas shocked the professional black basketball world and leased his team to his greatest competitor, Abe Saperstein.[47] Under Saperstein the Rens became the undercard team for the Harlem Globetrotters. Only one or two of the Rens' players under Saperstein had played with Douglas's Rens, as many others retired from basketball or joined other teams. Unable to accept his Rens' two-year decline in prestige under Saperstein, though, Douglas brought them back to New York in 1951. Retaining ownership of the team name, Douglas hired Johnny Walker, manager of the amateur Snookies and Sugar Bowl Five, and Pete Petroupolos, head of Greater New York Sports Promotions, to rebuild his Rens.[48] The rebuilt Rens then barnstormed in the Northeast until the mid-1950s. From 1952 to 1954 the *New York Amsterdam News* reported on the "Original Renaissance Five" just five times.[49] In 1950, as the NBA integrated, *New York Amsterdam News* sportswriter Joe Bostic suggested that professional basketball hire Bob Douglas as a scout and adviser for African American players, but Douglas never received such an offer.[50] Instead he remained as manager of the Renaissance Ballroom for the next twenty-one years, until 1971, when he was eighty-nine years of age.

Under Douglas's tutelage the Renaissance Ballroom continued to serve as the site of a wide variety of events, from dinners, dances, and celebrations to amateur basketball games, wrestling contests, and amateur boxing bouts.[51] Much to Douglas's delight, the Boys of Yesteryear and Old Timers basketball organization held most of its games and socials at the Renaissance, and the events frequently served as fundraisers for youth. Douglas had been a founding member of the Boys of Yesteryear, a nonprofit organization incorporated in the midst of the Depression whose goals were to run sports programs for youth and award college scholarships.[52] Both Olie Edinboro, a popular community worker in Harlem, and Eric Illidge, the former Rens traveling secretary, were honored at the Renaissance, in 1965 and 1967 respectively, by the Boys of Yesteryear for their longtime work with the organization's youth basketball teams.[53] Former Rens, such as Puggy Bell and John Isaacs, played in Oldtimers basketball games at the Renaissance, and the Harlem YMCA staged doubleheader basketball games and dances for its scholarship fund at the Renaissance as well.[54]

Throughout the 1960s and 1970s Bob Douglas and his Rens received many accolades. In April 1969 Douglas was honored by the Basketball Old Timers at their thirty-first annual gathering, with Joe Lapchick and Nat Holman, friends of Douglas and former Original Celtic players, as the main speakers. In late 1971 upon Douglas's retirement as manager of the Renaissance Casino, the Boys of Yesteryear held a buffet luncheon in his honor at their clubhouse on West 139th Street, just two blocks from the Renaissance Ballroom. Several colleagues spoke highly of Douglas.[55]

A year later, in October 1972, Douglas and the Rens were inducted into Harlem's Hall of Fame. This Hall of Fame was established by the Harlem Professionals, which conducted the annual outdoor professional league.[56] Fourteen prominent black athletes were enshrined in the Black Athletes Hall of Fame at Caesar's Palace Hotel in Las Vegas on March 13, 1975. At the elite $100-a-plate affair, Joe Yancey accepted the award for ninety-one-year-old Douglas, who was unable to attend.[57] On April 12, 1975, the New York Old Timers Athletic Association honored the 1938–39 World Professional Championship Renaissance basketball team after the annual East vs. West All-Star game at Brandeis High School in Manhattan. And in May 1976, at ninety-three years of age, Douglas was one of three longtime residents of New York City to receive "the Most Excellent Order of the British Empire by command of her Majesty Queen Elizabeth II."[58]

But the three most coveted awards likely came in 1963, 1972, and 1977, when Douglas and his Rens received recognition that would last in perpetuity. In December 1963 the New York Renaissance basketball team was elected into the four-year-old Basketball Hall of Fame in Springfield, Massachusetts, the first black team enshrined.[59] The celebration for this accomplishment occurred five months later in May 1964, when nearly eight hundred friends gathered from around the country to honor Douglas and his Rens in a testimonial dinner at the Americana Hotel in New York City. William P. Young, Pennsylvania's secretary of labor, the first black to serve in that position, compared Douglas to such athletic figures as Cumberland Posey, Rube Foster, and Paul Robeson. William Mokray, chairman of the Honors Committee of the Basketball Hall of Fame, presented Basketball Hall of Fame awards to Douglas and the members of his 1932–36 team, as well as manager Eric Illidge. Joe Lapchick, basketball coach at St. John's University; Joe Yancey, New York Pioneer Club track coach; J. Foster Phillips of the Spartan Field Club; Bill Yancey, former Renaissance player and scout for the New York Yankees; and many others spoke on Douglas's behalf. Nat Holman, former basketball coach at the City College of New York, presented Douglas with a plaque from the Committee of Friends, with other plaques presented by the Boys of Yesteryear and the Sons and Daughters of St. Christopher.[60]

Nine years later, on April 20, 1972, Bob Douglas gained enshrinement as a contributor into the Basketball Hall of Fame in Springfield, Massachusetts, the first black individual to be so honored.[61] The Hall's selection committee received several endorsements for Douglas's enshrinement. Probably the most poignant, however, came from Nat Holman, who stated the following:

> No man's life has been more dedicated to the game of basketball for more than half a century. [Douglas's] contribution to basketball isn't measurable. The tendency is to look back at the record of achievement, but no applicant, I am sure, has made greater progress under greater odds. When one considers the exhausting, backbreaking pace his teams had to go through, having been the target for discrimination in the early days of the sport—his leadership, his integrity, his intelligence [qualify] Bob Douglas for a place in the Hall of Fame. His greatest reward is written in the hearts of his players. His influence in the black community on both amateur and professional players will remain long after he and the rest of us are forgotten and he will not be forgotten for a long time. I have always appreciated loyalty to one's friends but loyalty to the game, that it be played properly, is one of the trademarks of this high minded, decent and enlightened citizen.[62]

Former Ren Bill Yancey wrote, "First, if Bob gave you his word or a hand shake it was better to me than any contract I have ever signed. He kept basketball alive for a number of years when it was really on the rocks. If any man belongs in the Hall that man is Bob Douglas."[63] Many people, black and white, held Douglas in high esteem for his honesty, integrity, and professionalism.

Douglas had made several trips to the Basketball Hall of Fame in Springfield, Massachusetts. The final trip occurred in 1977, when he presented one of his star Renaissance players, Charles "Tarzan" Cooper, for enshrinement. Having first observed Cooper in 1930 in a game in Philadelphia, Douglas immediately signed him to the Rens, where he played for eleven years. Cooper led the Rens to their eighty-eight-game win streak in 1933 and the 1939 World Professional Championship title.[64]

On June 3, 1979, the John Hunter Memorial Camp Fund held its seventh annual Hall of Fame Luncheon at the Manhattan Holiday Inn. John Woodruff, Alice Coachman, and Walter "Longie" Sanders were inducted into the Bob Douglas Hall of Fame and photographed with a ninety-six-year-old smiling Bob Douglas. The John Hunter Camp Fund was organized in 1972 to increase the awareness of black history and to provide scholarships to inner city youth to attend summer camp; the luncheon serves as an annual gathering for former Harlem athletes, some nationally known, as well as some local celebrities. Douglas, the New York Rens, and Holcombe Rucker served as the first inductees into what was then called the "Harlem Professional Hall of Fame" in 1972. In 1978, however, the name was changed to the Bob Douglas Hall of Fame.[65] It was only appropriate that the last event Douglas attended was a hall of fame named in his honor.

Six weeks later, in the early morning hours of July 16, Bob Douglas died quietly in his sleep in his apartment on West 135th Street, with his wife of eighteen years, Cora, by his side. In bed most of the previous day and appearing to be very tired and nervous, Douglas just glanced up at Cora, unable to speak. "He was a great individual with a vision in the 1920s that propelled him heads and shoulders above any other sports entrepreneur of his time," wrote Howie

Evans, *New York Amsterdam News* sports editor and good friend of Bob Douglas. "For sure he has left a legacy that will outlive the game itself. Rest in peace, Mr. Douglas, it is well-deserved." Funeral services for Bob Douglas were held on Thursday, July 19, at St. Martin's Episcopal Church in Harlem, with rites conducted by his good friend, the Reverend John H. Johnson. Dozens of friends, former players, and basketball personalities attended what Les Matthews called "a sports reunion." Douglas was buried in Paramus, New Jersey.[66]

### Legacy

Robert L. "Bob" Douglas touched hundreds of lives during his ninety-six years. He possessed a unique ability to maintain a professional black basketball team at a time of legal segregation and through a depression and world war. Beyond his tremendous acumen for business, his hard work and persistence, and his remarkable ability to market his teams, it was Douglas's innate character and personality, philosophy of basketball and life, commitment to community, and support from friends and colleagues that allowed him to achieve success throughout his life.

Friends, players, and relatives remembered Bob Douglas with affection. The Reverend David Johnson, who followed his father, the Reverend John H. Johnson, as rector of St. Martin's, viewed Douglas as a second father, one who was loveable and old-fashioned, a talkative "gregarious fellow" from the old school who enjoyed "hobnobbing in the sports world." Richard Lapchick first met Douglas in August 1970 at his father's (Joe Lapchick's) funeral. Lapchick came to know an elderly Douglas well in the 1970s, describing the Renaissance owner as not only gentle, soft-spoken, and kind but also bold, courageous, and innovative. Pop Gates, who joined the Rens in the late 1930s and was enshrined in the Basketball Hall of Fame in 1999, recollected Douglas as a good businessman, one who knew what he was doing, and a nice person. Former Ren John Isaacs agreed with Gates, adding that Douglas was a handshake man: "His handshake was his word." James Douglas remembered his half brother Bob as a personable man: "His nickname was 'Smiling' Bob Douglas—he always had a smile for you."[67]

Douglas had been married to his first wife, Sadie, for several years. The couple never had children. Instead Douglas filled the void with his players and many friends. According to grandniece Gloria Vanterpool, Douglas felt warmth from his professional life and was viewed as a mentor by many. Vanterpool recalled that her "Uncle Bobby" was not close with his father, perhaps because Douglas's father was absent much of the time while he was growing up. Ultimately Douglas's world was basketball, and when that disappeared it was tough for him.[68]

Sadie passed away at the Douglas home of a cardiac condition on February 20, 1958, at the age of seventy-three, after several years of illness. Two years later Douglas married Cora Dismond.[69] Over the next nineteen years Bob and Cora were sighted at social events such as the NAACP Benefit Yacht Party in June 1961. The couple took several vacations to the Caribbean and Martha's Vineyard, where they reportedly made "a peach of a pair swimming together" on their belated honeymoon.[70]

Douglas's knowledge of basketball stretched back to the early years of the century and of the game. He had watched, participated in, coached, and managed thousands of games. The strategy he taught his Rens—one of lightning quick passes, teamwork, and staying within ten points of an opponent—guaranteed fans and repeat business. Douglas scheduled the toughest teams for his Rens, most of them white, and his Rens established rivalries with the Original Celtics, the Visitations, the SPHAs, and others. Douglas teams played the game seriously, as he refused to allow them to mimic the stereotype that many whites believed about blacks as lazy and childish or the type of entertaining play that Abe Saperstein required of his Harlem Globetrotters.

Image was just as important to Douglas and the Rens as hard work, talent, and ability. Douglas recruited players who were not only top athletes but also role models off the court. Players unable to meet his standards were suspended or cut from the team. By February 1926, in just their third season, Romeo Dougherty referred to the Rens as "an institution in Harlem."[71] Douglas and Dougherty knew that if the Rens could succeed on the basketball court, they could encourage other African Americans to do so in other areas of life. In the 1930s Douglas put team captain Fats Jenkins and road manager Eric Illidge in charge of discipline on the road, recalled John Isaacs, who called Illidge "I spy." Nothing escaped the astute Illidge, who served as Douglas's eyes on the many barnstorming tours.[72] In return, however, Douglas served as a mentor, a surrogate father of sorts to his players, purchasing them well-tailored suits after each season and varsity jackets after their 1939 win of the World Professional Championship.[73]

Douglas was a man dedicated to his Harlem community, and his Rens played charity or benefit games often, beginning in 1925 for the New York American Christmas Fund and extending through the 1940s. Other noteworthy causes included organizations such as the Boy Scouts of Harlem, the Welfare Fund of Philadelphia Sports Writers Association, the Scottsboro Defense Fund, and the African Academy of Arts and Research.[74] Douglas also created, coached, or supported youth teams during this time. Established by Douglas in 1925, the amateur Eastern Colored League teams played preliminary basketball games to the Rens' games every Sunday night for over five years.[75] In the mid-1930s Douglas organized and coached two amateur basketball teams, the Rens Cubs and Rens Juniors, at the Renaissance Ballroom. The Cubs and Juniors played one game a month at the ballroom and drew future Rens players such as John Isaacs.[76]

In the face of a legally segregated America, Douglas and his colleagues Joe Yancey and William Culbreath organized the New York Pioneer Club in 1936 in order to "promote higher education for Harlem youth and to advance racial understanding." As such, it served as one of the first interracial athletic clubs in any sport, putting a dent in the color line. Pioneer Club athletes participated in track and field, road running, and race walking. The club promoted a philosophy of equality and never turned an athlete away because of race, creed, or lack of ability. From 1948 to 1976 the Pioneer Club sent at least one athlete to the Olympic Games.[77]

In addition to the Reverend John H. Johnson at St. Martin's, Douglas received support from several black sportswriters, such as Romeo Dougherty. Dougherty and Douglas shared a cultural background, as both had emigrated from the British West Indies and both possessed a business-oriented mind. The *New York Amsterdam News* hired Dougherty, the "Sage of Union Hall Street," as its first sports and theater editor, and in this position he became acquainted with many celebrities. With a desire to help black athletes and artists through his writing, Dougherty used his position to promote his favorite sporting teams, including Douglas's Spartan Braves and Rens.[78] Dougherty not only congratulated Douglas but also applauded him and his actions in sports and at Renaissance Ballroom events.

Despite the social mores of the day, what began as a rivalry on the basketball court between a black team and a white team transformed into lifelong friendships off the court among Bob Douglas, Joe Lapchick, and Nat Holman. "Lapchick was one of Douglas's good friends," recalled James Douglas. "When the Celtics would play the Rens, Lapchick would tell the promoter, 'Look, you pay him first and then you pay me.' Bobby always remembered that about Lapchick. Nat Holman was a good friend as well." Lapchick displayed his affection for the Renaissance team when he kissed Tarzan Cooper on the cheek on the basketball floor in a very segregated Louisville, Kentucky. And he supported the Rens application to the BAA, though most of the owners had turned Douglas and his team away. Nat Holman wrote eloquently about Douglas in his letter advocating Douglas's enshrinement into the Basketball Hall of Fame.[79]

Back in May 1964, at the testimonial dinner to honor Douglas and his newly enshrined Hall of Fame Rens, William P. Young, had stated, "Douglas featured basketball as it was meant to be played. No clowning, but he presented an aristocracy on the court. He was an architect of men."[80] Young was right. Against seemingly insurmountable odds, this immigrant from St. Kitts without a high school or college education, this thin and wiry 5-foot-8, 150-pound man, had created the top professional basketball team in the country and in the process had molded generations of men.

### Notes

The subtitle of this chapter comes from the words of William P. Young, cited in *New York Amsterdam News*, May 9, 1964, 5.

1. Richard Montgomery, nomination form for Robert L. Douglas, Robert L. Douglas File, Naismith Memorial Basketball Hall of Fame, Springfield, Massachusetts.

2. James Douglas, phone interview with the author, June 26, 1994.

3. Bruce Newman, "Yesterday," *Sports Illustrated*, October 22, 1979, 101; Howie Evans, "Bob Douglas: A Legend Dies," *New York Amsterdam News*, July 21, 1979, 64.

4. Gilbert Osofsky, *Harlem: The Making of a Ghetto* (New York: Harper and Row, 1963), 131–33.

5. Osofsky, *Harlem*, 135.

6. Reverend David Johnson, interview with the author, Harlem, New York, July 5, 1994.

7. Howie Evans, "Bob Douglas: A Legend Dies," *New York Amsterdam News*, July 21, 1979, 10.

8. Edna and Art Rust, *Art Rust's Illustrated History of the Black Athlete* (Garden City NY: Doubleday, 1985), 288; *New York Amsterdam News*, June 12, 1948, 26.

9. *New York Age*, December 11, 1921, 6, and April 9, 1921, 6.

10. *New York Age*, December 17, 1921, 6.

11. *New York Age*, January 7, 1922, 6, and January 28, 1922, 6.

12. *Chicago Defender*, January 28, 1922, 10; *New York Age*, February 28, 1922, 7, and March 4, 1922, 6.

13. *Chicago Defender*, October 7, 1922, 10; *New York Age*, November 4, 1922, 6.

14. *New York Amsterdam News*, December 6, 1922, 5, and December 13, 1922, 9; *Chicago Defender*, December 9, 1922, 10, and December 20, 1922, 4.

15. *New York Amsterdam News*, January 3, 1923, 5.

16. *New York Age*, January 13, 1923, 1; *Chicago Defender*, March 3, 1923, 10.

17. *New York Amsterdam News*, October 24, 1923, 4; Newman, "Yesterday," 101.

18. *New York Amsterdam News*, November 7, 1923, 4.

19. *New York Amsterdam News*, December 23, 1925, 6.

20. *New York Amsterdam News*, September 11, 1929, 15, and October 23, 1929, 12–13.

21. See Susan Rayl, "African American Ownership: Bob Douglas and the Rens," in *Basketball Jones*, ed. Todd Boyd and Kenneth L. Shropshire (New York: New York University Press, 2000), 104–22.

22. John Isaacs, interview with the author, Bronx, New York, May 14, 1994.

23. Newman, "Yesterday," 101; *News Chronicle* (Moorestown NJ), July 25, 1963, 20.

24. *Chicago Defender*, January 28, 1933, 9, and February 4, 1933, 8–9; *New York Amsterdam News*, February 1, 1933, 9; *Pittsburgh Courier*, February 4, 1933, sec. 2, 4.

25. *New York Amsterdam News*, February 22, 1933, 9; March 1, 1933, 9; March 22, 1933, 9; *Pittsburgh Courier*, March 4, 1933, sec. 2, 5; *Cleveland Plain Dealer*, June 5, 1977, sec. 3, 2.

26. *New York Amsterdam News*, March 29, 1933, 9, and April 5, 1933, 9.

27. John Isaacs, presentations at Cortland College, New York, April 1987 and May 1988.

28. *New York Amsterdam News*, January 23, 1937, 14; John Isaacs, interview with the author, Bronx, New York, May 14, 1994.

29. *Chicago Herald and Examiner*, March 15, 1939, 26, and March 25, 1939, 23; *Sheboygan Press*, March 22, 1939, 10.

30. *Chicago Daily Tribune*, March 28, 1939, 19; *Pittsburgh Courier*, April 1, 1939, 16, and April 8, 1939, 17; *Chicago Defender*, April 1, 1939, 8.

31. *Chicago Herald and Examiner*, March 29, 1939, 23; *Chicago Daily Tribune*, March 29, 1939, 21.

32. *Chicago Defender*, April 8, 1939, 10; *New York Amsterdam News*, April 8, 1939, 18–19.

33. *Pittsburgh Courier*, April 10, 1943, 19.

34. *Oshkosh Daily Northwestern*, March 18, 1943, 21; *New York Amsterdam News*, March 27, 1943, 15.

35. *Chicago Defender*, March 27, 1943, 25; Douglas cited in *Pittsburgh Courier*, April 10, 1943, 19.

36. *People's Voice*, December 11, 1943, 32.

37. *New York Amsterdam News*, January 27, 1945, 7-B, and October 19, 1946, 12; *Chicago Defender*, December 7, 1946, 10.

38. *New York Amsterdam News*, December 21, 1946, 12.

39. *Pittsburgh Courier*, February 15, 1947, 16.

40. Richard E. Lapchick, *Five Minutes to Midnight: Race and Sport in the 1990s* (New York: Madison Books, 1991), 194–96; Newman, "Yesterday," 101–6.

41. *New York Amsterdam News*, April 3, 1948, 26, and April 17, 1948, 26; *Oshkosh Daily Northwestern*, April 7, 1948, 17.

42. *New York Amsterdam News*, October 23, 1948, 29, and November 6, 1948, 29.

43. NBL "Dayton Rens" program, William "Pop" Gates File, Naismith Memorial Basketball Hall of Fame Library, Springfield, Massachusetts.

44. *New York Amsterdam News*, December 25, 1948, 13; Pop Gates, phone interview with the author, July 21, 1994; John Isaacs, interview with the author, Bronx, New York, May 14, 1994.

45. *Dayton Herald Journal*, February 9, 1949, 9; February 10, 1949, 10; February 14, 1949, 6; February 19, 1949, 8; March 24, 1949, 8.

46. *Oshkosh Daily Northwestern*, April 1, 1949, 11; *Chicago Defender*, May 28, 1949, 15; Pop Gates, phone interview with the author, July 21, 1994.

47. *Chicago Defender*, May 28, 1949, 15; James Douglas, telephone interview with the author, June 26, 1994.

48. N.Y. Rens vs. Eastern College All-Stars program, November 4, 1952, 4, Johnny Walker File, Schomburg Center for Research in Black Culture, New York; Pop Gates, phone interview with the author, November 15, 1995.

49. See *New York Amsterdam News*, March 8, 1952, 29; November 29, 1952, 26; January 10, 1953, 25; January 31, 1953, 27; December 19, 1953, 32.

50. *New York Amsterdam News*, June 17, 1950, 31.

51. See, for example, *New York Amsterdam News*, February 18, 1950; February 23, 1963, 12; February 8, 1969, 8.

52. http://www.nydailynews.com/archives/news/men-fade-ideas-don-article -1.773777 (accessed July 7, 2014).

53. *New York Amsterdam News*, April 3, 1965, 30, and June 10, 1967, 48.

54. *New York Amsterdam News*, March 5, 1966, 31, and December 24, 1966, 38.

55. *New York Amsterdam News*, April 26, 1969, 40, and November 27, 1971, A1.

56. *New York Amsterdam News*, October 21, 1972, D10.

57. *Afro-American* (Baltimore), March 22, 1975, 9.

58. *New York Amsterdam News*, April 9, 1975, C15, and May 29, 1976, A1.

59. *New York Amsterdam News*, December 14, 1963, 40.

60. *New York Amsterdam News*, April 18, 1964, 7, and May 9, 1964, 5.

61. *New York Amsterdam News*, May 6, 1972, D12; "5th Annual Enshrinement Dinner" program, Robert L. Douglas File, Naismith Memorial Hall of Fame Library, Springfield, Massachusetts.

62. Nat Holman, letter to the Basketball Hall of Fame Honors Committee, June 25, 1969, Robert L. Douglas File, Naismith Memorial Basketball Hall of Fame Library, Springfield, Massachusetts.

63. Bill Yancey, letter to Lee Williams, June 25, 1969, Robert L. Douglas File, Naismith Memorial Basketball Hall of Fame Library, Springfield, Massachusetts.

64. *New York Amsterdam News*, May 14, 1977, C1, http://www.hoophall.com /hall-of-famers/tag/charles-t-cooper (accessed August 7, 2014).

65. *New York Amsterdam News*, June 9, 1979, 16; "John Hunter Camp Fund, Inc. Sixth Annual Hall of Fame Luncheon" program, June 4, 1978, author's files.

66. *New York Amsterdam News*, July 21, 1979, 60, 64, and July 28, 1979, 51; *Afro-American*, July 28, 1979, 9.

67. Reverend David Johnson, interview with the author, Harlem, New York, July 5, 1994; Richard Lapchick, phone interview with the author, January 10, 1996; William "Pop" Gates, phone interview with the author, July 21, 1994; James Douglas, phone interview with the author, June 26, 1994.

68. Gloria Vanterpool, phone interviews with the author, July 28, 2013, and January 17, 2014.

69. *New York Amsterdam News*, March 1, 1958, 4, and August 20, 1960, 9; James Douglas, phone interview with the author, June 26, 1994.

70. *New York Amsterdam News*, June 17, 1961, 14; August 19, 1961, 25; February 8, 1964, 12; August 21, 1971, B1

71. *New York Amsterdam News*, February 10, 1926, 6.

72. John Isaacs, interview with the author, Bronx, New York, May 14, 1994.

73. John Isaacs, phone interview with the author, August 17, 1995.

74. *New York Amsterdam News*, December 16, 1925, 6–7, and March 24, 1934, 10; *New York Age*, April 23, 1932, 6; *Pittsburgh Courier*, March 17, 1934, sec. 2, 4; *People's Voice*, March 1, 1947, 29.

75. *New York Amsterdam News*, December 23, 1925, 6; December 30, 1925, 6; March 26, 1930, 12; October 15, 1930, 17.

76. *New York Amsterdam News*, January 19, 1935, 11; February 2, 1935, 11; February 9, 1935, 1.

77. *New York Times*, April 27, 1975, sec. 5, 2, http://www.tedcorbitt.com/New YorkPioneerClub.html (accessed June 21, 2014).

78. *New York Amsterdam News*, December 16, 1944, 1A.

79. James Douglas, phone interview with the author, July 26 1994; Richard Lapchick, topic expert, "Lapchick and Sweetwater: Breaking Barriers," MSG documentary, 2008; Nat Holman, letter to the Basketball Hall of Fame Honors Committee, June 25, 1969.

80. Cited in *New York Amsterdam News*, May 9, 1964, 5.

## EIGHT

# Isadore Channels

*The Recovered Life of a Great African American Sports Star*

ROBERT PRUTER

Isadore Channels is commonly recognized in all the histories of African American tennis and basketball as one of the greats of both games. She established her reputation in Chicago, emerging at the beginning of the 1920s and sustaining herself for more than a decade as both a top basketball star for the Roamers team and a top tennis star, winning four national singles titles. Despite the tremendous legacy Channels established in African American sports and her frequent notation in the histories of both African American basketball and tennis, virtually nothing had been known about her outside her principal athletic achievements.

### The Mysterious Isadore Channels

The unfortunate aspect in assessing Channels's role in the history of African American sports is that despite the flowering of research in African American sports history in the past quarter century since the publication of Arthur Ashe's pioneering three-volume history of black Americans in sports, *A Hard Road to Glory* (1988), Channels's personal life has been a complete mystery. Nothing has been known about her beyond her primary recorded achievements—not where and when she was born, not where she went to school, nothing on her career and life after she retired from sports, and nothing on where and when she died.[1]

This lack of basic biographical facts on Isadore Channels has acted as a kind of vacuum, sucking in a lot of erroneous and (dare I say) invented information to describe her career. Thus I find it essential first to establish what is not true about her career so as to provide a proper biography. Sport historians have rendered her basketball career abysmally, but they have accurately presented her tennis career, probably based on the published records of achievements in the American Tennis Association tournaments. But their accounts have been no more than a sentence or two, despite her four national singles titles. For example, the one notable history on African American tennis, Sundiata Djata's two-volume history, *Blacks at the Net: Black Achievement in the History of Tennis* (2006, 2008), briefly and indirectly mentions Isadore Channels and her four singles titles, with only twenty-three words, in a brief paragraph on African American sports stars who played more than one sport.[2]

The basic basketball information on Channels is that she was a member of the Roamers, a top African American women's team in Chicago during the 1920s, playing in the central AAU men's-rule women's amateur competition. Yet in an examination of the published record on Channels and the Roamers, in print and online, one finds an immense amount of erroneous information. Most notably amateur historian Helen Wheelock has published online a women's basketball timeline, and for 1931 she has this curious write-up:

> During the 1930s, two women's black barnstorming teams feature two of America's best athletes. Organized by Edward "Sol" Butler, the Chicago Romas' star player Isadore Channels was also a four-time winner of the American Tennis Association (ATA) Women's title. The Romas, who played against both male and female teams, went undefeated between 1939–45. The Romas' chief rival was the Philadelphia Tribunes, also known [as] the Philly Tribune Girls, sponsored by the black newspaper of the same name. The team's star player Ora Mae Washington won eight ATA titles.[3]

To summarize the many errors: (1) The Roamers played during the 1920s and barely into the 1930s, let alone the 1940s; (2) The Roamers were never called the Romas, and in fact the name cannot be found in any contemporary report; (3) the Roamers barnstormed only one year, in 1933; (4) the Roamers never played the Philadelphia Tribunes.

This misinformation has been repeated on innumerable popular history websites and in print publications. But some academic historians have contributed misinformation on the Roamers as well. For example, Susan K. Cahn's otherwise extraordinary book, *Coming on Strong*, slips a bit when she says the Roamers team was undefeated for six seasons. The Roamers may have been undefeated for six seasons against other black teams, but they lost a number of games to white teams. One sport historian got the story of Isadore Channels and the Roamers correct, however—namely, Gerald Gems, in his 1995 essay, "Blocked Shot: The Development of Basketball in the African-American Community of Chicago." Both Gems and Cahn note the alternate Romas name, but each place this information in a footnote as though they distrust it.[4]

### Early Biography

I have uncovered the basic outline of Channels's life, but significant gaps remain, and at the end of this essay her life will still remain sketchy. She was born Isadore Channels (not Isadora Channels, as she was often called throughout her life) on February 1, 1900, in Louisville, Kentucky, to a farm laborer, Allen Channels, and his wife Fannie (nee Adams). Isadore was their only child. While Allen could not read or write, Fannie was listed in the census as literate. For some years the family lived in Louisville; the length of time we do not know. The family does not appear or cannot be found in the censuses of 1910 and 1920, although there is a 1910 listing of an illiterate Allen Channels living alone in the area and working as a gardener who may be Isadore's father. At some point, possibly before 1910, Allen and Fannie were divorced.[5]

Isadore Channels was located in Chicago by at least late 1916, judging by an item listing in the *Chicago Defender* that reported that the sixteen-year-old, along with her friend Vivian Moss, gave a dancing party on New Year's Day in 1917. By 1919 it is fairly definite that Isadore was playing on African American tennis courts in the city.[6]

In her migration to Chicago (possibly accompanying her mother)

Channels was one of more than fifty-six thousand African Americans who left the South to settle in the city seeking freedom and opportunity between 1910 and 1920. She was also numbered among the 3,164 Kentucky-born migrants to the city. This migration helped to explode Chicago's African American population in that period from 44,103 (2 percent of the total population) to 109,458 (4 percent). The African American population inflow into Chicago was part of what is called the Great Migration, a massive movement of blacks from the South to the North from World War I to the end of the 1920s—half a million from 1916 to 1919 and close to another million during the 1920s. Hand in hand with this migration was the explosion in the national circulation of the *Chicago Defender*, which endlessly reported on the lynchings and everyday social and economic oppression in the South, luring blacks to the North by painting a dramatic contrast to life in the South with reports of freedom and economic opportunity in the North and particularly in Chicago. Isadore Channels, undoubtedly hearing the siren calls from the North, should be counted as among the pioneers in the Great Migration.[7]

### Becoming a Tennis Star

Isadore Channels made the most of her freedom and opportunity in Chicago by developing into a national tennis star, learning her sport in a private club owned by African Americans. Such an establishment and the opportunity it presented for blacks would have been unimaginable in the South. Sometime in 1919 Channels began training at the Prairie Tennis Club, perhaps an indication of her middle-class aspirations. The club's co-owner was Mary Ann Seames, usually referred to as Mrs. C. O. Seames but fondly known as Mother Seames because she was considered to be the founder of African American tennis in Chicago. Seames was thirty-seven years old when she was introduced to tennis in 1906. She was in ill health and decided to take up the sport to help her get stronger and well. At the time there were only a handful of black players in the city, one of them being A. L. Turner (father of future tennis star Douglas Turner), who taught Seames the game. She became hugely enthusiastic over the sport and worked avidly to spread its benefits to Chicago's black community.

The sport received a considerable boost in black Chicago in 1912, when Seames with her husband, Charles O. Seames, and three other African American women formed the Prairie Tennis Club. The initial officers of the club were all men, however—notably Nathan E. Caldwell (an official in the local NAACP) as the first president. The club was originally located at a dirt and clay court at Prairie Avenue and Thirty-Seventh Street, but after three years the Seames relocated the court to Thirty-Fifth Street and Giles Avenue (both locations in the heart of the growing Black Belt).[8]

By the time Channels arrived at the club in 1919, Mother Seames was the reigning queen of African American tennis in Chicago, consistently winning the city's women's singles title every year. The Prairie Tennis Club presented a great opportunity for Channels as it had all the top African American tennis players in the city, and with the best teachers she was sure to blossom into a top player if she had the native athletic ability and the will to learn and work.[9]

The Prairie Tennis Club was a member of a larger organization of African American tennis clubs called the American Tennis Association (ATA). The ATA was formed in 1916, and what led up to its founding was a long history of segregated tennis in which the national governing body in the United States, the U.S. Lawn Tennis Association (USLTA, formed in 1881) and its member clubs practiced racial exclusion from their inception. African Americans, as they had in other sports (most notably baseball), were thus forced to build their own institutions to play competitive tennis. During 1890–95 Tuskegee Institute claimed the lead in pioneering tennis among African Americans in black colleges and universities. But tennis during the 1890s was primarily developed among the African American social elite, who proceeded to build courts and form tennis clubs, and by the end of the century a number had been formed, primarily in the mid-Atlantic states and New England. The most notable pioneering black club was the Chautauqua Tennis Club in Philadelphia, which under the leadership of the Reverend W. W. Walker held the first tournament for African Americans in 1898.[10] Despite ostracism in polite white society, sports such as tennis and golf thus served as a means toward gaining social capital within black culture. W. E. B.

Du Bois claimed that a talented tenth of blacks could compete with whites if given such opportunities, and national tournaments put such prowess on public display.

By the time of World War I tennis among African Americans was spreading beyond the eastern cities, notably with the emergence of an African American tennis scene in Chicago, with the founding of the Prairie Tennis Club. This expansion set the stage for the formation of the ATA in November 1916 in Washington DC. The organizers set up headquarters in New York City, however, where a large proportion of the African American tennis clubs was located. The following year the ATA held its first national tournament, sponsored by the Monumental Club in Baltimore, involving twelve clubs and three events—men's singles, women's singles, and men's doubles. Each year the tournament grew so that by the 1920s Channels, with the competitive opportunities provided by the ATA, was able to become a major champion and a significant athletic figure for her race. Her adoption of tennis would significantly help to socially advance her from a child of an illiterate farm laborer to a middle-class status in African American society.[11]

The ATA at its founding dedicated itself with providing learning opportunities and competitive opportunities in tennis for African Americans. More important, tennis was viewed by African Americans as a vehicle to advance the race. The black elite saw tennis as a sport of gentlemen and ladies, as it was played by the white elite. A. L. Jackson, writing in the *Chicago Defender* in 1923, reflected this viewpoint:

> We as a Race are developing rapidly in many directions and we note with particular gratification the strides made in sports like tennis and golf. During the recent matches held under the auspices of the American Tennis Association we were as much interested in the manners and deportment of the players and officials as we were in their form on the courts. For here were what the man in the street would regard as examples of our best. It is rather difficult for us at this stage of the game to build a real aristocracy on the basis of blood ancestry or money, but it is certainly possible to build one on a sure foundation of brains, manners, and character.[12]

Some blacks aspired to white social norms because they were the only ones that the dominant mainstream white society would respect. Blacks had to accept and demonstrate that they had reached acceptable levels of "civilization." In that sense the genteel sport of tennis spoke much louder than the victories of black boxers.

The ATA nationals in 1921 represented the advent of Chicago into the competition, and the city had some players that would surprise the East—notably the unknown Isadore Channels. The progress of Channels had been rapid before her debut in the 1921 nationals, where Chicago was attempting to make an impact by sending five players. By July 1920 she had won the African American championship for Chicago, dethroning Mother Seames, who reportedly had been women's singles champion for eight straight years. Seames was due to lose; she was forty-five years old. In 1921 Channels repeated as Chicago champion and then surprised the experts in the East when she took second place in the ATA in the women's singles national championship in September. In the ATA's first national ratings for women, released the previous April, Channels was not listed among the top ten women, all of whom were from a small mid-Atlantic coast section—New York, New Jersey, Philadelphia, and Baltimore. In the nationals, held in Washington DC, Channels upset the field, easily beating her opponent in the first round with her "clever stroking and brilliant ground play," then "overwhelming" the number two–ranked player, Lottie Wade of New York, so that when she lost the finals match in three sets to Lucy Slowe of Baltimore, observers almost considered it an upset by Slowe. The *Chicago Defender* commented that despite the final match loss, "Miss Channels has undoubtedly the best command of her racquet of any female player seen on the courts."[13]

The *Chicago Defender* exclaimed in early 1922, "The rise of Isadore Channels of Chicago is most remarkable. Three years ago this young girl knew nothing of the game, but under the tutorship of two of Chicago's best gentlemen players she rapidly developed." The *Defender* report unfortunately does not give the names of the "gentlemen players." In terms of African American women's tennis Channels helped develop it into a more national scope by making Chicago a factor in black tennis competition. Her teammate from Chicago at the 1921 nationals, Dr. O. B. Williams, likewise helped establish the city's reputation by taking second in the men's singles.[14]

In 1922 at the ATA nationals in Philadelphia, Channels took her first national women's title by beating Lottie Wade of New York, thus ending the eastern states' dominance of the tournament. Thirty women competed in the meet that year. Her success and the lesser success of other Chicago tennis players were influential factors in the ATA's awarding the national championship tournament to Chicago for 1923. (By this time the Prairie Tennis Club had upgraded to new courts at Thirty-Second Street and Vernon Avenue.) It was the first time the ATA had held its national tournament outside the East, a significant civic recognition for black society in Chicago as it began to assert itself as a challenger to Harlem's cultural leadership in the African American community.

Channels was known for her highly athletic game, as indicated by the following description from Frank Young of the *Chicago Defender* evaluating her chances before the 1923 championship: "Miss Isadore, with her mean back-hand and her cross-court drives, her ability to play the net as well as the back court, makes her the strongest contender for the national honors." In the championship match, which, according to the *Chicago Defender*, was played before the largest crowd ever to see such an ATA, Channels again defeated Lottie Wade.[15]

When hailing the achievements of their African American sports heroes, the black newspapers of the day in discussing ATA tennis were always painfully conscious that their top players were not being given the opportunity to show their abilities and skills against white opposition. Edgar G. Brown, then one of the country's top African American tennis players, used his column in Baltimore's *Afro-American* to extol African American players and suggest that they could compete against the very best of what the white world could offer given the opportunity in equivalent training or competition. Brown, like many of his fellow journalists and the African American public as well, would often confer upon exceptional black entertainers and sports stars sobriquets that would associate them with their white counterparts in achievement. For example, nineteenth-century African American opera singer Matilda Sissieretta Joyner Jones was famously called "the black Patti" after the famed Italian opera singer Adelina Patti. A notable black football player of the 1920s, Franz "Jazz" Byrd of Lincoln College, was commonly referred to as "the black Red Grange."[16] Even granting such a comparison threatened the whites' belief in their physical and social superiority.

Channels was receiving the same kind of recognition in the black press when the *Chicago Defender* gave her the sobriquet "the Bronze Helen Wills," after the U.S. top woman tennis player.[17] In his column for the *Afro-American* on the 1923 nationals, Brown, while not directly using a sobriquet, referred to Channels as "our own Mme. Lenglen," to compare Channels to the great French tennis star Suzanne Lenglen. He said that Channels

> demonstrated unmistakable right to the premier honors when she overcame the five-two, set point lead of Mrs. Wade, New York State champion. Those fortunate enough to see that match will not concede many equal to the smoking drives and uncanny volleying of our own Mme. Lenglen. I think Miss Channels would hold her own with the best tournament players of the world and I hope to see the day come when she will be competing for the great lawn tennis trophy pitted in the finals against [Mme.] Lenglen, the so far invincible French woman."[18]

Ironically it was in Paris where many black boxers, the great dancer Josephine Baker, and pilot Bessie Coleman went to find greater freedom and acceptance. Unfortunately Brown would never see the day he described. Later, in writing for the *Chicago Defender*, Brown noted that the 1923 championship by Channels made her a "fit competitor for Miss Helen Wills."[19]

Channels's career peaked in the 1924 nationals, at the Monumental Club in Baltimore, where she not only won the singles for the third consecutive year but also won women's doubles and took second in mixed doubles. In the singles title game Channels beat a new tennis star from Philadelphia, Lulu Ballard, a one-hundred-pound sixteen-year-old schoolgirl from Germantown High School. This victory was no sure thing, however, because a week earlier in a Philadelphia tournament, Channels had been upset by Ballard in straight sets—certainly an intimation of things to come in Channels's tennis future. Channels was teamed up with a New Yorker, Miss Leonard, in doubles, and the pair coasted to the championship, beating an all-Chicago pairing of Dorothy Radcliff and Mrs. C. O. Seames. In mixed doubles Channels was teamed up with another Chicagoan, Richard Hudlin, and lost a close battle for the championship. Channels led a Chicago contingent that emphatically reinforced that the East was no longer dominant.[20] Rube Foster, another Chicagoan, had already formed the Negro National Baseball League to display black talents. Sport triumphs, thus combined with an emergent music scene of blues and jazz, helped to designate Chicago as a leader in black popular cultural life.

The ATA by 1924 had grown substantially from a handful of eastern "local associations" in 1917 to a total of seventy-nine local associations and clubs from twenty-five states coast to coast. The Baltimore tournament attracted 142 men's singles, 38 women's singles, 63 men's doubles, 18 women's doubles, 40 mixed doubles, and 12 junior singles. There were a total of 276 individuals competing, giving tournament attendees 310 matches to watch. The finals were played before two thousand people. Probably the one damper on the turnout was the low number of junior players participating. Channels was undoubtedly honored to be a part of such a large sporting show, in which African Americans excluded from the mainstream world of tennis could feel proud at their presentation of such a magnificent event.[21]

### Becoming a Basketball Star

Channels was also building a reputation as one of the top amateur women basketball players in the city. She was one of the founding members of the Roamer Girls, which formed during the 1920–21 season. The amateur women's basketball scene in Chicago was ramping up at that time, and in the African American community the first notable women's teams were the Roamers, organized by famed black athlete Sol Butler, who coached the team. Butler was one of the most renowned multi-sports stars in the African American community, an Olympian with many track titles to his credit.[22]

Chicago was some years behind the East Coast in developing women's basketball teams in the African American community. As early as 1911 in the New York boroughs, such women's teams as the New York Girls and the Spartan Athletic Club girls' team were competing for the metropolitan championship. In Washington DC the African American YWCA sponsored a women's team as early as the 1911–12 season.[23]

The first black women's teams in Chicago came out of the church. The Roamers were formed from a group of girls in the Grace Presbyterian Sunday School (when Sunday schools served children until adulthood), probably in 1920, and initially went by the name Roamers Athletic Club. Their closest rival in the black community was the Olivet Cosmopolitans, who were from the Olivet Church Sunday School.[24]

The Roamers played a brand of women's basketball that was highly athletic, under men's rules, supported and sponsored by the Central Amateur Athletic Union (AAU). In most other parts of the country the AAU sponsored the women's competition under the far more tame women's line game (in which the court was divided into three sections so that one defender and one offensive player in each of the sections competed for the ball). Each team had six players—two guards, two forwards, and two centers. A game in late March 1921 showed how great an athlete Channels had already become when she contributed twenty of the team's twenty-six points to beat the Roamer Girls' closest competitors, the Olivet Cosmopolitans.[25]

That Channels competed in amateur basketball in Chicago is significant in evaluating her legacy as an athlete. Chicago in the 1920s produced a flourishing amateur women's basketball scene by men's rules, which demanded far more athleticism, running, dribbling of the ball, and a level of aggressiveness and scrappiness not found in the line game. The origins of men's-rules basketball for women in Chicago go back to the formation of the Chicago Hebrew Institute (later called the Jewish People's Institute) girls' team in the fall of 1916 by Rose Rodkin. She prevailed on four other institutions to form teams to launch a first season of competition in 1916–17. The use of men's rules for the women's game rapidly caught on throughout the

Chicago area among the club and amateur teams. The Central AAU, headquartered in Chicago, took notice and, unlike its AAU counterparts elsewhere, chose to sponsor women's basketball under the men's rules. In 1919 it sponsored its first women's city championship, selecting two top teams to compete for the title.[26]

In 1922 the Central AAU sponsored its first full tournament competition, recruiting "twenty or more" women's teams. The push for the women's game continued the following year, when the *Chicago Tribune* reported that "Stress this year is being placed on the women's games by the AAU, and, according to officials, the girls, playing under boys' rules, will feature the meet." The Central AAU had no color line for its competition, and amateur African American teams competed in both its tournament and league competitions. Although local high schools had integrated teams, there does not appear to be any evidence of integrated teams in the AAU amateur scene. Also outside the AAU African American teams in Chicago often competed independently against white teams.[27]

### Basketball at Phillips High

While Channels was competing on a high-level amateur basketball team and winning national tennis titles, she was working as a "packer" (possibly in the stockyards), according to *Polk's Chicago Directory* of 1923. However, she left the job the following year to return to high school at an advanced age of twenty-four, attending Phillips High on the city's South Side during the 1924–25 and 1925–26 school years.[28]

While some other Chicago high schools had girls' teams that competed interscholastically, Phillips did not. The Chicago Public High School League officially barred interscholastic basketball games for girls, but many of the schools that had intramural basketball programs ignored the ban and engaged in occasional outside contests. A group of high schools on the South Side even formed a league for a few years. Phillips not only did not have a team that played outside contests, but the school did not even have an intramural program. The lack of an intramural program is a bit mystifying, but more understandable is why Phillips did not sponsor an outside team. Being the only predominantly African American school in the city, the school authorities were well aware that Phillips was under extra scrutiny from administrators, who historically had presumed a greater propensity for African Americans to skirt and break the rules.[29]

In her junior year at the school, in 1925, Channels served as captain on the captain basketball team. Captain basketball was played without a basket. It was basically a passing game in which the players on each team would advance the ball from each of their three sectors to get the ball to the captain, who was standing under where the basket would be to catch the ball for a winning point. This type of game showed the disparity between educators and the amateur sports world in the 1920s. Channels was playing in Chicago's highly competitive amateur basketball scene, playing a rough and tumble aggressive men's game, while educators at Phillips and some other Chicago high schools had Channels playing this tame exercise.[30]

When Phillips High played a big intersectional game or a cross-state game, as against Armstrong from Washington DC and Peoria Spalding from central Illinois, the game was usually preceded by the Roamers playing another amateur team. Preceding the Armstrong game in February 1925, for example, Channels led the Roamer Girls to a 29–3 victory over a white team from the suburbs, the Harvey Bloomers, scoring 19 of her team's points. Her performance was described in the *Chicago Defender*: "Scoring and passing at will and even at times joking with the Harvey girls, she played a game far above the heads of her opponents and far in advance of her colleagues."[31]

As much as Channels and the Roamer Girls easily handled some of the white teams in the Chicago area, they were rarely competitive with the big three in Chicago—the Brownies, the Taylor Trunks, and the Jewish People's Institute Girls—and were always eliminated before the finals of the Central AAU women's basketball championships. The Roamer Girls were also the first African American team to compete in one of the many leagues in which white teams competed, the Windy City Basketball League, but performed only so-so in competition. For example, in December 1924 the Roamers were defeated by the Welles Park Arrows (with the great Violet Krubaeck), 12–4, all the Roamers' points being scored by Channels. On the other hand, in two Windy City contests against the Bethlehem Community Center, the Roamer Girls won both contests, in December 1924 and January 1925. Channels, playing forward, contributed points in both games but was not the leading scorer. In March 1926 the Roamers competed against one of the big three, the Jewish People's Institute Girls, in a preliminary game prior to the Phillips High–Peoria Spaulding game, and lost, 20–8. Channels, who was a senior at Phillips High, was cited as "the best player" for the Roamers. Later in March, in the Central AAU tournament, the Roamers were eliminated by the top team in Chicago, the Tri-Chis (who changed their name to Taylor Trunks the following year) by an embarrassing score of 24–2.[32]

The Roamers ended the 1926 basketball season with a game in April against their longtime rivals, the Olivet Cosmopolitans. The contest was played at the Eighth Regiment Armory before a record crowd, and the Roamers edged out a victory in overtime, 16–15, when Channels made the winning basket with one of her "famous long shots from near the center." The *Chicago Defender* noted that the game demonstrated the "girls can charge and play as hard at basketball as boys." It also chided the audience for the amount of overt gambling going on, a reflection of the intense interest in the black community that the game aroused.[33]

Channels also served on the school's athletic council, which was a student organization that promoted and supported sports at Phillips, mostly boys' interschool competition. The girls on the council worked to raise funds by selling tickets. In 1925 Channels took second in ticket sales, selling twenty-five dollars' worth for the Armstrong-Phillips game. The school also had a girls' tennis club, which competed intramurally, but no contests were permitted with outside schools, as many other Chicago high schools allowed then. About a dozen Chicago high schools competed in tennis in the dual meet and tournament competition sponsored by the Chicago Public High School League. Channels served as coach of the team, and the yearbook proudly noted that she was "national champion." It is not clear whether she competed against the other girls or not, but she probably did not, given she was probably far above her fellow students in talent. It is tempting to speculate that had Channels participated and had Phillips fielded a team for outside competition, the African American tennis phenom could have made league history.[34]

Channels graduated from Phillips High in June 1926 (at the ripe age of twenty-six) and at this time retired from basketball, ending her career with the Roamers, at least for a while. Following her departure, the Roamers disbanded, with most of the members founding a new team, the Community Girls.[35]

Then the Roamer Girls came together again for the 1927–28 season. The Roamer Girls—with some of the top players in black Chicago—competed in an African American league and took the championship but for some reason disbanded again at the end of the season. But for the 1929–30 season the Roamers reconstituted themselves again, and Channels returned to play. She was the only elite player on the team, but it was enough for the team to win a tournament in February 1930. Again the Roamer Girls disbanded at the end of the season. In the next season, 1930–31, Channels, along with another outstanding tennis player, Lulu Porter, were playing with a team called the Val Donnas.[36]

### Final Years in Sports, 1925–33

In her tennis career things were not going well for Channels in 1925. Her reign as three-time national champion in women's singles was looking seriously imperiled as the summer wore on. At the ATA's New York State Tennis Championships in August, Channels was eliminated in a first-round match in three sets to rising tennis star Ora Mae Washington of Philadelphia. Washington would eventually emerge as the preeminent female tennis and basketball star in the black sports world, seriously diminishing by contrast the sports legacy of Channels. Washington won eight consecutive national singles tennis titles from 1929 to 1937 and was the star of the top black women's basketball team in the nation, the Philadelphia Tribunes, from 1932 to the late 1940s. In 1925 at the nationals in Bordentown, New Jersey, Channels again met high school phenom Lulu Ballard, whom she had conquered the previous year. But this return meeting proved different, as Channels succumbed to Ballard in two quick sets. Edgar G. Brown used his column in the *Afro-American* to extol

Ballard's virtues, but he also lamented that Ballard, as true of most African American athletes, did not have the scientific training that her white counterparts had gotten, such as Helen Wills. Brown speculated that had Ballard had the same kind of training, she would have been able to beat the great Wills.[37]

Upon her graduation from Phillips in June 1926, Channels concentrated on honing her tennis game during the summer and was able to regain her national tennis singles championship in August in St. Louis, getting her revenge on Ballard in a close match. Thereafter, however, Channels never won another ATA singles title. Nonetheless, by winning a fourth singles title, she cemented her legacy as one of the great African American female tennis players of all time.[38]

In July 1927 Channels moved to Roanoke, Virginia, to pursue a nursing education. Her training was apparently partially completed by at least 1929 because she is listed in the Richmond, Virginia, directory as a nurse, working at Memorial Hospital, perhaps serving a residency. In her new career of nursing Channels did not leave the world of discrimination and segregation. If she had read the *Chicago Defender* from October 1928, she might have noticed a story on an African American nurse who was accepted for a job at a New York hospital by mail, but when she arrived, she was barred from employment. While the tennis tournament reports listed Channels as being from Roanoke during her schooling, her permanent address, according to the 1930 census, was Chicago, where she and her mother were lodgers in the residence of a playground instructor, La Fern G. Davis.[39]

While Channels no longer was winning national singles titles, she was still one of the top players in the late 1920s, taking second in singles to Lula Ballard in the nationals in both 1927 and 1928 and taking second in women's doubles in 1927. Her career was in decline, however, judging from national rankings, which are usually released in March or April before the season begins and which reflect the previous year's activity. Channels was listed fourth in women's singles in 1929 and fifth in 1930. In the 1931 rankings Channels was not even listed in the women's singles, probably indicating that she had largely withdrawn from singles competition in 1930. She maintained a third-place ranking in women's doubles and a fourth-place ranking in mixed doubles.[40]

For a time Channels boarded with the Dunham family in Chicago, and Caldwell Dunham fondly remembers as a youngster her coming into the household always carrying her tennis rackets. He did not recall much, but one rumor about Channels stuck in his mind: "My older sister remembers an incident that would suggest that [Channels] was a lesbian." Perhaps pertaining to this possibility, *Chicago Defender* columnist Dan Burley commented in 1959, "She sat in front of me in high school. . . . Man, I was afraid of her. . . . And you would have been too! . . . Isadore was muscular and could use that muscle too."[41] Burley's coded language is unmistakable.

Channels was from an era when it was extremely rare for any public individual—athlete, entertainer, or politician—to voluntarily reveal a sexual orientation different from the norm. To do so would bring on ruination of one's career and public shame and humiliation. Homosexuality was held so beyond the pale that Channels would find those of her orientation in her everyday world assailed with such ugly terms as "degenerates," "queers," "perverts," and "deviants." The *Chicago Defender* and mainstream newspapers rarely mentioned homosexuality and usually would abjure the word itself for such circumlocutory words as "unnatural" and "perversion." It was also extremely rare for members of the media to "out" a figure whom insiders knew was homosexual. Channels, like the great Bill Tilden during his heyday and other notable athletes of the time, never revealed her sexual orientation, and the press during her career never mentioned it or even hinted at it.[42]

Early in 1933 Channels was again competing in basketball in yet another reconstituted Roamer Girls team. The Roamers apparently became a barnstorming team for the first time, as evident by a report of a game on January 17, playing and losing to a local white men's team in Wakefield, Michigan. Besides Channels, other members were two players from Chicago's Crane Junior College team—her old playing pal Lulu Porter and, remarkably, Ora Washington (who was a member of the famed Philadelphia Tribunes). The Roamers were built up in the local press as "the outstanding women's basketball team in the

United States." Ten days later Channels and Ora Washington were both back east, competing against each other—Channels playing with the St. Nicholas Harlem Big Five team of New York City (managed by Channels's former playing partner in Chicago, Blanche Wilson), and Ora Washington playing for the Philadelphia Tribunes. Playing in Philadelphia, the Harlem Big Five found the Ora Washington–led team was too much for them and were shellacked 30–5. The Harlem Big Five may have been the last basketball team on which Channels played, as she was thirty-three at the time.[43]

Sometime in 1933 Channels was back in Roanoke, Virginia, which served as her base for a limited competitive schedule. In tennis she occasionally competed at a high level—for example, taking second in a singles championship to Ora Washington at the Midwest Tennis Tournament in 1933. Her last national ranking listing in any category, however, dated back to March 1931.[44]

### Nurse in Obscurity

By 1934 Channels was working as a hospital nurse in Atlanta, and she was out of tennis by that time. Channels had certainly risen to a middle-class existence, from her birth to an illiterate farm laborer in the South to a nationally known tennis star working at a respectable profession. There were no reports of Channels competing in 1934.[45]

In 1935 Channels was working in hospitals in Knoxville, Tennessee, where she stayed the next five years. In every city Channels worked, she brought her mother along, but in July 1936 that arrangement ended when Fannie died at the age of seventy. Channels had no family at this point. She was well retired from tennis competition when in a newspaper report on the ATA nationals in 1937 she was listed as one of the former champion spectators. In 1940 Channels moved to St. Louis to work as a nurse. That same year the great Mother Seames, or Mary Ann Seames, who had helped Channels develop into a national champion, died in Chicago. Whether Channels was still connected enough to the tennis world to be aware of her death we do not know.[46]

In 1947 Channels moved to the small city of Sikeston in southeastern Missouri. With her registered nursing degree she got a position as public health nurse in the District No. 2 Health Office, where she originally served the African American population of Scott and Mississippi Counties. By 1953 she was working in the Sikeston school system, serving as the school nurse for Lincoln School. Notices in the local newspaper mentioned Channels's positions and some community activities but made no mention of her previous status as an African American tennis champion. Channels possibly never mentioned her previous tennis fame.[47]

We do not know whether or not Isadore Channels was keeping abreast of what was happening in the world of tennis during the 1950s, a world she had left behind some twenty years earlier. But if she was still keeping up, she was probably thrilled over the breaking of the color line during that decade, notably with the success of Althea Gibson. The rising young ATA star had been knocking on the door for some time when in 1950 Alice Marble wrote a letter that was published in *American Lawn Tennis* (the official publication of the USLTA) harshly criticizing the organization for excluding Gibson from its tournaments. Marble directly said, "She is not being judged by the yardstick of ability but by . . . her pigmentation." The letter shamed the USLTA into allowing Gibson into its prestigious competitions, and gradually other African Americans were allowed to compete as well.[48]

When Gibson won singles at the French championship in 1956, Wimbledon in 1956 and 1957, and the U.S. National in 1957 and 1958, did Channels salute her achievements and think of herself as the Althea Gibson of her day? Possibly not, as Channels never had the opportunity to compete against the reigning queens of tennis in the 1920s, Suzanne Lenglen and Helen Wills; unlike Althea Gibson, who never had to receive a sobriquet like "the black Maureen Connelly" (referring to the reigning white tennis star of that era), one would like to think that Channels would have compared herself to Gibson, but we'll never know. Channels during the 1950s was completely isolated from the African American sports world and almost completely forgotten.[49]

During her last decade of life Channels had health issues and was frequently in and out of hospitals. In June and August 1953 she was in the local hospital for surgery (reasons unknown). She was admitted to the hospital again in January 1957. The last mention of Channels appeared in the local Sikeston newspaper in June 1958, when it reported that she had been admitted into the local hospital. Channels was suffering from complications due to diabetes at this time, and while bedridden at home, she developed bronchial pneumonia and died a year later, on June 30, 1959. Her death certificate shows no known relatives. Her death went unreported in any kind of press, black or white, and remained unknown for decades afterward.[50]

Isadore Channels was one of the great African American athletes of the 1920s. While she has not been elected to any basketball hall of fame, she was elected to the Black Tennis Hall of Fame in 2011. Many mysteries about her life still remain—notably the fact that she attended Phillips High until the age of twenty-six and the void in her biography from her birth in 1900 and her appearance in Chicago in 1917. Isadore Channels was neglected and forgotten during her lifetime and afterward and overlooked by the public and chroniclers. Her life is now partly recovered, and deservingly in future years her achievements and legacy will be more richly remembered and celebrated in African American sports history.

## Notes

1. Arthur R. Ashe Jr., *A Hard Road to Glory*, vol. 1: *A History of the African-American Athlete, 1619–1918*; vol. 2: *A History of the African-American Athlete, 1919–1945*; vol. 3: *A History of the African-American Athlete, 1946–1986* (New York: Warner Books, 1988).

2. Sundiata Djata, *Blacks at the Net: Black Achievement in the History of Tennis*, vol. 1 (Syracuse NY: Syracuse University Press, 2006), 8.

3. Helen Wheelock, "Women's Basketball Timeline—Since 1891," http://womens hoopsblog.wordpress.com/womens-basketball-timeline-since-1891 (accessed 2013).

4. Susan K. Cahn, *Coming On Strong: Gender and Sexuality in Twentieth-Century Women's Sport* (New York: Free Press, 1994), 37, 292; Gerald R. Gems, "Blocked Shot: The Development of Basketball in the African-American Community of Chicago," *Journal of Sport History* 22, no. 2 (Summer 1995): 141.

5. "United States Census, 1900," index and images, *FamilySearch*, https://family search.org/pal:/MM9.1.1/M94V-K5N (accessed October 9, 2012), Isadore Channels in household of Allen Channels, ED 5 Magisterial District 5, Precinct 6 Louisville city Ward 1, Jefferson, Kentucky, United States; citing sheet 11B, family 224, NARA

microfilm publication T623, FHL microfilm 1240528; "Kentucky Births and Chris-tenings, 1839–1960," index, *FamilySearch*, https://familysearch.org/pal:/MM9.1.1 /FWNP-PYS (accessed May 14, 2014), Allen Channels, 01 Feb 1900; citing Louis-ville, Jefferson, Kentucky, reference Vol. 1, Pg. 168; FHL microfilm 209689 (Isadore is incorrectly listed as Allen, but it is clearly the birth record for her); Missouri Division of Health, Standard Certificate of Death, Isadora M. Channels, 16 July 1959; *United States Census, 1910*; Allen Channels, Census Place: Harrods Creek, Jefferson, Kentucky; Roll: T624_483; Page: 6A; Enumeration District: 0005; FHL microfilm: 1374496; Ancestry.com. *1910 United States Federal Census* (database online). Provo UT: Ancestry.com, Operations, 2006 (accessed May 16, 2014). The 1910 listing differs on two facts: two years' difference in birth year and the listing as "widowed," but the latter might be because the illiterate Allen did not under-stand what "widowed" meant.

6. "Society," *Chicago Defender*, January 13, 1917. I have qualified my comment with "fairly definite" on when Channels began learning tennis at the Prairie Ten-nis Club because the date was based on an article on Channels from 1922 that said she had been with the club for three years.

7. James R. Grossman, *Land of Hope: Chicago, Black Southerners, and the Great Migration* (Chicago: University of Chicago Press, 1989), 3–4, 81–82, 269–70; Bureau of the Census, *Thirteenth Census of the United States Taken in the Year 1910*, vol. 2: *Population 1910, Alabama-Montana* (Washington DC: Government Printing Office, 1913), 504, and *Fourteenth Census of the United States Taken in the Year 1920*, vol. 3: *Population 1920* (Washington DC: Government Printing Office, 1922), 261.

8. "CPTC History," Chicago Prairie Tennis Club (http://www.cptc.com), 2013; "Mary Ann Seames Mother of Tennis Buried in Chicago," *Chicago Defender* (nat. ed.), March 30, 1940; Edwin B. Henderson, *The Negro in Sports* (Washington DC: Associated Publishers, 1949, rev, ed.), 217.

9. Henderson, *The Negro in Sports*, 217.

10. Djata, *Blacks at the Net*, 3–5; Frank A. Young, "National Net Play at Saint Louis," *Chicago Defender* (nat. ed.), August 7, 1926; Henderson, *The Negro in Sports*, 204.

11. Henderson, *The Negro in Sports*, 206; Djata, *Blacks at the Net*, 4.

12. A. L. Jackson, "The Onlooker: A Popular Champion," *Chicago Defender* (nat. ed.), September 1, 1923.

13. "Washington Gets National Tennis Championships; Ratings Given Out," *Chicago Defender* (nat. ed.), April 9, 1921; "Woman's Championship Goes to Miss I. Channels," *Chicago Defender* (nat. ed.), July 21, 1920; "Isadora Channells [*sic*] Wins Tennis Championship," *Chicago Defender* (nat. ed.), July 30, 1921; "Tennis Stars in Washington for Big Tournament," *Chicago Defender* (nat. ed.), August 20, 1921; Gerald F. Norman, "Tally Holmes Wins National Tennis Championship Title," *Chicago Defender* (nat. ed.), September 3, 1921.

14. "Tennis Ass'n Ratings for 1921 Given Out," *Chicago Defender* (nat. ed.), Feb-ruary 18, 1922; Frank Young, "City Tennis Championship Causes Many Big Sur-prises," *Chicago Defender* (nat. ed.), August 12, 1922; Norman, "Tally Holmes Wins."

15. "National Woman's Tennis Champion" (caption), *Chicago Defender* (nat. ed.), September 2, 1922; "Chicago Gets 1923 National Tennis Championship Meet," *Chicago Defender* (nat. ed.), August 26, 1922; Frank Young, "National Tennis Tournament News," *Chicago Defender* (nat. ed.), August 11, 1923; "Chicagoans Win Two Tennis Titles," *Chicago Defender* (nat. ed.), September 1, 1923.

16. John Graziano, "The Early Life and Career of the 'Black Patti': The Odyssey of an African American Singer in the Late Nineteenth Century," *Journal of the American Musicological Society* 53, no. 3 (Autumn 2000): 566; Raymond Schmidt, *Shaping College Football: The Transformation of an American Sport, 1919–1930* (Syracuse NY: Syracuse University Press, 2007), 135.

17. "The Bronze Helen Wills" (caption), *Chicago Defender* (nat. ed.), August 30, 1924.

18. Edgar G. Brown, "Our Women Tennis Players Rank High," *Afro-American* (Baltimore), May 18, 1923.

19. Edgar G. Brown, "Kemp and Miss Channels Best Tennis Players of 1923, Says Edgar Brown," *Chicago Defender* (nat. ed.), April 19, 1924.

20. "100-Pound Lulu Ballard Beats Channels in PA," *Chicago Defender* (nat. ed.), August 23, 1924; "Miss Channels Wins National Women's Tennis Championship," *Chicago Defender* (nat. ed.), August 30, 1924.

21. Gerald Norman, "The American Tennis Association," *Crisis*, November 1924, 22–23.

22. James Odenkirk, "Sol Butler," in *African Americans in Sports*, ed. David K. Wiggins (Armonk NY: M. E. Sharpe, 2004), 55.

23. Edwin B. Henderson and William A. Joiner, eds., *Official Handbook: Inter-Scholastic Athletic Association of Middle Atlantic States 1911* (New York: American Sports Publishing, 1911), 44 and 58; Edwin B. Henderson and Garnet C. Wilkinson, eds., *Official Handbook: Inter-Scholastic Athletic Association of Middle Atlantic States 1912* (New York: American Sports Publishing, 1912), 102.

24. "Pollie Richman Leads Roamer Girls to Victory" (headline misleading), *Chicago Defender*, March 26, 1921; "Roamer Girls after Games Present a Strong Lineup," *Chicago Defender*, October 22, 1921.

25. "Pollie Richman Leads Roamer Girls to Victory."

26. Harland Rohm, "Boys' Rules Speed Girls' Basket Games," *Chicago Tribune*, December 27, 1926; Walter Eckersall, "New London Five Puts Out IAC in Basket Meet," *Chicago Tribune*, March 12, 1919.

27. Chicago Teams to Play in AAU Cage Tourney," *Chicago Tribune*, February 12, 1922; "Brownie Girls Down Institute; AAU Fives Reach Semifinals," *Chicago Tribune*, March 4, 1922; "Girl Quintets to Meet Here in CAAU Tourney," *Chicago Tribune*, February 4, 1923; "Drawings Made for CAAU Cage Event," *Chicago Tribune*, March 11, 1923; "Roamers Win and Lose; Will Meet Olivet Five," *Chicago Defender*, December 20, 1924; "Roamer Girls Win in Third Overtime Period," *Chicago Defender* (nat. ed.), January 24, 1925; "Roamer Girls Lose to Tri-Chis, 24 to 2," *Chicago Defender*, March 20, 1926.

28. *Polk's Chicago Directory 1923* (Chicago: R. L. Polk, 1923), 1080.

29. "Basketball," *Centurion 1922* (Chicago: Senn High School, 1922), 149; "Basketball," *Schurzone 1926* (Chicago: Schurz High School, February 1926), 125; *The Red and Black, June, 1925* (Chicago: Phillips High School, June 1925), 161–64.

30. "The Captainball Team," *The Red and Black, June, 1925* (Chicago: Phillips High School, 1925), 162–63.

31. J. Wm. Jesse Lovell, "Phillips Takes Basketball Game from Armstrong by 25–15 Score before 4,500," *Chicago Defender* (nat. ed.), February 21, 1925.

32. "Roamers Win and Lose; Will Meet Olivet Five," *Chicago Defender*, December 20, 1924; "Roamer Girls Win in Third Overtime Period," *Chicago Defender* (nat. ed.), January 24, 1925; "Roamer Girls Meet Bethlehems Tuesday," *Chicago Defender*, January 16, 1926; "Peoria Hi Beats Phillips Five," *Chicago Defender*, March 6, 1926; "Roamer Girls Lose to Tri-Chis, 24–2," *Chicago Defender*, March 20, 1926.

33. "Izzy Channels' Basket in Closing Seconds of Play Beats Olivet Church Five," *Chicago Defender*, April 17, 1926.

34. "The Athletic Council," *The Red and Black, June, 1925* (Chicago: Phillips High School, 1925), 160–61; "The Girls' Tennis Club," *The Red and Black, June, 1925* (Chicago: Phillips High School, 1925), 164; "Girls Tennis Stars to Play in Annual Tennis Tournament," *Harrison Herald*, May 14, 1926; "Lindblom Girls Win City Prep Tennis Tourney," *Chicago Tribune*, June 17, 1926.

35. *Proceedings, July 8, 1925, to June 23, 1926* (Chicago: Board of Education, 1926), 1817.

36. "Girl Cage Stars Sign with Mid-City Outfit," *Chicago Defender*, October 23, 1926; "Roamers Win," *Chicago Defender*, February 8, 1930; "Val Donnas Lose," *Chicago Defender*, February 8, 1931.

37. "Miss Isadora Channels Is Beaten in First Round by Ora Washington of Phila.," *New York Age*, August 22, 1925; "Thompson Beats Brown for Net Crown," *Chicago Defender* (nat. ed.), September 5, 1925; Leslie Heaphy, "Ora Mae Washington: Tennis and Basketball Queen," *Black Sports, the Magazine*, February 2007, 36–37; Pamela Grundy, "Ora Washington: The First Black Female Athletic Star," in *Out of the Shadows: A Biographical History of African American Athletes*, ed. David K. Wiggins (Fayetteville: University of Arkansas Press, 2006), 79–92; Edgar G. Brown, "Miss Ballard Touted to Beat Woman's Tennis Champion," *Afro-American*, September 4, 1925.

38. Frank A. Young: "National Net Play at Saint Louis," *Chicago Defender* (nat. ed.), August 7, 1926, and "Saitch Wins National Net Crown," *Chicago Defender* (nat. ed.), August 28, 1926.

39. *Hill's Roanoke Salem and Vinton Virginia City Directory 1927*, 164, Ancestry.com. U.S. Directories, 1821–1989 (beta) (database online), Provo UT, Ancestry.com Operations, 2011; "The Week," *Chicago Defender* (nat. ed.), October 13, 1928; *Hill's Richmond Virginia City Directory 1929*, 380, Ancestry.com. U.S. Directories, 1821–1989 (beta) (database online), Provo UT, Ancestry.com Operations, 2011; "United States Census, 1930," index and images, *FamilySearch*, https://family

search.org/pal:/MM9.1.1/XSTQ-JVQ (accessed October 9, 2012), Isadora Channels in household of La Fern G. Davis, Chicago (Districts 0001-0250), Cook, Illinois; citing enumeration district (ED) 0146, sheet 24B, family 262, NARA microfilm publication T626, roll 421.

40. "Finals of the National Women's Doubles," *Chicago Defender* (nat. ed.), September 3, 1927; "Edgar Brown Regains Net Crown," *Chicago Defender* (nat. ed.), September 1, 1928; "Doctor to Enter Final Play for Tennis Laurels" (unidentified African American newspaper clip), August 1931; "1929 Tennis Ratings Show Many Shifts among Stars," *Afro-American*, March 8, 1930; "Doug Turner, Ora Washington Lead Men and Women Tennis Players in Ratings of 1930," *Chicago Defender*, March 14, 1931.

41. Caldwell Dunham, email to author, December 8, 2008; Dan Burley, "What's Wrong with Women," *Chicago Defender*, September 1, 1959.

42. "Orgies Ruin Characters in Los Angeles Colony," *Chicago Defender* (nat. ed.), September 20, 1930; "Pastor Reveals Divorce Charges: Wife Unnatural, Says Rev. Spencer Carpenter," *Chicago Defender* (nat. ed.), August 1, 1931; "Undertaker Is Acquitted by Judge in Private Hearing," *Chicago Defender* (nat. ed.), March 13, 1932; Frank Deford, *Big Bill Tilden: The Triumphs and the Tragedy* (New York: Simon and Shuster, 1976), 40–41.

43. "Mentors Book Colored Girls," *Ironwood Daily Globe*, January 10, 1933; "Mentors Will Play Colored Women's Team," *Wakefield News*, January 14, 1933; "Mentors Win Contest from Colored Quintet," *Ironwood Daily Globe*, January 17, 1933; Randy Dixon, "Philly Girls Seek to Bring to Philly Undisputed National Crown," *Philadelphia Tribune*, January 19, 1933; "N.Y. Girls Bow to Philly," *Pittsburgh Courier*, January 28, 1933. Some of the players on this Roamers team in 1934 formed the Club Store Co-Eds team, which from 1935 through 1938 barnstormed largely in the West as the Roamers Girls while retaining its Club Store identity in Chicago. See, for example, "Dusty Roamer Girls Will Play Phantoms," *Bismarck Tribune*, March 7, 1935; "Girls Basketball Team Will Meet Lucerne Club," *Logansport Pharos-Tribune*, January 7, 1938.

44. Chas. H. Williams, "Hampton Prepares for Annual Clay Tennis Tourney," *Chicago Defender* (nat. ed.), August 5, 1933; Ralph Brown, "Hudlin Retains Midwest Tennis Crown," *Chicago Defender* (nat. ed.), September 9, 1933.

45. Arthur P. Chippey, "Jackson Boys Hold Top in Annual Net Ratings," *Chicago Defender* (nat. ed.), April 13, 1935; *Atlanta, Georgia, City Directory, 1934*, 279, Ancestry.com. U.S. Directories, 1821–1989 (beta) (database online), Provo UT, Ancestry.com Operations, 2011.

46. *Knoxville, Tennessee, City Directory, 1935*, 746, Ancestry.com. U.S. Directories, 1821–1989 (beta) (database online), Provo UT, Ancestry.com Operations, 2011; Tennessee State Library and Archives, Nashville TN; *Tennessee Death Records, 1909–1959*; Roll #11, Certificate #32694, Ancestry.com. Tennessee, Death Records, 1908–1951 (database online), Provo UT, Ancestry.com Operations, 2011; *Knoxville, Tennessee, City Directory, 1940*, 785, Ancestry.com. U.S. Directories, 1821–

1989 (beta) (database online), Provo UT, Ancestry.com Operations, 2011; "Walker Beats Scott in Net Title Tourney," *Chicago Defender* (nat. ed.), August 28, 1937; "Mary Ann Seames Mother of Tennis Buried in Chicago," *Chicago Defender* (nat. ed.), March 30, 1940.

47. "United States Census, 1940," index and images, *FamilySearch*, https://family search.org/pal:/MM9.1.1/K7H3-K6Q (accessed October 9, 2012), Isadora Channels, Ward 17, St. Louis, St. Louis City, Missouri, United States; citing enumeration district (ED) 96-424, sheet 14B, family, NARA digital publication T627, roll 2198; *St. Louis, Missouri, City Directory, 1944*, Ancestry.com. U.S. Directories, 1821–1989 (beta) (database online), Provo UT, Ancestry.com Operations, 2011; "Public Health Nursing Week Set for Apr. 20–26," *Sikeston Standard*, April 22, 1947; "Health Office Will Be Closed Next Week," *Sikeston Herald*, April 20, 1950; "Mild Influenza Epidemic Hits City Schools," *Sikeston Daily Standard*, January 13, 1953; "Most of Sikeston's Teachers Have Been Hired for Next Year," *Sikeston Herald*, June 2, 1954.

48. Cited in Sue Davidson, *Changing the Game: The Stories of Tennis Champions Alice Marble and Althea Gibson* (Seattle: Seal Press, 1997), 113–14.

49. Davidson, *Changing the Game*, 167–68.

50. "Hospital Notes," *Sikeston Daily Standard*, June 16, 19, 25, 1953; June 25, 1953; August 13, 19, 1953; January 21, 1957; and June 26, 1958; Missouri Division of Health, Standard Certificate of Death, Isadora M. Channels, July 16, 1959.

working laborers, and southern migrants unfamiliar with a more sophisticated urban lifestyle. Small homes were owned or rented by families, most of the small businesses were black-owned, and there was a plethora of black cultural centers for art and music, mostly a variety of clubs where music played most nights into the wee hours.[3] Chicago seemed to be a city of promise for African Americans; it was the home of heavyweight boxing champion Jack Johnson and football star Fritz Pollard, the place where Rube Foster founded the Negro National League, and the headquarters of the *Chicago Defender*, the most popular black newspaper in the United States. More than 100,000 blacks had migrated to the city by 1920 and about 234,000 a decade later.[4] But the lack of full acceptance and the increasing segregation forced African Americans to develop their own parallel popular culture in which both sport and music played a large part.

Tommy Brookins featured prominently in both spheres. Brookins lived at 3734 Wabash Avenue, on the edge of Bronzeville. He likely attended Coleman Elementary School, formerly at Forty-Second and State, five blocks away.[5] From his early years he played basketball, likely on the courts of Douglass Park at Thirty-Third and Calumet, when he could squeeze into a game with the bigger and better players from Bronzeville and beyond. This playground court was one of a number of courts (Carter, Calumet, and Forestville, among others) on the South Side of Chicago, where players both honed their skills and clashed with the top black players in the city (a practice still evident today, especially on the public courts of cities like New York and Chicago).[6] Around 1921 Brookins entered Wendell Phillips High School, less than a half-mile from his home, as a freshman. He does not seem to have played on the lightweight basketball team his first or second years in high school before becoming a member of the heavyweight squad as a junior. The distinction was based on actual weight (130 or 135 pounds was the cutoff), not age or ability, an administrative distinction intended to equalize competition and illustrating the differences in the way basketball was viewed and played then compared to today. Brookins and some of his friends played in local gyms and playgrounds before joining the Phillips basketball team. Brookins also played in his early teen years for St. Mark's

AME Church on the 125-pound team in the old church league. One of his teammates was Junie Rutledge, who would later be an opponent on the Hyde Park High team.[7] In addition, Brookins was busy as a young singer, observing in some of the local nightclubs and singing with local bands or groups. Bands and basketball teams then operated in conjunction, as ballrooms hired musical groups for introductory entertainment and regularly scheduled postgame dances.

Basketball at this time was a relatively young sport, having been invented in 1891 and then rapidly spreading through YMCAs, settlement houses, and other training schools. Rules were highly regional, if not localized, because of the various venues and diverse interpretations. By 1915 there were sharp divisions between collegiate and Amateur Athletic Union (AAU) rules, as well as with professional, so-called national, rules. At that time the AAU, YMCA, and colleges formed a joint committee to try to create uniformity in rules and enforcement. The results of that joint committee were that basketball was more clearly "translated" from region to region, and this translation led to an increase in the popularity of the game and a greater willingness to have intercity or regional competitions.[8] Some of the later rules specified give some indication of the "diversity" and need for standardization of the game: "Rule I (a) A backboard is now compulsory. It is not sufficient to paint a 6x4 rectangle on the wall. This means that the end walls on every court are out of bounds, and that 'running up the wall' is impossible, for as soon as a player with the ball touches the wall he has carried the ball out of bounds."[9]

There was still a great deal of latitude in the venue, as evidenced by Rule 1, Section 1: "The Playing Court shall be a rectangular surface, free from obstructions, the maximum dimensions of which shall be 90 feet in length by 50 feet in width, and the minimum dimensions of which shall be 60 feet in length by 35 feet in width."[10]

One other rule that should be noted, Rule 14, Section 8, ultimately led to Brookins's success as a leader on the court: "There shall be no coaching from the sidelines during the progress of the game by anyone officially connected with either team, nor shall any person go on the court during the progress of the game except with the permission of the referee or umpire."[11]

Almost from basketball's earliest days, teams formed along ethnic, vocational, or religious lines, playing locally and sometimes touring a region and playing local squads in return for a percentage of the gate receipts. Early squads like Basloe's Globetrotters, who were touring the New York region as early as 1904, and the Buffalo Germans, considered the first great team in basketball, starting in about 1900, made barnstorming in basketball relatively common by the 1920s.[12] By that time a national black basketball circuit had developed between New York, Washington DC, and Chicago. In Chicago the Wabash YMCA Outlaws represented the segregated black community but defeated numerous white teams in interracial games during the 1915–16 season.[13] Many African American teams were also touring by the 1920s, often as a result of the influence of Edwin Henderson, who introduced basketball to Washington DC's public schools and organized the city's athletic league.[14] Claude Johnson has chronicled the Alpha Physical Culture Club's play from 1904 to 1923, but other great black teams included the Chicago Crusaders, the Loendi club of Pittsburgh, the Cleveland Pennzoils, and, beginning in the early 1920s, the New York Renaissance.[15] All of these teams either started or became professional squads, despite hardly ever making more than expenses. They played as far west as the Midwest regularly, so they and other pro barnstorming teams would have been known to young men like Tommy Brookins at least as existing, if not in the details of their team makeup.

These top teams relied on passing, running, and rugged physical defense. There was no shot clock, no three-second prohibition in the lane rule, no three-point shot, no jump shot, and nothing even close to dunking. Players hardly left their feet "since a player didn't know if his feet would be knocked out while he was in the air."[16] Barney Sedran, one of the greatest of the early 1900s players and a member of the Naismith Memorial Basketball Hall of Fame, recalled, "Don't imagine that in my time, we didn't think of the jump shot, the bread and butter shot of today. But it was suicide to shoot for the basket with your feet off the ground because you'd be lucky to come down alive. So for self-preservation, we had to keep our feet on the floor while making a shot."[17]

Thus basketball at the time was a fast-paced, rugged game that relied on swift movement, deceptive passing, and hard picks on opponents. It was not uncommon for the ball to be moved around for minutes at a time until a wide-open shot was taken, almost always by the forwards. Guards and centers were more known for doing the picking, the passing, and rugged defending. Games were usually under an hour, but the bruises lasted much longer.

Hard and even illegal contact was commonplace in interracial games as the white working-class ethnic groups already situated in their communal neighborhoods perceived the increasing and encroaching blacks as usurpers and competitors for their jobs. Blacks comprised 25 percent of the stockyards employees, a major industry in the city, and the race riots of 1919 that cost thirty-eight lives signaled a transition in the previously harmonious race relations.[18]

Brookins began play on the Wendell Phillips High School heavyweights with the 1923–24 season. There is no record of him on the lightweights or heavyweights the prior season, and only two players from the 1922–23 team appear on the roster the following season. One lightweight player, June Rutledge, played on the 1922–23 Phillips lightweights but then appeared on the Hyde Park High lightweights the next year. Since Chicago did not have open enrollment, except for Lane Tech (North Side boys) or Chicago Vocational (South Side boys), Rutledge's family must have moved, still on the South Side, possibly still in Bronzeville, but across the district lines from Phillips to Hyde Park. The addition of Brookins, plus Simpson, Spears, and Wright and the continued presence of Johnson and Phillips much improved the team. Playing in the South Central section of Chicago's public high school division, the Red and Black of Phillips crept up on Bowen High after losing to Crane Tech. In the latter game Brookins had just four points in the 18–12 loss, played at the Jewish People's Institute, but in the former game, a 37–10 romp by Phillips, Brookins led with fourteen points on seven baskets, with the rest of the scoring line (Simpson, twelve, and Spears, eleven) rounding out the team scoring. The lightweights featured Randolph Ramsey as their center, with seven points. He would replace Reuben Spears the next year as the heavyweight center.[19]

An interesting aside: the *Chicago Defender* had an article in December 1923 noting that Ethel Waters was coming to the Avenue Theatre in the Bronzeville area.[20] By this time in his life Brookins was singing at clubs, and it was not unlikely that he was able to see Waters at this one-week engagement, a foreshadowing of his future in about twenty years. Louis Armstrong was playing in Chicago in 1922, and Brookins first went to the Royal Gardens, a famous jazz locale on East Thirty-First Street, at about this time also, an early indication of his dual interests. "The news spread like wildfire among the musicians who hurried that same evening to Lincoln Gardens. It wasn't that Louis's name was then known, but the musicians were aware of the fact that a young trumpet player had just arrived from New Orleans and was playing with Oliver. This was King Oliver (leader of a well known jazz band)."[21] "Toward 1923, I was still a little kid, and I was in school in Chicago where the kids were talking about Joe Oliver and his Creole Jazz Band. I went to the Royal Gardens for the first time. But I was still too young and wearing short pants so I had to borrow a pair of pants long enough to have some hope of getting in, but with those pants and the help of a doorman, I did."[22]

Chicago had blossomed into a center of black sport and black music during the 1920s. It featured many black and tan cabarets, where whites often composed the majority of patrons. Radio popularized the new music as ragtime, which had migrated from the South and evolved into new forms, such as the blues, gospel, and jazz. Chicago soon became a major conduit for the recording industry with production studios that attracted many musicians and singers.

In his high school years, however, Brookins's major focus remained on basketball. Directly after the Bowen victory, Phillips played and lost to Lane Tech, 16–12, with Brookins scoring only one point. Spears had five to lead the Red and Black. Lane's top scorer—and only African American player—was its center, Bill Watson, who led Lane with eight points.[23]

After the holiday break Phillips returned to the court to crush Lindblom High's heavyweights by a score of 32–8. Brookins scored fourteen points to top all scorers and was ably complemented by Spears with nine. Phillips was "led by Brookins, one of the best forwards seen this season, and Spears, all Chicago center of 1922." It was also noted that "Brookins, who got away with seven baskets, is a real find."[24]

So Brookins, now around six feet or six feet one and exceptionally fast, had been discovered, at least by the *Defender*, which gave him national press. It would be interesting to see how he responded. The next week Phillips beat Hyde Park, its closest competitor geographically, in the Phillips gymnasium. The score was 20–4, and Brookins had just two free throws for the game. Spears was the big scorer, with eight points. Phillips defeated Tilden High on January 21 in a game that Frank "Fay" Young, the *Defender*'s sports editor, found notable for the poor officiating, small gym, and slippery floor. Young did not often cover high school sports, so his presence was a testimonial to the accolades that the Phillips teams was drawing. The score was 19–16, with Spears and Brookins each scoring nine points.[25] Both players were extolled by the *Defender*, as they brought racial pride to the community. But Phillips, which was the only all-black high school in the city, was special to Bronzeville and the black community. Its victories were felt way beyond the school itself.

The next week Tilden played turnabout, topping Phillips, 15–14. Brookins and Spears were again the offense, scoring six and seven points respectively, but even with the loss Phillips had already clinched the South-Central championship since this was its first loss in City Public High School League (Public League) play. There was no "finger-pointing" in the loss, as the *Defender* noted that "the officiating was the best of the season."[26]

Such black victories enhanced black pride but also exacerbated racial tensions and hard feelings when whites lost. As Jack Johnson had shown, whites did not take kindly to the overturning of their Social Darwinian beliefs. The Phillips players were met with bricks at Tilden High School, accosted at Lindblom High, and engaged in a fight with the opponents at Englewood High. The *Defender*'s opinion of the officiating referred to the phantom calls often made by white referees to aid losing white teams.[27] Brookins no doubt noticed that whereas basketball required a direct confrontation of physical prowess, blacks were always allowed to entertain whites in their musical pursuits, as they apparently posed no threat to white notions of superiority.

On February 24 Phillips faced Englewood High, the South-Central runner-up for the right to play in the city finals, and for the third time Phillips was victorious "before over 3,000 fans who were packed like dried prunes in the enclosure" (the Parker High gym). The score was 17–10, and Brookins led his team with eight points. Illustrating the difference in game "management" from today's contests, "There wasn't a substitution on either side. Time was taken out once by Phillips and twice by Englewood." Frank Young went on to give an entire rundown of the game's action, ending with "Bring on Lane or Crane for the city title! Phillips is ready."[28]

The contest would be against Lane, to whom the Phillips team had lost in late December by 16–12. The championship game was not nearly as close, as Lane triumphed, 18–4. Played at Loyola University's gymnasium on March 7, the game was a rout from the beginning, as Phillips had no points until the fourth quarter and Lane had no personal fouls called on its players (Phillips had eight). Frank Young asserted that the "referee broke the morale of the team in the first three minutes" by taking away a Phillips's basket and calling two questionable fouls on Spears. Bill Watson was the high scorer with six points, and both the *Chicago Tribune* and the *Chicago Defender* noted that he was the only "colored player" (*Tribune*) and "the star; the rest of the boys were white."[29]

In a review thirty-four years later, Dan Burley saw the game as one that was greatly hampered by bad, one might say prejudiced, calls by a referee who gave Phillips' three top players three fouls before the end of the first quarter. Burley also viewed Bill Watson of Lane as a secret weapon that was not really known before; but that simply wasn't so, as Watson had been the leading scorer in the Lane-Phillips game the previous December. Nevertheless, there was no denying the greatness of the Phillips squad, as subsequent years would prove.[30]

The loss to Lane was crushing to the Phillips squad, the high school, and the African American community of Chicago, especially Bronzeville, but even before the Lane contest, a game between Phillips and Lincoln High of Kansas City, Missouri, had been arranged for an unofficial midwestern black high school championship. The *Defender*, in hyping the game on March 15, noted that "Spears and

Brookins lead the Chicago High School heavyweights in scoring."[31] Also on that day the *Defender* reported on the all-star city high school squad selected by the *Chicago Daily News*. Both Spears and Brookins had been selected, as well as Bill Watson of Lane. The *Defender* noted, "For the first time in the history of Chicago prep basketball, three members of our group have been selected as representatives on the all-star city high school heavyweight basketball quintet of the *Chicago Daily News* . . . . Watson and Spears were awarded berths on the first team, while Brookins was given a place on the second team."[32]

So the news of the day was bittersweet with the loss but buoyed by the success of Spears and Brookins and the promise of more glory in Kansas City. Two weeks later the Phillips team traveled to Kansas City, where the players were treated like visiting dignitaries by the African American community of that city. They then proceeded to be "bad guests" by defeating Lincoln High by a score of 23–13 before a crowd of seven thousand in Kansas City's Convention Hall, as reported on page one of the *Defender*. Simpson led the team with seven points, and Spears contributed six. Brookins was not listed in the lineup, and the article explained his absence with a suggestion of his future actions: "Brookins was left in Chicago because he has attended school three days since March 7. His excuse was that he was down hearted [sic] because Lane defeated Phillips. . . . Perhaps Phillips' victory will teach Brookins, who is very young, a lesson. We hope so. He is too good a basketball player to kill his future by allowing the 'little glory' already won to run away with his head. Brookins is back in school now, a sorry but a wiser kid. He is studying day and night to make good."[33]

Sportswriter T. E. Gaillard's observations may have been true, but Brookins managed to make the best of his "forced exile." On the night of the Kansas City game Brookins played for the Eighth Regiment Lights in a doubleheader on the Regiment court, at Thirty-Fifth and Giles; the occasion pitted the Eighth Regiment Heavyweights in a featured contest against the famous Pittsburgh Loendi squad of Cumberland Posey, before nine hundred fans. The Eighth heavyweights upset Loendi, 29–22, but the biggest splash was made in the lightweight game, where the Eighth squad topped Jefferson Park, 37–

17. The leading scorer was Tommy Brookins, who had thirteen baskets and two free throws for twenty-eight points for the victors.[34]

The end of the basketball season did not mean that Brookins would be devoted just to his studies since he was still busy singing and playing baseball. In a 1985 interview with Franklin Brison, Brookins casually mentioned that he played second base on the Chicago Giants, who were a founding member of the Negro National League in 1920 and existed until 1952. Brookins would not have been playing for them until at least 1926, but he would have to have played a lot of baseball prior to that to be considered for the Giants, who won Negro League pennants in 1920, 1921, and 1922.[35] So his summer activities were most likely baseball and singing, as well as visiting nightclubs (when he could sneak in) to observe the greats of the jazz era.

Brookins apparently did his homework, literally and figuratively, to prepare for his senior season in basketball. Chicago public schools required that each athlete carry four "solid" subjects and have passing grades in all of them in order to retain eligibility, so Brookins must have done that.[36]

The 1925 Public League basketball season opened on January 7 for Phillips with a win over Tilden, 28–8. Brookins and the new center, Ramsey, led all scoring with twelve each, before 1,200 students at the Eighth Regiment Armory.[37] In late December 1924 the team had lost to an alumni squad, 27–24. Brookins led Phillips with eleven points, and the alumni were led by his old teammate, Spears, who was now a freshman at Howard University, with seventeen points. Still the *Defender* felt that Phillips "showed that they had a winning combination."[38]

The Phillips team lost to Lindblom, 17–15, in their second league contest, and Jesse Lovell of the *Defender* was adamant in his accusations of incompetence (or worse) on the part of the referee, A. E. Barnum, who was white. According to Lovell, Barnum, "continuously and successively fouled the Phillips team when Lindblom was behind in the score."[39] When Phillips led 13–6 in the third quarter, Barnum called a technical, then an offensive foul on Brookins, then, after two missed free throws, said that the Phillips rooters were too loud and had the free throws shot again, with one made. The Lindblom timers, according to Lovell, then ended the game with a minute to play. Despite the loss, Lovell noted that "the sterling work of Brookins was especially commendable." He had eleven of the fifteen points for Phillips, with Ramsey getting the other four.[40]

Phillips then lost badly to Hyde Park, 24–18, and to Englewood High, 29–15. Brookins had just two points, and Eaves led the team with nine. The Hyde Park defeat was seen by Lovell as decisive, and he pronounced Hyde Park the better team. Brookins tied for game honors with Cockrell of Hyde Park, each with eight points. Lovell noted that "Brookins was the star of the contest, as usual, until he was put out of the game via the personal foul route. The fast forward scored four field goals, more than the total number made by the Hyde Park cagers, but was unable at all times to control his speed." Brookins's fouling caused him to sit for a time, and "this was a severe blow to the Phillips five, who suffered much the loss of the great forward."[41] White referees, as noted above, sometimes called an inordinate number of fouls on black teams and awarded free throws to whites or disallowed the baskets scored by black players for alleged technicalities.[42]

Four days later Phillips managed to escape Tilden in overtime by a score of 21–19. Five Phillips players scored; Ramsey led with six, Eaves had five, and Brookins, four. Then Phillips played Lindblom at home and avenged its earlier defeat with a 22–13 victory. Brookins had ten points to lead all scorers, with support from Eaves (four) and Ramsey (four).[43] The *Defender*, in reporting the Lindblom contest, noted, "Brookins was in his best form and shot from difficult angles."[44]

At this point Phillips had three league losses, and its record of 3-3 had it in third in the division, behind Englewood and Hyde Park, each with records of 4-2. The next contest with Hyde Park would largely determine whether Phillips would return to the Public League playoffs. On February 3 the two squads met at the Eighth Regiment Armory, and Hyde Park eked out a 14–12 victory, despite seven points from Brookins. The loss eliminated Phillips from all city playoffs but did not mean that its season was over.[45] Instead it was scheduled to play another intersectional game against Armstrong Technical High School of Washington DC for the unofficial national high school cage title among black high schools. It was also scheduled to play Englewood a second time, on February 6, to close the Public League season, but that game was forfeited by Phillips on February 5. Phillips players had been tripped and kicked at Lindblom, and whites had picked a fight with the Phillips players at Englewood.[46] "Recent attacks on officials of the City Public high school basketball league and clashes between students of Wendell Phillips High and opposing schools during league basketball games have led Principal W. A. Evans of Phillips to order withdrawal of his school's quintet for the rest of the season. . . . [This] comes as a result of disturbances at Hyde Park and Lindblom High School during basketball games."[47]

It is interesting that this story went unreported in the *Chicago Defender*, as that newspaper focused on the upcoming clash between Phillips and Armstrong. The departure of Armstrong's team for Chicago warranted an article detailing the Washington team's itinerary and review of the previous year's game, in which Phillips traveled to Washington to win 17–10 against Armstrong. The Washington team would take the train from Washington via Harper's Ferry, West Virginia, and Pittsburgh before arriving in Chicago. Tip-off for the game was scheduled for February 12.[48]

The game made the front page of the *Chicago Defender* after Phillips defeated Armstrong by a score of 25–15 before 4,500 at the Eighth Regiment Armory. It was more than a game; rather it was an event with bands, decorations galore at the Armory, "pretty girl ushers in evening gowns," "the elite of Chicago's business and social world," and dancing. The closing hour of the Eighth Regiment Armory afterward "[brought] down the curtain of one of the greatest spectacles to be recorded in basketball history."[49] Such events served as community festivals marking the blossoming of the parallel black national sporting culture in which African Americans displayed their finery, their support, and their pride in an affair arranged and orchestrated without white support or administration.

The game itself was a showcase, largely for Brookins and Ramsey:

Thomas Brookins led the offensive attack for the Phillips five with truly sensational and extremely difficult shooting and field work, although Randolph Ramsey was the actual star of the game. Brookins' goals were made from nearly every conceivable angle and from some which were inconceivable. . . . At times, the big forward ran wild and, when the Armstrong guards were expecting him to dribble nearer the goal or pass the ball, he leaped into his sensational shooting pose and delivered the shot with almost mathematical accuracy, the ball never touching the rim or the basket.[50]

Lest they get swelled heads after the big victory, the next week the *Defender* published an admonition to Brookins and Ramsey regarding their futures, which, rumor had it, were to be professional basketball for the Eighth Regiment team. The piece sought to discourage this action, which would make them professionals, whether they were paid or not, and it went on to clarify what constituted amateurism and professionalism in the sport. "We are against any set of young men, who, under the guise of amateurs are professionals, and we warn players who are members of college teams who wish to play with other clubs here that playing against any professional team BARS [*sic*] you from athletic competition in any school of standing. The same goes for high school players."[51]

Such pronouncements exemplified the black middle-class acceptance of and aspirations to white values in the ongoing quest for acceptance. Sport provided a proving ground through a very public display of progress toward that objective. Both Brookins and Ramsey seemed to take this warning to heart, at least for a while.

In the fall of 1925 the two were part of an amateur team, put together largely by Brookins, called the Chicago Flashes. The team began in October, and the *Defender* said that the team "promises to be the fastest team of its weight in the city." The team included Lester Johnson, formerly of Phillips and recently of Howard University; "Walter Wright of last year's Phillips team[;] and Joe Higgins and Bob Harness, also two former stars from Phillips."[52] The team was eager to take on all comers and began traveling beyond the city early in 1926. A trip to St. Louis saw the Flashes defeat a high school team and lose to the St. Louis Y team. They came apart some time after that, and the next month saw Brookins playing on another squad, the Wabash YMCA All Stars, also called the Chicago All-Stars. In November they lost to another newly formed squad, the Chicagoans, led by old nemesis Bill Watson from Lane. The score was 26–19, with Watson leading with twelve points. Brookins had six for the All Stars.[53]

In February the All Stars journeyed north to the North Avenue Y to play the Larrabee Five (Larrabee is about 700 West, and North Avenue is 1600 North and once was the northern boundary of the city but is now, and was then, the near North Side). Brookins, however, was the only holdover from the All Stars of January. The remainder were distinctly Phillips in origin. The Wabash quint won by a 41–24 score, and Brookins (eleven) and Randolph Ramsey (sixteen) led the scoring. Of the three other starters, Troutman and Rutledge also had Phillips ties, the former having played with Brookins and Ramsey and the latter having been a lightweight for Phillips before moving to the Hyde Park district. The *Defender* noted that "the team work of the winning five was by far the feature of the game," and this was characteristic of Phillips High basketball.[54]

Brookins and his mates left the team before a scheduled game in March. With the end of the basketball season there was no clarification on what happened, but it may have been that Brookins and his pals, ostensibly amateurs, were getting some sort of cut from receipts and the deal fell apart. It may have been that they were offered something more to play elsewhere, but in the fall of 1926 a new team, organized by Dick Hudson as manager and captained by Brookins, was formed, playing out of the Eighth Regiment Armory as the Giles Post American Legion team. Brookins was joined by Wright, Johnson, and Ramsey once again.[55]

In late December this team began an eighteen-game tour of Wisconsin towns, booked most likely (according to Ben Green) by Abe Saperstein for Hudson. The Giles Post team lost in Clintonville, 28–14, and, after a short rest in Chicago later in January, returned to Wisconsin to continue the tour.[56] In February the Giles Post team defeated Fisher Body of Janesville, 41–17, after topping Watertown, 50–16, and the Reedsburg Flashes, 56–23. The lineup was Brookins, Ramsey, Wright, Johnson, and Fisher; Fisher was not from Phillips but from Evanston, but he led in scoring against Fisher Body with sixteen. Ramsey had twelve and Brookins six.[57]

Upon the return of the Giles Post team, a conflict arose between Hudson and Frank "Fay" Young, ostensibly about Hudson's use of the name without the permission of the Post commander and about the inflation of players' credentials (advertisements likely attributed to Abe Saperstein, hired as tour promoter), which claimed that they were former college stars when in fact none had ever been in college. Such subterfuge was a common ploy of the trickster in black oral culture and in musical renderings and was no doubt meant as a marketing strategy to increase attendance and revenue. Young's earlier concern about the mixing of amateurs and professionals seems to have been forgotten. Nevertheless, the tiff forced Hudson to find a new sponsor for his squad, and the newly opened Savoy Ballroom at Forty-Seventh and South Parkway proved to be that. Hudson's team was now the Savoy Bearcats, but that soon was altered to just the Savoy Big Five.[58]

The Big Five debuted at the Savoy Ballroom on January 3, 1928, against the Howard University team, and the result was a victory for the Savoy Big Five. Brookins and Joe Lillard, who had been a top football, baseball, and basketball player in Mason City, Iowa, each scored sixteen points in the 42–29 win. Ramsey had two, Wright, one, and Johnson, three to complete the Phillips alumni scoring. Bill Watson had two, and a new young man, Inman Jackson, also supposedly a former Lane student like Watson, had two. *Defender* writer David Kellum made no mention of Howard's playing semiprofessionals.[59]

The two teams played again later in the week, but it was not reported in the *Defender*, although there was a later reference to a Howard loss after that team went on to Atlanta to meet other college squads, Morehouse and Morris Brown. The Savoy team next played the Elgin YMCA on January 16 and defeated it for its first loss, 44–23, at Savoy. Lillard had fourteen points and Brookins eight to lead the scoring. Ramsey had five, Johnson, six, and Wright, four, to round out the Phillips contributions.[60] Three nights later the Savoy Five met Wilberforce College and were upset by the college lads in the last minute of play, 32–28. Lillard was the big scorer for Savoy with eighteen, while the Phillips group had Brookins with only two, as he and Lester Johnson were both fouled out of the contest with the maximum four fouls. Johnson had one point, Wright, one, and Ramsey, five. Brookins was referred to as the Savoy's star player, and he was now the captain of the team.[61]

The Savoy Five defeated the Pittsburgh Loendi club of owner/manager/player Cumberland Posey in two weekend games on February 11 and 12. The first game was 24–17, and the second, 30–24. Both games were quite rough; the *Defender* called them "the roughest games seen on a local floor this year." One reason might have been the agreement to not disqualify a player on the basis of four fouls but rather to use the professional rules, wherein a player could be tossed at any time if a referee felt that the player was too rough. Thus Hampton of Loendi had eleven fouls on Saturday and another twelve on Sunday. Brookins picked up six in the Sunday contest, while Watson and Wright had four each in that game. Brookins had five points on Saturday (behind Lillard's eight and Watson's six) and eight on Sunday (behind Watson's nine).[62]

The Savoy Five absorbed its second defeat, again to Wilberforce, on Monday, February 20, 29–18, before more than two thousand fans at Savoy. Newly acquired "Rock" Anderson (eight), Lillard (six), and Brookins (four) were the only Savoy scorers in the loss. Brookins, clearly annoyed at the outcome of the game, threw a Wilberforce player to the floor while he was shooting near the end of the contest and was immediately pulled out of the game by the Savoy coach, amid boos and hisses directed at Brookins.[63]

Two nights later Savoys topped Lincoln University, playing at the end of a six-game tour in which the college team had won its previous five contests. The score was 36–31, and Watson and Lillard led the scoring with ten points each, while Brookins had six and Ramsey, eight.[64] The Savoys followed this with a win over DeHart Hubbard's Cincinnati Comets but without Brookins and Wright, who had "quit the team following a row last week over their pay checks." This "row" would be the beginning of a series of differences that would ultimately lead to Brookins' taking his Phillips pals to go off on their own—but not quite yet.[65] De Hart Hubbard, a national and Olympic track star, the first African American to win a gold medal in the Olympic games (in 1924 in Paris as a long jumper), held a measure of social capital. Such celebrity athletes often played other sports year round, and their names attracted larger crowds anxious to witness their physical prowess.

There was at least a temporary truce a week later when the Savoys played the Chicago Bruins of owner George Halas (also the owner of the Chicago Bears). The Bruins were members of the American Basketball League and were populated with some of the top players in all of basketball. The great Johnny Beckman, formerly of the champion New York Celtics, was at one forward. John (Honey) Russell was a guard. (Both were later elected to the Naismith Memorial Basketball Hall of Fame.) Milo "Slim" Schoun was a center approximately seven feet tall. The Bruins won, 29–25, but the game wasn't as close as it seemed, with the Bruins taking an 11–0 lead and then toying with the Savoys the rest of the way. Brookins had four points and Ramsey did not score. Lillard with eight and Anderson with six led the Savoy scoring.[66]

The Savoy Five won the rest of their games with smaller crowds coming to see games against less challenging opponents like the Irving Cohn Jewelers in late March, whom the Savoys beat 37–30, with balanced scoring from Brookins (six), Lillard (nine), Jackson (six), Ramsey (six), and Anderson (ten).[67] Anderson had come from Cincinnati and had beaten out Lester Wright as a starter, causing Wright to quit the Savoys and move to the Fort Dearborn Elks.[68] Shortly after Joe Lillard and Rock Anderson left the team for spring practice with their baseball teams, Lillard with the Chicago American Giants and Anderson likely with the Birmingham Black Barons. Their departure meant more playing time for the other starters and fewer divisions of the game receipts among the players. On April 14 the *Defender* announced an upcoming contest that week against the Evanston Y, noting that Fisher, the Savoys' big center, had formerly played for the Evanston team and that both Lillard and Anderson were expected back for the game. The possible return of Lillard and Anderson seemed to be a new source of contention for Brookins and his cohorts, Ramsey, Jackson, and Wright, who quit the team, leaving the Savoys a bit shorthanded for the Evanston game. It didn't seem to matter as the Savoys still dominated Evanston for a 33–12 victory after snaring some other locals to fill out the Savoy squad. Anderson and Fisher led the scoring with fifteen and six respectively. The account of the game noted that there was no Brookins, Ramsey, Wright, and Jackson, who had "quit the team because they were unable to reach an agreement with manager Faggin."[69] Ironically it was Lillard's baseball playing that got him declared ineligible for college football after he returned to the University of Oregon in 1930 and played freshman football, then played two games for the varsity the next season, before losing his eligibility. He played for the Chicago Cardinals in 1932 and 1933 (one of only two African Americans in the NFL) but lost his position on the roster, allegedly due to his pride and violent responses to racial slurs, forcing his white coach, Paul Schissler, to remove him from the game.[70]

At the end of the season the Savoys were "in complete disarray," with Joe Lillard as the only remaining player on the roster who had been on it when the season opened.[71] Brookins, meanwhile, had been busy with singing dates in various clubs around the city, so he was much better off financially than his teammates, as well as in high demand. Other well-known African American athletes, such as Paul Robeson and Fritz Pollard, eventually eschewed their athletic careers to enter the entertainment industry, which was less physically demanding and promised greater longevity.

In November 1928 the opening of practice saw a completely different Savoy team as Tommy Brookins had organized his own squad, the Tommy Brookins Globe Trotters. This team would have Randolph Ramsey, Lester Wright, Inman Jackson, Bill Watson, Willis Oliver (another former Phillips player), and Bobby Anderson, a former Savoy assistant coach. They would play at the Eighth Regiment Armory. But both Jackson and Watson must have had second thoughts and returned to the Savoys before the first Globe Trotters contest. The Savoys continued to draw big crowds to the Savoy Ballroom, as well as beat top teams. Their games were generally covered in the *Defender*.

For Brookins and his squad the opponents and the coverage were hit or miss. In early February the *Defender* headlined the upcoming contests between the Globe Trotters and Morgan College, noting that the Brookins team consisted of four former Phillips players—Brookins, Ramsey, Johnson, and Wright. The article also noted that "several of the players were members of last year's Savoy Big Five" and that "the Globe Trotters have recently returned from a trip through Southern Illinois where they made an excellent showing, winning seven games and losing two."[72]

The Globe Trotters and Morgan split their two games, with Morgan winning the opener at the Eighth Regiment court, 19–17, and the Globe Trotters winning the next night at St. Elizabeth's Hall, at Forty-First and State, 30–17. Brookins, Ramsey, and Johnson were joined by Harper, another former Phillips player. Brookins had two points in the first game and thirteen in the second, to lead all scorers. In the latter game Ramsey had five, Johnson, five, and Harper, five.[73]

The Globe Trotters disappear from the *Defender*'s pages, and their future, as well as that of Brookins, is fuzzier. By this time Brookins had married Ruth Albright, when he was twenty-one and she was only seventeen. Three years later they had a son, Thomas Jr., and they were living in the heart of Bronzeville, on Forty-Fourth Street, with Brookins's in-laws and Ruth's twenty-three-year-old brother. Brookins stated that he was an employed theatrical entertainer on the 1930 census, an indication that his identity from athlete to entertainer had taken root.[74] The best account of what then transpired for the team and Brookins comes from interviews with Brookins in about 1973 with a sportswriter for the *New York Times*, Michael Strauss. (The most unusual and extensive of these interviews was on a beach in St. Maarten, and some were in Brookins's restaurant.) Strauss's account was published in *Sports Quarterly Basketball Special, 1973–74*, and Ben Green used that and a subsequent interview with Strauss in about 2001 as the sources for his conclusion of how the Harlem Globetrotters began.[75]

According to Strauss and assertions by a Globetrotter researcher whom Green tracked down, Brookins and Hudson, back together with the Globe Trotters, wanted to do a 1929 tour of Michigan and Wisconsin, as in 1927, but neither felt that he could take the time to do the bookings, so they hired Abe Saperstein, a white, local, would-be promoter of black league teams, as well as a forester in Chicago, working a patronage job with the Chicago Park District. The tour for the Brookins Globe Trotters went along successfully until it was discovered that Saperstein had booked two teams for tours of Michigan and Wisconsin (claiming both were the Brookins Globe Trotters) and, when confronted by Brookins, admitted to doing so.

By that time Brookins had introduced entertainment between

games, according to Strauss, although such entertainment had been offered other places with other teams. Brookins, however, made it a regular part of the Globe Trotter games, and both he and Ramsey were part of the entertainment, Brookins as a singer and Ramsey as a banjoist and comedian.[76] Brookins said, "One of the songs that I used to sing was none other than 'Sweet Georgia Brown'—the same one that the Harlem Globe Trotters [*sic*] have used as their theme song for years."[77]

The disclosure of Saperstein's double-dealing led to a confrontation between Brookins and Saperstein, the former feeling that the latter had not treated the players fairly, and it resulted in Saperstein's shrugging and saying essentially, "What's done is done; what can I do?" Brookins shrugged also and saw this double-dealing as the impetus he needed to leave the team, a move that he had been contemplating for a while, in order to concentrate on his singing career. He was making $75 a week at the Regal Theatre (in Chicago at Forty-Seventh and South Parkway, now known as Martin Luther King Boulevard), and it was much better money and steadier work than basketball touring. Plus he said that his mother was sick and he wanted to stay closer to her.

There were no hard feelings, although over the years Brookins was disturbed that he never received the credit for originating the Globetrotters and that a myth arose about the origin of Saperstein's Globetrotters—that is, that they came to be when playing a Hinckley, Illinois, team. This myth was perpetuated by Saperstein, who may have simply conflated the 1927 tour that he first promoted with the later actual play in Hinckley, documented in a box score from 1929. In a later meeting Brookins got Saperstein to promise to keep his "original team"—mostly the Phillips gang plus Jackson—as part of the team, and Brookins gave Saperstein three sets of old Globe Trotter uniforms. Green notes that Brookins's version of the team's origin has fewer inconsistencies than Saperstein's and "meshes with the chronology of events that can be documented."[78]

Brookins still played occasionally on the Chicago teams of Dick Hudson in the next couple of years, but basically his basketball career had ended and his entertainment career took off.[79] As for the

Globetrotters, they went on to the fame that they have today after their glorious eighty-five-year history. Brookins and Saperstein (the Jewish booking agent/manager who died in 1966) never had anything to do with each other again. Brookins said, "We just didn't have anything in common."[80] (From the earliest years of basketball, blacks and Jews were seen as superior players at the game. They also were the regular targets of discrimination in many aspects of American society, including sports. Thus there were mutual understandings between the two ethnic groups that led to cooperation in basketball. Nevertheless, ethnic pride and striving were apparent for each group—at the expense of the other if necessary, which resulted in the Brookins-Saperstein split.)

Although Brookins moved on to singing and basketball was left behind, his contributions to the game as a player, leader, organizer, and entrepreneur should be seen in light of the early development of the game. Brookins was a swift, aggressive player who knew how to use the backboard in shooting from various angles. He was a noted high scorer in high school and as a touring player, and his exploits were well known within the African American communities across the nation, largely because of the *Chicago Defender*'s national dissemination and its pioneering sports editor, Frank Young. In a game where speed and power trumped mere height, Brookins was a star. As big men (those six feet five and over) became more agile, the game evolved toward more offensive inside play, more than just tip-ins, but by that time Brookins had become less prominent as a basketball player as he pursued his singing career, though he still dabbled in the game as well as in baseball. He was not, however, gone from the headlines. In 1932 he played baseball for the famed Gilkerson Giants team, and during the winter the Giants organized a formidable basketball team with Brookins at forward and Sol Butler, who was a member of the 1920 Olympic team, at guard.[81]

### Brookins the Entertainer

Tracing Tommy Brookins's career as an entertainer is much more difficult than tracing his basketball career because as an independent agent, he moved around with various bands until becoming an act of his own in the 1930s. He noted that he sang at Kelly's on the North Side of Chicago for about a year, then "I was hired at the Eldorado Club at the corner of Fifty-Fifth Street and Garfield Boulevard. The Eldorado was in a cellar and Jimmie Noone had the orchestra there."[82] Noone was from Louisiana and was playing the clarinet professionally in New Orleans at age eighteen (1913). He moved to Chicago in 1918 and played professionally at the Royal Gardens. In 1926 he started leading the band at the Apex Club at 330 West Thirty-Fifth Street until it was raided and shut down in 1929 (this was the era of Prohibition). He then played at various locations around Chicago, and Brookins would sing with the band. In the early 1930s Noone went to New York, and Brookins went with him.[83]

Once Brookins was in New York, he began going around to the various nightclubs seeking jobs. In 1933 he hooked up with Arnold Wiley and Jesse Oliver to form a dance and singing trio. "The act is one of the best seen as a trio, according to reports if [sic] the critics of the R-K-O circuit."[84] They also were a hit on the Keith circuit (another group of theaters).[85] Although on the move, Brookins maintained an address at the Dewey Square Hotel at 117 Seventh Avenue (now Adam Clayton Powell Boulevard) and 117th Street in Harlem.

Brookins was hired by Fletcher Henderson and toured Europe with Henderson and his band. According to Brookins, he was paid round-trip ship fare plus a salary on a six-week contract, but he decided to stay in Europe, primarily England, for seven years, until sometime in the late 1930s. He played in Australia briefly, throughout Scandinavia, and in the late 1930s in Antwerp, Belgium. Also around this period he met Sammy Van, and he and Brookins began a successful nightclub act as dancers, comedians, and singers. Usually Brookins played the piano and sang, and Van danced, while the two often stopped for comedy routines.[86] They were reviewed favorably in many venues throughout Europe. Most echoed the comments found in *The Stage* regarding their show in Belfast: "Brookins and Van are two smart colored artists. . . . They certainly are a pair of very entertaining comedians and cause a good deal of fun."[87]

In 1936 Brookins played on a BBC Channel 2 show, following Paul Robeson, who made the biggest impression on him of anyone he ever met. Such admiration is not surprising since Robeson, ten years Brookins's senior, was a dynamic force who exuded power, confidence, and respect, but for Brookins it was probably even more meaningful because of the parallels in their lives. Robeson, of course, had been an All-American football player and had played basketball at Rutgers before attaining a law degree from Columbia and then fully pursuing a singing and acting career.[88]

Brookins had met Sammy Van on the European club circuit and they began their partnership around 1933, but they left Europe around 1939 as Europe came closer and closer to war following the appointment of Adolf Hitler as German chancellor in 1933 and the creation of the Axis between Italy and Germany in November 1936. The *New York Amsterdam News*, a black newspaper, explained that many "American-born Negro show folk were reluctant to return to the United State until things broke better for them [but] the war is now raging."[89] Brookins and Van were only two of the many African American entertainers who had sought a better life in Europe, but the eruption of World War II disrupted their good fortune. Brookins had been so successful that in his "most prosperous days as an entertainer, he owned a luxurious Hispano Suiza, a foreign car that cost him $17,000. In 1939 he brought it back with him on the *Île de France* (considered the most luxurious ship in the world at that time) and drove it to Chicago."[90]

Brookins and Van made short films (probably for showing between or before feature films), toured, and also played separately. In July 1943 Al Monroe noted in his *Chicago Defender* column, "Tommy Brookins, who formerly played basketball in Chicago and then went on to the stage, is the latest heart-beat of the sensational Ethel Waters with plenty cash and property deeds to prove it, they are saying."[91] By late 1943 Brookins was on a tour that featured Waters, about eight years his senior but someone whom he had first seen and admired when he was in high school twenty years earlier in Chicago. Donald Bogle states the following:

> Brookins looked like a smooth operator, with his athletic build, quick smile, well-trimmed mustache, and friendly eyes-eyes that focused

on Ethel (then about 47), who, in turn, focused hers right back on him. He appeared giddy whenever he and Ethel were together in public. Before Ethel could say much, the press were calling Brookins her "latest heart-beat." . . . Within a few months, there would be talk of "trousseau shopping" and not long afterward, Tommy would be referred to as another of her husbands (she had three, legally). . . . But Ethel was too much on the move to pant too hard for young Brookins.[92]

At Christmas in 1943 Brookins accompanied Waters and her secretary to a dinner given in her honor at the Philadelphia home of her half brother, Benjamin Waters. On her way back to Los Angeles, "Waters departed the train to make a stop in Chicago, where she was the guest of honor at the launching of a new nightclub, Cabin in the Sky, at Sixty-Fourth and Cottage Grove. Run by none other than Tommy Brookins, the club was a kind of homage to Ethel—in part Ethel's homage to herself, because she had poured money into the establishment."[93]

Waters and Brookins were obviously lovers who enjoyed each other very much, but no announcement of an impending marriage ever came. The club put Waters heavily into debt and never succeeded in turning a real profit. Even Waters failed to appear there, choosing instead "to star in a Broadway nightery."[94] Brookins and Waters kept up a long-term relationship, but that relationship eventually fizzled out. "The restaurant was never the success that Ethel had hoped for. A new owner came in, and the establishment eventually folded."[95] Then came another announcement: "They're saying Ethel Waters has called it quits in her romance with Tommy Brookins who is operating the Cabin in the Sky drinkery in Chicago on what's left of an originally heavy bankroll."[96]

In 1948 Brookins and Van were touring again, having reunited for a time, but the demise of the Cabin in the Sky club gave Brookins no reason to stay in Chicago—or in the United States for that matter.[97] He had enjoyed his time in Europe very much and returned there in late 1948. He played in clubs for the next few years, returning to the United States in the early 1950s. He debuted a new act in late 1951 in Paris; the act caught the attention of the African American press but, despite promise, never seemed to make it to the United States.

> Paris—Brookins and Laureen Fresno are creating a sensation here where they have been entertaining for several months in some of the smartest spots. The team is believed to be the only one of its kind in the entertainment world—a Negro man and a white girl in a sophisticated act—and they will open Christmas Day at one of France's most famous winter resorts.
>
> Because the team is a mixed one and this type of act has never been presented to an American audience, Tommy and Laureen decided to try it out abroad before offering it to night clubs and theatres in America. They expect to return to the States, however, to try their fortune some time next year.[98]

A more acceptable combination occurred around 1957, as Brookins became a regular in a St. Louis club, where, according to Brookins, the Musial family came by on Saturday nights and Stan, who played the banjo, watched Brookins to see how to play the piano. Musial thus learned and played it by ear. Brookins often traveled back to Chicago and referred to himself as "'the world's most well traveled Negro' in regards to his getting around as a top-flight entertainer."[99]

In the late 1950s and early 1960s Brookins lived and played clubs in Hawaii, right after it became a state in 1959. He became politically active and worked for Neil Blaisdell in his election campaigns for mayor of Honolulu, asserted Brookins in the 1985 interview with Franklin Brison. He then returned to Chicago in the early 1960s and was appointed acting director of urban progress programs in the city under Mayor Richard J. Daley.[100] These programs were funded by the Urban Renewal Act of 1965 as part of the War on Poverty and were forerunners of the Model Cities Programs, which encouraged wide discretion in efforts to reinvigorate urban neighborhoods.[101] Why Brookins was appointed is not clear, but there is no question that the appointment was one of political patronage, as attested by former reformist alderman Dick Simpson, now a professor of political science at the University of Illinois at Chicago. He referred to such appointments as "havens of patronage."[102] Like many African

Americans who had to survive in a society dominated by whites, Brookins used his talents, social skills, and professional contacts to forge a successful life in a variety of roles.

Brookins moved to St. Maarten in 1969 and sometime after that purchased the Portofino restaurants, which specialized in pizza. He returned to the United States regularly but spent almost all his time in his adopted home.[103] He owned the restaurants at the time of his death in a St. Maarten hospital in June 1988.

Brookins was a nationally famous basketball player and is now credited with beginning the team that became the Harlem Globetrotters in 1928. He became internationally known for his singing, piano playing, and comedy act with Sammy Van in the 1930s. His romance with Ethel Waters gained him attention and a nightclub in Chicago in the 1940s, during World War II. He later returned to the piano and stage, playing and living in Europe, before ending his stage career in the 1950s. His contacts in Chicago were obviously instrumental in his political appointment to the urban progress programs in the mid-1960s. Tiring of big city life and cold winters, Brookins emigrated to St. Maarten in about 1969, where he lived quietly for the last nineteen years of his life.

Ironically the Harlem Globetrotters, which slipped from Brookins's fingers in 1929, were purchased by Mannie Jackson, a former star at the University of Illinois (and one of the school's first African American players) and former Globetrotter who had succeeded as a corporate executive with Honeywell. By that time greater opportunities existed for African Americans, but those opportunities started with the efforts of Tommy Brookins and others who confronted and overcame the racial barriers of previous eras.

### Notes

I gratefully acknowledge the assistance of Robert Pruter for his help in providing and copying materials, as well as his insight and encouragement. I also thank Amanda Maple of Penn State Libraries for her assistance in tracking down musical references. Gerald Gems edited the manuscript and added very useful sections.

1. Katherine Johnson, "My Ancestor, Tommy Brookins, the Original Globetrotter," originally posted May 9, 2012, http://www.pbs.org/wnet/finding-your-roots

/stories/famous-relatives/mu-ancestor-tommy-brookins-the-orignial-globe trotter/ (accessed June 20, 2014). Johnson says Brookins died in 1987, but a *Chicago Tribune* death notice puts his death as June 1988. Kenan Heise, "Ex-Jazz Singer, Thomas Brookins, 81," *Chicago Tribune*, http://articles.chicagotribune.com/1988-06-05/news/8801040962_1_caribbean-island-urban-progress (accessed June 30, 2014).

2. In their column "Netschpicking," *Chicago Tribune*, February 9, 1986, Michael Sneed and Kathy O'Malley noted that the following Tuesday (February 13) was Tommy Brookins's eightieth birthday.

3. Much of the personal information on Tommy Brookins is drawn from an interview in 1985 (or 1987) by Franklin Brison for the St. Maarten newspaper *Today*. Brison was a prominent member of the St. Maarten Chamber of Commerce in later years. Some of the data that Brookins provided are not exactly correct, but that is not unusual for oral history interviews of persons of his age. Even his age, however, is not entirely without question.

4. Allen H. Spear, *Black Chicago: The Making of a Negro Ghetto* (Chicago: University of Chicago Press, 1967), 12.

5. That school was torn down in the 1990s and replaced by a new Coleman School at Forty-Sixth and Dearborn.

6. Taylor Bell, "Black Basketball—A Proud History," *Chicago Sun-Times*, March 6, 1988, 74–75.

7. Dan Burley, "The Way of Sports . . . ," *Chicago Defender*, September 23, 1958, A22.

8. "The Second Year of Uniform Rules for Basket Ball," *Spalding's Official 1916–17 Basket Ball Guide* (New York: American Sports Publishing, 1916), 4.

9. "The Second Year of Uniform Rules for Basket Ball," 5.

10. "The Second Year of Uniform Rules for Basket Ball," 7.

11. "The Second Year of Uniform Rules for Basket Ball," 24.

12. See Frank Basloe, *I Grew Up with Basketball: Twenty Years of Barnstorming with Cage Greats of Yesterday* (New York: Greenberg, 1952, 2012). The Buffalo Germans won the Pan American championship in 1901 and the AAU title in St. Louis at the Olympics, when basketball was a demonstration sport.

13. Gerald Gems, "Blocked Shot: The Development of Basketball in the African-American Community of Chicago," *Journal of Sport History* 22, no. 2 (Summer 1995): 138–40.

14. David K. Wiggins, "Edward Bancroft Henderson, African-American Athletes and the Writing of Sport History," in *Sport and the Color Line: Black Athletes and Race Relations in Twentieth-Century America*, ed. Patrick B. Miller and David K. Wiggins (New York: Routledge, 2004), 271–88.

15. Claude Johnson, *Black Fives: The Alpha Physical Culture Club's Pioneering African American Basketball Team, 1904–1923* (Greenwich CT: Black Fives Publishing, 2012).

16. Murry Nelson, *The Originals: The New York Celtics Invent Modern Basketball* (Bowling Green OH: Bowling Green Popular Press, 1999), 49–50.

17. Cited in Bernard Postal, Jesse Silver, and Roy Silver, "Sedran Barney," in Postal, Silver, and Silver, *Encyclopedia of Jews in Sports* (New York: Bloch Publishing, 1965).

18. Spear, *Black Chicago*, 46–47.

19. "Phillips Five Divides" and "Bowen Bows to Phillips," *Chicago Defender*, December 22, 1923, pt. 1, 10. Unlike most other high school leagues, that of the Chicago Public Schools played four seven-minute quarters, making for very fast contests, both in style of play and length of games.

20. "Ethel Waters Coming to the Avenue Theatre," *Chicago Defender*, December 29, 1923, pt. 1, 5.

21. Max Jones and John Chilton, *Louis: The Louis Armstrong Story, 1900–1971* (London: Da Capo Press, 1971), 65.

22. Cited in Nat Shapiro and Nat Hentoff, eds., *Hear Me Talkin' to Ya* (New York: Rinehart, 1952), 98.

23. "Lane and W. Split," *Chicago Defender*, December 29, 1923, pt. 1, 6.

24. "Phillips High Quints Split with Lindblom," *Chicago Defender*, January 12, 1924, pt. 1, 8.

25. Frank Young, "Phillips Heavies Defeat Tilden in League Game," *Chicago Defender*, January 26, 1924, pt. 1, 10.

26. "Phillips Beaten by Tilden Tech, Upsetting Dope," *Chicago Defender*, February 2, 1924, pt. 1, 10.

27. Gems, "Blocked Shot," 143–44.

28. "Phillips High Quintet Wins Way to Finals," *Chicago Defender*, March 1, 1924, pt. 1, 10.

29. Frank Young, "Phillips Loses City Championship to Lane Tech," *Chicago Defender*, March 18, 1924, pt. 1, 9. "Lane Wins City Title; Harrison Lights Triumph," *Chicago Tribune*, March 8, 1924, 16.

30. Dan Burley, "That 1924 Night When Phillips Played Lane," *Chicago Defender*, April 14, 1958, A 22.

31. "Phillips High 5 to Play Kansas City, Mo., Mar. 31," *Chicago Defender*, March 15, 1924, pt. 1, 10.

32. "Spears, Watson and Brookins Make Daily News All-Star Five," *Chicago Defender*, March 15, 1924, pt. 1, 9.

33. T. E. Gaillard, "Chicago in Win over Kansas City 5," *Chicago Defender*, April 6, 1924, pt. 1, 1.

34. The box scores appear in the *Chicago Defender*, April 6, 1924, pt. 1, 10.

35. There is no mention of Brookins in Thomas Loverro's *Encyclopedia of Negro League Baseball* (published by Facts on File in 2003), but players often used aliases to safeguard their amateur status.

36. George Shaffer, "Prep Basket Teams of 100 Pounds Voted Too Light by League," *Chicago Tribune*, December 19, 1919, 15.

37. David Kellum, "Phillips High Beats Tilden in First League Game," *Chicago Defender*, January 10, 1925, pt. 1, 10.

38. "Spears Leads Alumni to Win over Phillips Cagers," *Chicago Defender*, December 27, 1924, pt. 1, 9.

39. J. Wm. Jesse Lovell, "Incompetent Referee and Lindblom Timers in Phillips High Defeat," *Chicago Defender*, January 17, 1925, pt. 1, 9.

40. J. Wm. Jesse Lovell, "Incompetent Referee and Lindblom Timers in Phillips High Defeat," *Chicago Defender*, January 17, 1925, pt. 1, 9.

41. J. Wm. Jesse Lovell, "Phillips Handed Bad 24–18 Defeat," *Chicago Defender*, January 24, 1925, pt. 1, 9.

42. Gems, "Blocked Shot," 144.

43. "Englewood 29, Phillips 15," *Chicago Tribune*, January 20, 1925, 15; "Phillips Jolts Tilden in Overtime," *Chicago Tribune*, January 24, 1925, 10; "Phillips 22, Lindblom 13," *Chicago Tribune*, January 28, 1925, 24.

44. J. Wm. Jesse Lovell, "Wendell Phillips Upsets Dope by Beating Lindblom and Tilden Tech High Fives," *Chicago Defender*, January 31, 1925, pt. 1, 9.

45. David Kellum, "Phillips High Cagers Lose to Hyde Park," *Chicago Defender*, February 7, 1925, pt. 1, 9.

46. Gems, "Blocked Shot," 144.

47. "Phillips Withdraws from Basket League," *Chicago Tribune*, February 6, 1925, 17.

48. J. Wm. Jesse Lovell, "Armstrong High Leaves for Chicago Where They Meet Wendell Phillips," *Chicago Defender*, February 7, 1925, pt. 1, 9.

49. "Wendell Phillips Defeats Armstrong," *Chicago Defender*, February 21, 1925, pt. 1, 1.

50. J. Wm. Jesse Lovell, "Phillips Takes Basketball Game from Armstrong by 25–15 Score before 4500," *Chicago Defender*, February 21, 1925, pt. 1, 10.

51. "Attention! Brookins-Ramsey," *Chicago Defender*, February 28, 1925, pt. 1, 9.

52. "Chicago Flashes Start Cage Practice," *Chicago Defender*, October 23, 1925, pt. 1, 9.

53. David Kellum, "Chicagoans Defeat Fast All Star Five 26 to 19," *Chicago Defender*, November 27, 1926, pt. 1, 9.

54. "Wabash Cagers Swamp Larrabee," *Chicago Defender*, February 20, 1926, pt. 1, 11.

55. Ben Green, *Spinning the Globe: The Rise, Fall and Return to Greatness of the Harlem Globetrotters* (New York: HarperCollins, 2005), 36.

56. Green, *Spinning the Globe*, 38.

57. "Giles Post Five Cops," *Chicago Defender*, February 5, 1927, pt. 1, 10.

58. Green, *Spinning the Globe*, 38–39; *Chicago Defender*, December 31, 1927, pt. 1, 10.

59. David Kellum, "Howard U Beaten in Chicago," *Chicago Defender*, January 7, 1928, pt. 1, 10.

60. "Savoy Five Winner over Elgin Quint," *Chicago Defender*, January 21, 1928, pt. 1, 9.

61. David Kellum, "Wilberforce Beats Savoy 5," *Chicago Defender*, January 21, 1928, pt. 1, 8.

62. "Loendi Club Beaten Twice by Savoy Five," *Chicago Defender*, February 18, 1928, pt. 1, 9.

63. David Kellum, "Wilberforce Again Beats Savoy," *Chicago Defender*, February 25, 1928, pt. 1, 8.

64. "Lincoln Five Falls before Savoy, 36 to 31," *Chicago Defender*, February 25, 1928, pt. 1, 9.

65. "DeHart's 5 Lose, 37–33, to Savoys," *Chicago Defender*, March 3, 1928, pt. 1, 9.

66. "Bruins Toy with Savoy Five, 29–25," *Chicago Defender*, March 10, 1928, pt. 1, 8.

67. "Savoy Quintet Beats Cohn," *Chicago Defender*, March 24, 1928, pt. 1, 8.

68. Green, *Spinning the Globe*, 42.

69. "Savoys Give Evanston a Good Licking," *Chicago Defender*, April 21, 1928, pt. 1, 9; Green, *Spinning the Globe*, 42.

70. http://www.aaregistry.org/historic_events/view/joe-lillard-was-stellar-athlete (accessed June 24, 2014).

71. http://www.aaregistry.org/historic_events/view/joe-lillard-was-stellar-athlete (accessed June 24, 2014).

72. "Globe Trotters Five to Play Morgan College Feb. 12–13," *Chicago Defender*, February 9, 1929, pt. 1, 9.

73. "Morgan College and Globe Trotters Split," *Chicago Defender*, February 23, 1929, pt. 1, 9.

74. U.S. Federal Census at Ancestry.com (accessed July 8, 2014).

75. Michael Strauss, "Real Founder of the Globe Trotters," *Sports Quarterly Basketball Special, 1973–74* (New York: Counterpoint Publishing, 1973), 58–59, 112–13; Green, *Spinning the Globe*, 45–50.

76. Strauss, "Real Founder of the Globe Trotters," 112. Also discussed by Brookins in the 1985 interview with Franklin Brison.

77. Cited in Strauss, "Real Founder of the Globe Trotters," 112. It would be feasible that Brookins sang "Sweet Georgia Brown" since the song was written and first recorded in 1925 and was the number one song in the country for five weeks in that year, as recorded by Ben Bernie and his Hotel Roosevelt Orchestra.

78. Green, *Spinning the Globe*, 48–49.

79. Green notes that Hudson started another team in 1930 called the Chicago Hottentots, which included Brookins and Ramsey (*Spinning the Globe*, 56). Joe Lillard played on another version of the Hottentots in the mid-1930s. Brookins also played for the Crusaders of Chicago and the Chicago Union Giants in 1931, usually leading his team in scoring. "Crusaders 28 Regal 20," *Chicago Defender*, January 3, 1931, 9, and "Union Giants Quint Defeated in St. Louis," *Chicago Defender*, January 24, 1931, 9.

80. Cited in Strauss, "Real Founder of the Globe Trotters," 113. Green provides more details and explanation about the Trotter formation in *Spinning the Globe*, 47–50.

81. "Gilkerson Giants to Play Here, Jan. 12," *Alton (IA) Democrat*, January 8, 1932.

82. Cited in Nat Shapiro and Nat Hentoff, eds., *The Story of Jazz as Told by the*

*Men Who Made It* (New York: Dover Publications, 1955), 113–14. The "Eldorado" undoubtedly was the El Rado Club at the Garfield Hotel, where Jimmie Noone and his orchestra played in the 1920s and 1930s, according to the archival site of the University of Chicago Library, http://www.lib.uchicago.edu/e/su/cja/mapkey.html (accessed June 30, 2014). The interviewers probably misunderstood what Brookins said, or he simply forgot the exact name of the club.

83. https://www.youtube.com/watch?v=2mCg6URSnWQ (accessed June 30, 2014).

84. Bessye Bearden, "Around New York," *Chicago Defender*, February 4, 1933, 5.

85. "Brookins and Wiley Hit," *Chicago Defender*, February 25, 1933, 5.

86. https://www.youtube.com/watch?v=LH0uDEGHNvA (accessed June 30, 2014). This clip runs just under four minutes but is one of the few remaining films of Brookins and Van doing their act and shows Brookins as a creative and capable pianist with a sweet tenor voice.

87. "Belfast," *The Stage*, issue 2916, February 1937, 13.

88. Brookins interview with Franklin Brison.

89. "War Catches Actors Unawares," *New York Amsterdam News*, September 9, 1939, 16.

90. Strauss, "Real Founder of the Globe Trotters," 113.

91. Al Monroe, "Swinging the News," *Chicago Defender*, July 3, 1943, 18.

92. Donald Bogle, *Heat Wave: The Life and Career of Ethel Waters* (New York: Harper, 2011), 395.

93. Bogle, *Heat Wave*, 408–9.

94. Al Monroe, "Swinging the News," *Chicago Defender*, January 9, 1944, 22.

95. Bogle, *Heat Wave*, 411.

96. "Dan Burley's Back Door Stuff," *New York Amsterdam News*, June 10, 1944, 6B.

97. The Brookins-Van act is cited in "Sam Price Lauds New Jazz Room at Delaney's," *New York Amsterdam News*, May 1, 1948, 23.

98. "Here's Something New in Show Biz!" *New York Amsterdam News*, December 22, 1951, 15.

99. Dan Burley, "The Ways of Sports . . . ," *Chicago Defender*, September 22, 1958, 22.

100. Brison interview, at http://articles.chicagotribune.com/1988-06-05/news/8801040962_1_caribbean-island-urban-progress (accessed June 30, 2014).

101. For example, the Woodlawn Progress Center had a program to improve the poise and development of teenage girls. Two other centers were in the Lawndale neighborhood on the West Side and the Pilsen Center, located in the Halsted Institutional Church at 1935 S. Halsted.

102. Email communiqué, Dick Simpson to Murry Nelson, July 4, 2014.

103. Alan McMillan, "On Broadway," *Philadelphia Tribune*, March 20, 1971, 23. Brookins attended the Frazier-Ali "Fight of the Century" in Madison Square Garden, March 8, 1971.

## TEN

# Tidye Pickett

*The Unfulfilled Aspirations of America's Pioneering*
*African American Female Track Star*

ROBERT PRUTER

Tidye Pickett is recognized in the history of African Americans sports as an outstanding female track and field runner of the 1930s. She emerged at a time when African American athletes were excluded from most amateur and professional sport competitions involving white athletes—except in high schools outside the South—but they were making significant breakthroughs in the 1930s, notably in track and field at the Olympics. Pickett and Louise Stokes of Massachusetts were the first African American women to be selected for a United States Olympic team when they won places on the track team in 1932. Pickett and Stokes were selected for the U.S. team for the 1936 Olympics, and Pickett became the first African American woman to actually compete in the Olympic Games. An increasing number of black male athletes had appeared on the U.S. Olympic teams in the 1920s, but African American women had even fewer opportunities to display their physical prowess. The career of Tidye Pickett significantly exemplifies these pioneering achievements for the African American athlete and for black America in general, breakthroughs that would eventually lead to the post–Civil Rights era of almost full legal and significant social integration into American society.

Tidye Pickett was born Theodora Ann Pickett on November 3, 1914, on the South Side of Chicago. Throughout her life she never used the name Theodora, and her nickname was variously rendered as either Tidye or Tydie. She had a distinctive name and was physically distinctive—short, light skinned, and somewhat Asian in her looks. She was the daughter of Louis and Sarah Pickett, her father working as a foreman in a foundry and her mother working as a clerk in a factory. They lived on the South Side in the Englewood community. She had an older brother (by two years) named Charlie, but it does not appear that he participated in athletics.[1]

### Early Development as a Track and Field Star

From the fall of 1930 to the spring of 1934 Tidye Pickett was a student at Englewood High School, an integrated institution that was about one-third black when she attended. At that time Chicago high schools did not sponsor interschool sports for girls, but they did sponsor an extensive number of intramural activities. Pickett, however, did not choose to join basketball, field hockey, tennis, golf, gymnastics, dance groups, or any other of the many intramural activities offered by the school for girls. Instead Pickett followed her sports interests outside the school—track, tennis, and basketball—in the city's great park and playground organizations and in the African American church-sponsored leagues. She probably found the level of competition not challenging enough for someone who had had considerable experience in the park district programs prior to high school.[2]

In terms of her development as a track star, Pickett was the product of Chicago's great park and school playground systems, which had produced many of the nation's top women track and field athletes in the previous decade. Chicago was a pioneer and leader in the development of municipal playgrounds or small parks, beginning in 1900, when it created five playgrounds. By 1916 the city was operating seventy-three small parks, seventy playgrounds (sixty-three of which were in schoolyards), three beaches, and four public pools. These playgrounds were supervised with trained directors and included field houses, gymnasiums, and athletic fields. Likewise the Chicago park system—the South Park, West Park, and Lincoln Park districts, each of which could tax and issue bonds for the building of field houses and facilities—provided a number of supervised playgrounds patterned after the municipal playgrounds. Both the municipal playgrounds and the large park districts created organized athletic programs that sponsored tournaments for boys (baseball, wrestling, skating, and track) and for girls (playground ball [softball], skating, and track). Most important, the playground competition was opened to all religions, ethnicities, and races. The park district playgrounds located in schoolyards came under the Chicago Board of Education control in 1921. During the 1920s and early 1930s, because of its park and playgrounds programs, Chicago produced a large share of the nation's top track and field athletes, especially women.[3]

Pickett began her running career at the South Park District–operated program in Washington Park, one of the largest parks in the city, just across from her home. She then entered races at picnics sponsored by the *Chicago Daily News*, winning some prizes. Her first organized team competition came when she joined the track team sponsored by the Carter School Playground in the Board of Education playgrounds program. She was a small athlete—five feet two and weighing only 104 pounds at the age of seventeen—but she exhibited remarkable speed from the time she started running in the program. She proceeded to compete in the various playground competitions and soon graduated to other track meets sponsored variously by athletic clubs, church organizations, and YMCAs. At a meet at an armory she met University of Chicago track star John Brooks, who became her trainer and mentor. Brooks, a rare African American athlete at the university, was serving a common role in the self-help communal strategies within the black community, which sought to improve the standing of blacks in America. When Pickett started making a mark as a significant track and field talent, she was running for the Board of Education playground team, which was a select group formed from all the school playgrounds.[4]

### A Church League Basketball Star

Pickett had a notable career in basketball, competing as a star player on some of the top African American women's teams in the city, but this part of her athletic endeavors has never been mentioned in any of the short biographies on her. The biggest sports organization in the African American community in Chicago was the Union Church League or, more formally, the Union Sunday School Athletic Association. The organization was an interdenominational group, formed back in 1913. During the 1920s with some twenty member churches, the league "fostered" baseball, bowling, tennis, track, and basketball play and also sponsored annual championship contests in baseball and bowling. In 1930 the Union Church League expanded its sponsorship of sports championships with the introduction of basketball competition in three leagues—men's heavyweight, men's lightweight, and women's. Unlike in other parts of the country, most of the women's amateur teams in Chicago played under men's rules and competed in an annual championship sponsored by the Central Amateur Athletic Union (Central AAU).[5]

The convergence of opportunities in Chicago and the ongoing and increasing arrival of African Americans from the South in the Great Migration created a vibrant and evolving black urban culture that propelled athletic and musical stars to achieve greater acceptance in mainstream society. Pickett's fellow Chicago tracksters Sol Butler, Fritz Pollard Jr., and Ralph Metcalfe; tennis great and basketball player Isadore Channels; aviator Bessie Coleman; and the great Harlem Globetrotters basketball team all achieved national renown. Pickett also grew up in a world of music and entertainment, where such jazz artists as Louis Armstrong, Earl Hines, and Cleo Brown and such blues greats as Big Bill Broonzy, Tampa Red, and Memphis Minnie filled the clubs and theaters in her neighborhood and spread the music nationwide through radio and recordings, while modernist African American painter Archibald Motley captured black music and dance in evocative paintings.

Pickett's first year in the Union Church League, at the age of fifteen, was in the winter season of 1929–30 as a member of the middling Quinn Chapel team. The following year she moved up to a more formidable team, the Bethesda Baptist Church, which contended for the league championship, and there Pickett got her first notices. She usually played forward. In the 1931–32 season Pickett served as captain of the team and was often the top scorer, significantly helping to make Bethesda one of the top teams in the league. The Bethesda team would disband after the 1931–32 season, and Pickett and a couple of other players on the Bethesda team would join the already formidable Pilgrim Baptist team for the 1932–33 season. The Pilgrim team, fortified by the addition of Pickett and other Bethesda players, easily swept through the Union League schedule undefeated. Pickett was considered the "floor general" of the team and was such a prolific scorer that at season's end she ranked second by only one point to teammate Ruth Reese among the league's scoring leaders.[6]

The Pilgrim team then played other Central AAU teams, including such notable white teams as the Baby Ruth Girls. In late March the girls competed in the *Chicago American*'s huge basketball tournament, which it sponsored each year in multiple classes. The tournament had three men's classes and four women's classes. The four women's classes were open, freelance, church, and girls' rules. (Girls' rules involved six players, three defensive only, three offensive only, and two each playing and confined in one of the three sections of the court.) In a *Chicago American* story on the tournament, the reporter singled out Tidye Pickett for mention, listing her with a side headline and discussing her Olympic and track achievements. The Pilgrim Baptist team made it to the title game in the church class, losing the championship to the Lamon Methodist Episcopal Church by only one point, 12–11. The tournament in all its classes included more than nine hundred teams, so this was an extraordinary feat by the Pilgrim Baptist team, providing recognition and evidence of black women's achievement in basketball to the white population of Chicago.[7]

The following year, Pickett's senior year, the Union Church League, while continuing the two men's classes, eliminated the women's class. There was no mention in the *Chicago Defender* as to why it did so, but as the Depression wore on, agencies and organizations were finding it harder and harder to sustain themselves at previous levels, and one sees a significant decline in women's teams at this time. At Englewood High School, for example, the school eliminated its annual yearbook for 1934, replacing it with a thin booklet that showed photos and names of all the seniors, not even giving mentions of their activities. Many seniors did not bother to get their photos taken for the booklet, among them Tidye Pickett. Pickett graduated in June

called run) established by Helen Filkey in 1928. The *Chicago Defender* hailed her achievement in a banner inch high headline—"Girl Ties World's Track Mark." The paper was proud of Pickett's achievement and repeatedly ran items and her picture almost weekly after her breakthrough 60-yard indoor record. The *Chicago Tribune* also made Pickett's achievement the headline for its story on the meet—"New Playground Star Ties National 60 Yard Record." The purpose of the meet was to discover Olympic prospects, and it certainly achieved its aim in finding Pickett, who was a seventeen-year-old student at Englewood High competing on the Board of Education playground team. In March, at the annual Illinois National Guard meet, Pickett again astounded the Chicago track world when she beat out two top veteran runners, Mary Terwilliger and Annette Rogers, in the 60-yard race.[10]

Pickett, based on her track achievements during the winter, was selected to compete in the trial races to be held in Chicago in mid-July for the upcoming Los Angeles Olympics. Based on their performances, she and Louise Stokes were selected to be on the women's track team. The *Chicago Defender* proudly covered the meet and made the point that Pickett and Stokes were racing against fellow white competitors, noting that "The prejudiced South would not have permitted these two stars to enter a race with their white sisters."[11]

The selection of the sixteen women for the Los Angeles Olympic Games, based on the trials, was far less set in stone than the newspaper reports indicated. The *New York Times* and other papers, using the AP reports, said that the results of the 100-meters produced six members of the team—the top three for the 100-meters event and the bottom three for the 400-meter relay event. That theoretically meant that Louise Stokes, who had tied with Mary Carew for fourth place, and Tidye Pickett, who had taken sixth place, qualified for the 400-meter event. Beat out and in seventh place was one of the top runners, Evelyn Furtsch, who had tripped and fallen on the uneven cinder surface while battling for the lead near the finish line. Theoretically she did not qualify, but at the behest of an influential team chaperone who appealed to the U.S. Olympics Committee, Furtsch was placed on the team while her teammates were on the train to Los Angeles. Another top Chicago athlete, Annette Rogers, made the Olympic team as a result of her third-place position in the high jump. But Rogers was also a top runner, and it appears that Olympic officials took that into account in her selection. The selection process was obviously fluid, but members of the Olympic team possibly had the impression that their places and the team were set and final. That impression would change once they got to Los Angeles.[12]

Despite the relative racial fairness in the North, the 1932 Olympics proved disappointing and humiliating to Pickett and Stokes and their sense of racial identity. On the train trip to Los Angeles the two faced their first humiliation when at the overnight stop in Denver at the Brown Palace Hotel they experienced various snubs and discriminations. The hotel honored the Olympic team with a banquet, but the two African American members were not allowed to share the experience, being forced to eat their meal in their room. And instead of being housed in the same area as the rest of the team, Pickett and Stokes were separated and placed in a room near a service area on an upper floor. Pickett said bitterly, "All the other girls had private rooms, went to the banquet, were interviewed by reporters. Louise and I shared a room in the attic and ate our dinners upstairs on trays." Olympic officials did not challenge the hotel's action. Back on the train, Pickett was doused by a pitcher of ice water while sleeping in her compartment by the racist and generally obnoxious Babe Didrikson, the highly talented all-around athlete who would win world fame at the Los Angeles Olympics. Notwithstanding that Didrikson was an equal-opportunity abuser of her teammates, her well-known racism and her particularly nasty attack on Pickett made it a racial humiliation. Pickett, who was interviewed by two Chicago papers in 1984, reported to the *Chicago Tribune* that "there were a few athletes and team officials who did not hide their bigotry." She told the *Chicago Sun-Times*, "We had a chaperone and a manager who were something else. They caused us quite a lot of concern."[13]

The greatest humiliation for Pickett and Stokes took place after the team arrived in Los Angeles. For two weeks the eight runners considered eligible for the 400-meter relay ran trial sprints under coach George Vreeland to select the four best runners. The final selection left both Pickett and Stokes designated as alternates and thus not competing in the games. They had to sit on the sidelines and watch their teammates win medals. Pickett and Stokes, and many black journalists, felt that two less qualified white runners (Mary Carew and Evelyn Furtsch) had been moved ahead of them in the selection process. According to historian Doris H. Pieroth, however, Carew and Furtsch had each demonstrated abilities that Vreeland was looking for—Carew, unusually quick starts and Furtsch, "speed and dexterity with the baton." The other selectees—Billie von Bremen and Annette Rogers—demonstrated the fastest speed. The assumption in the African American community at the time was that the exclusion of Pickett and Stokes was for racial reasons. Years later Pickett was quoted as saying that "I knew I was better than some of them. It was politics. Politics and sports, sports and politics, they've always gone together"—"politics" obviously being her code word for racial discrimination. The woman sportswriter for the *Afro-American*, Ivora King, commented at the time, "For us to be considered, we have to be ten times as good as those of the other race." She noted that whereas Ralph Metcalfe and Eddie Tolan had demonstrated clear superiority over their white counterparts, Pickett and Stokes had demonstrated only similar but not outstanding performance and thus were vulnerable to racial exclusion. Given King had built a national reputation as a strong advocate for sport for black women, her moderate tone over the "exclusion" is thus all that more persuasive.[14]

Black baseball players echoed such sentiments for decades thereafter, claiming that they had to amass a batting average at least twenty points higher than their white teammates to break through into a lineup. Sport historian Gerald R. Gems suggests that Stokes and Pickett faced an early form of "stacking," where talented black athletes were assigned to positions behind or backing up each other instead of being allowed to compete for leadership or more central team roles.[15]

King saw the situation perhaps more clearly than many of her fellow African American journalists, suggesting that Pickett and Stokes were not clearly superior enough as to make a solid case for racial injustice. An examination of the records during the year and the Olympic trials shows that Pickett and Stokes were roughly equal to their white counterparts, but based on results where one-tenth of a second could be used to determine who was in or who was out, their white counterparts had a slight edge. Aside from their achievements during the two weeks of trials in LA, during the year both Furtsch and Carew had produced better times than Pickett and Stokes in both the 100-meter and the 100-yard races, as had Rogers and Von Bremen. Peiroth, who interviewed all the still living participants in the 400-meter drama, felt that it was not possible to make a black-and-white judgment (so to speak) on the question as to whether racial discrimination played a part: "Given the prevailing racial attitudes and practices of 1932, the possibility of discrimination, however subtle, makes a final answer to the question unlikely."[16] Racism was an endemic situation in the United States of 1932, and there was undeniable racism that Pickett and Stokes both encountered in their Olympics Games experience. The standard narrative that has come down regarding their exclusion from participation as being based on racism, however, cannot be sustained based on the facts. Nonetheless, this narrative has become almost an article of faith in the histories of African American sports. David K. Wiggins in 1982 asserted that Pickett had been "dismissed" from the team because of her "color." As recently as 2013 Helen Jefferson Lenskyj in her *Gender Politics and the Olympic Industry* ascribed the demotion of Pickett and Stokes to reserves as an example of racism trumping "medal-winning potential." A. D. Emerson in her book on African American women's medal achievement in the Olympics, *Olympians against the Wind*, starts with the 1948 Olympics but discusses the 1932 exclusion as an issue of "politics" and "racial tensions" and says it was a "pivotal point in Olympic history." She remarks that African American women competitors in the 1948 Olympics "carried the spirit of Tidye Pickett and Louise Stokes with them as they competed against the wind of expectation to attain an Olympic medal.[17]

### Competing between the Two Olympics

Despite her disappointment after the 1932 Olympics, Pickett continued to be engaged in athletics in Chicago. She joined the Algonquin Athletic Club, became its vice president, and hosted a meeting of the club at her South Side home. Most of the members appeared to be her fellow basketball players—Mattie Steele, Zadie Lloyd, and Rosa Reese notably. Pickett's mentor and track star John Brooks dropped in on the meeting. During the winter of 1932–33 she was competing in playground track competition as well as in national AAU meets. At that time more than seven hundred girls were participating in indoor track in the South Park District, which sponsored sports at eighteen playgrounds. In February Pickett was one of five girls from the South Park District at the national AAU indoor meet at Madison Square Garden, where she competed for the Carter Playground. Pickett did not have a good season in 1933, beginning with her elimination from the finals in the 50-meter dash at the national indoors. In the National AAU outdoor meet, held in Soldier Field in July, she was shut out in all her sprint events, while her fellow African American teammate from 1932, Louise Stokes, took first in the 50-yard and second in the 100-yard. Pickett was active in tennis during these years, although she never competed at the level of Chicago's elite African American players. She hosted and helped form a tennis club in August 1933, in which John Brooks was elected president.[18]

Possibly because of her disappointing track season the previous year in the sprints, Pickett in the winter of 1933–34 began to train and compete in hurdles. She trained for months in the Eighth Regiment Armory with her coach, John Brooks. In April Pickett, competing as part of a combined entry of the Lincoln Park and South Park Districts, ran in the women's National AAU indoor competition in Brooklyn. She did poorly, however, finishing fourth in the 50-meter hurdles. In the last indoor meet of the season, however, in Chicago, at the annual regimental track and field championship, Pickett set a world mark for a 40-yard dash, a success that anticipated an excellent summer for her.[19]

Compared to the previous year, Pickett had a great competitive summer in 1934, beginning as a member of a combined Chicago team, the Highland Park Athletic Club, which competed at the Toronto centennial games. There Pickett broke the Canadian record in the broad jump, clearing an impressive 18 feet, 1½ inches; she ran on the Chicago relay team that set a new Canadian record, won the 60-meter dash, and finished second in the 80-meter hurdles. The broad jump achievement put Picket among the best in the world. At the Central AAU meet in August Pickett, representing South Park, took the broad jump, the 80-meter hurdles, and the 100-meter run. The 100-meter victory was especially satisfying, as Pickett beat two runners whom she had always trailed, Annette Rogers and Mary Terwilliger. For Pickett 1934 was a very good year.[20]

In 1935 Pickett continued her stellar performances, first with three outstanding indoor meets—the Central AAU annual indoor in Chicago and two indoor meets in Hamilton and Toronto, Canada. In Chicago Pickett won the 100-meter in 12.4 seconds, took the 80-meter in 12.1 seconds, and captured the broad jump in 16 feet, 4 inches. At Hamilton and Toronto the Chicago team, competing as the Highland Park Athletic Club, won both meets. Pickett teamed up with Annette Rogers, Doris Anderson, and Mary Terwilliger to twice set a world's record in the 440-yard relay—first in Hamilton at 52.2 seconds and then in Toronto at 51.8 seconds. Pickett's individual achievements included winning the 50-yard races at both Hamilton and Toronto, gaining the Hamilton victory in a Canadian record of 7.7 seconds. Tidye Pickett did not compete in the AAU indoor national at St. Louis in 1935. In an amazing move that showed the dominant strength of Chicago's women's track, the Chicago Park District split up its team—half to compete in St. Louis and half to compete in Canada—and both teams won their meets. At the Central AAU outdoor meet in August, Pickett took second behind Annette Rogers in the 100-meters and finished first in the 80-meter hurdles. Pickett had established herself as one of the top female runners in the country and a strong prospect for the 1936 Olympics. During the summer the African American elite in Chicago gave Pickett an elaborate "testimonial tea," with entertainment by an orchestra and glee club, in recognition of her track achievements, which made her fellow black citizens proud. The testimonial was also to help raise funds for Pickett to attend the American Physical Education College (track bigwig and American Olympic Committee president Avery Brundage was a contributor).[21] For African Americans sport afforded one of the few means to positive national recognition, and athletes were held in great esteem by the black community.

Pickett launched her 1936 track season most auspiciously when at the indoor nationals in St. Louis in February—which the Chicago Park District won for the third year in a row—she brought points to her team in winning the 50-meter hurdles. At the Central AAU indoor meet, however, Pickett experienced a slight dip when she took fourth in the 50-meter dash behind Helen Stephens, Annette Rogers, and Mary Terwilliger; she took second in her new specialty, the 50-meter low hurdles, to veteran runner Evelyn Hall. Pickett recovered her excellence in the Central AAU outdoor meet at Stagg Field in Chicago, winning the 50-meter dash and the long jump (with a stellar 17¾ feet). She took second to Evelyn Hall in the 80-meter hurdles, however.[22]

At the national outdoor championship at Brown University in Providence, Rhode Island, which also served as the Olympic trials, Pickett earned a sure spot on the Olympic team by taking second in the 80-meter hurdles, and she was expected to compete in the 100-meter dash and the 400-meter relay. Her achievement in the hurdles was especially impressive because she severely bruised the ankle on her trailing foot on the seventh hurdle. This would prove ominous for Pickett at the Games in Berlin, Germany.[23]

### The 1936 Olympic Games in Berlin

The 1936 Berlin Olympics were perhaps the most controversial of all the Games, as they were hosted by a violent and totalitarian regime under the aggressively anti-Semitic and racist Nazi leader Adolf Hitler. Leading up to the Games, contentious debates swirled around in Western democracies, notably the United States, over whether or not to boycott the Games. Eventually the United States chose to participate, and the 1936 Olympics became a stage by which the black athletes from the United States, led by Jesse Owens (from Ohio), excelled and thereby were remembered famously as rebuffing the racial theories of Nazism. Tidye Pickett was surely no stranger to the larger politics, as in the African American press a raging debate arose, reflecting the same division in the mainstream press, over whether or not the United States should participate. Her hometown paper, the *Chicago Defender*, had regularly covered the German Nazi regime since the assent of Adolf Hitler in 1933, often referring to "Nazi racial hatred." Such reporting heated up in June 1936, just prior to the Berlin Games, in the coverage of the first Joe Louis–Max Schmeling fight, as the *Defender* and other black papers reported on Nazi racial attitudes regarding Joe Louis and blacks in America. The Nazi attitudes became especially hurtful after Louis was knocked out in his first match with Schmeling. The concern before the Olympics was on how the German regime would treat the African American athletes at the Games. The *Defender* and other black papers often reminded white Americans that in their defense of the Jews, they should not forget the racism in the United States regarding the Olympic Games. The *Defender* cited the exclusion of two black athletes on the U.S. relay teams in 1932, Jimmy Johnson and Tidye Pickett, as examples of home country racism.[24]

Leading up to the Olympics blacks expressed some concern about how their athletes would be treated in Germany, but much to their surprise and delight, the black athletes were treated well by the German people. The black athletes—who notably included Jesse Owens, Ralph Metcalfe, Mack Robinson (Jackie Robinson's brother), as well as Pickett—discovered that the German people were "extremely courteous and hospitable" to them the whole time they were there. Also the German authorities serving as hosts, whatever their views on African Americans, were correct and cordial to the black athletes. The *Chicago Defender* in an article entitled "Olympic Stars Given Welcome in Berlin; Prejudice Missing as Athletes Arrive," explained that the Nazis serving as hosts were on their best behavior because for "a group of members to be slighted, segregated, or discriminated against would be a blot on the international sports horizon which might bring about political complications." In the few interviews conducted with Pickett, she never mentioned encountering any racial problems in Germany.[25]

The Olympic Games became especially notable in black America because Hitler supposedly snubbed Jesse Owens, who among all the African American athletes achieved the most by winning four gold medals—in the 100- and 200-meter runs, long jump, and 400-meter relay. The coverage of the achievements of the African Americans, especially those of Owens, in the *Chicago Defender* and other black newspapers was extraordinary and was as much as they had devoted to the Louis-Schmeling fight earlier in June. In the Games, which Hitler attended daily, he made it a practice to meet with the winning athletes in his box afterward and congratulate them. The day after Owens won the 100-meter run Hitler did not congratulate him, and the African American press was enraged, indicative of the headlines in the *Cleveland Call and Post* ("Hitler Snubs Jesse!") and *Chicago Defender* ("Owens Humiliated in Hitler's Land"). According to historian David Clay Large, author of *Nazi Games: The Olympics of 1936*, however, the Hitler snub of Owens did not happen. The day before, the first day of competition, Hitler was congratulating all the winners in his box, but he failed to congratulate the three American high-jump medalists (two of whom were black). But, as with most field events, the competition went on a long time past dusk, and Hitler retired from the stadium after the German competitors were eliminated, and it remained an all-American affair. Here some observers saw a snub, believing that Hitler had retired from the stadium when it was evident to him that he would have to congratulate two African American track men. Olympic officials took note of Hitler's behavior and told him that it was not customary for the host country leader to personally congratulate winners, but if he was going to make it a practice, he must congratulate all of them or otherwise end the practice. Hitler willingly assented to ending his congratulations, and thereafter no winners, including Jesse Owens, received the dictator's personal accolades.[26]

As in 1932 Pickett and Louise Stokes were the only African American women selected for the team; unlike in Los Angeles, Pickett competed, but Stokes was again relegated to the reserves. Pickett was one of four women competitors to have had her voyage fare to Germany sponsored. Said Pickett in 1984, "I had my fare paid in 1936, so they must have thought I was good. They were depending on me to win." Pickett was scheduled to compete in the hurdles, the sprint relay, and the 100-meter run and was expected to pick up some medals. Unfortunately an accident in the semifinals of the hurdles ended her Olympic career. In the hurdle races Pickett had been catching hurdles with her trailing foot and was working to correct the problem with fellow competitors Ralph Metcalfe and Jesse Owens. While the hurdles in the United States would fall over if she caught one with her trailing foot, the ones in the Berlin Olympics did not. In the semifinals Pickett not only caught her foot on one of the hurdles, but she also broke it while falling down in the race, ending her Olympic participation.[27]

Pickett noticed a difference in the way she was treated by U.S. Olympic officials in 1932 and 1936. Again Louise Stokes was the only other black female track Olympian, and Pickett told the *Chicago Tribune* in 1984: "It was better in 1936 than in '32. The coaches and all of them in charge were different in 1936, and they were nicer to us."[28]

A year after finishing high school, Pickett had entered Illinois State Normal University in Bloomington, Illinois, in the fall of 1935. Her initial plans to attend the American Physical Education College were put aside for a more upscale institution. Her major was health and physical education. Like most institutions of higher learning, Normal did not sponsor outside competitive teams for women but did provide an extensive intramural program. Pickett surprisingly did not participate on the basketball team but was a member of the field hockey team. In the first term of her junior year Pickett served as the student head of all women's athletic activities. She was also a member and served as secretary for the Orchesis, the school's interpretative dance group. During her freshman year Pickett helped prepare for the Olympics by working with the Illinois State men's track coach, Joe Cogdal. She also raced in exhibitions at that time, such as at the Walther Lutheran League annual track meet, when she raced against the male president of the Walter Lutheran League. Pickett dropped out of Normal during the spring semester of her junior year. In September 1939 the *Chicago Defender*, in a story on what had become of the 1936 black Olympians, reported that Pickett was unemployed and lacked the money to finish her last year at Illinois Normal.[29]

### Barnstorming with the Coeds Basketball Team

Pickett's track career was over after the 1936 Olympics, although she participated in a few meets. But she resumed her basketball playing in 1939, joining the Bivins All Stars, a team that had evolved from the

Club Store Coeds, the team she had briefly joined when it had come together in December 1934. The Coeds under promoter and coach Dick Hudson soon emerged as the top African American female team in Chicago. Hudson turned the team into a barnstorming pro team, and one can liken the barnstorming Club Store Coeds as a female Harlem Globetrotters. When the team went on the road, Hudson redesignated his team as the "Roamer Girls," naming them after the legendary female black team from Chicago of the 1920s and early 1930s. From 1935 through 1938 Hudson's team regularly made trips through the western half of the United States, hitting small towns and billed as "national colored girl champions" or some variation. Hudson's big drawing card was his six-foot-seven-and-a-half player Helen "Streamline" Smith (from Lemoyne College), whom he usually billed as being seven feet tall. This team played both men's and women's teams.[30]

In December 1939, when Pickett joined the team, it had a new sponsor, Matthew Bivins Jr., and a new name, the Bivins All Stars. Bivins was a flashy sporting figure in Chicago, called the "Playboy of Policy," operating three policy wheels—Whirl-away, Alabama-Georgia, and Jackpot (policy was one of many illegal gambling rackets in the city). Like a number of top policy-wheel operators he was heavily engaged in golf, winning, for example, the 1937 midwestern golf championship and heading various golf associations. He owned and operated a legitimate business, Bivins Van Lines. Bivins sent the Bivins All Stars barnstorming in Wisconsin, Iowa, and Michigan during the winter of 1939–40. In addition to Pickett, the other members were Helen Smith, Kate Bard (Lincoln University), Louise Hill (Howard University), Naomi Stokes (Western College), Bernice Marshall (Crane College), and former tennis great Lula Porter (Crane College). Pickett was incorrectly designated as coming from the University of Chicago. A local newspaper reporter in Escanaba, Michigan, wrote that the previous year the team had played only men's teams, playing by men's rules, and that its record was 51-33. Typically the Bivins All Stars billed themselves as the "women's world champion basketball team" (as they had done when Dick Hudson was promoting the team).[31]

The following year the Bivins All Stars came under new sponsorship and adopted the name "Co-eds" or "Chicago Co-eds." In January 1941, for example, the team playing under the banner "Chicago Co-eds" competed in a number of games against men's teams in small communities in Alberta, Canada, chiefly around the city of Lethbridge. In its first game against the Cardston Leafs, which the Co-eds lost, the team was praised by the local Lethbridge paper, which noted, "The dusky maidens from over the border put on a display of sharpshooting seldom equaled by any men's teams that have played here on previous occasions." The paper reported that 1936 Olympian Tidye Pickett at half time gave a "sprint demonstration." In a report on the next game, against the Raymond Union Jacks, the Lethbridge paper gullibly asserted that Helen Smith was seven feet tall and the "tallest lady in the world." Pickett was the only other player mentioned, described as the "fastest girl runner in the world" and an "all-American forward" from 1934 through 1937. The Co-eds were easily defeated by both the Leafs and the Union Jacks and lost a third game to another local team, the Magrath Lions, who "toyed" with the girls.[32]

Within weeks on the barnstorming tour the Coeds changed the team name to the Chocolate Coeds. The era was such that in the world of sports and entertainment, black entertainers and sporting figures took names that identified them by race—for example, boxer Kid Chocolate, the Ink Spots singing quartet, and notoriously the blues singer Black Boy Shine. In the pre-television era marketing and show business were all-important to get crowds to come see a barnstorming squad they had never heard of before. Such teams were expected to be interesting, exhibit dazzling skills, and sometimes bring a comic touch to the game. The Chocolate Coeds were selling themselves as such a novelty—all of which rested on their being black, being girls, being physically distinctive, playing men, and being highly skilled (an attribute that in itself was considered a novelty). The most famous barnstorming female basketball team, the All-American Redheads, likewise marketed itself under similar categories (the players' red hair, dyed or not, being their physical distinctiveness). The Chocolate Coeds would be classed as a show team, to join such black barnstorming men's basketball teams of that ilk as the Harlem Globetrotters (most notably), the Broadway Clowns, the Iowa Colored Ghosts, and the notoriously named Hottentots. Perhaps traveling under the almost generic "Coeds" name was deemed insufficient for marketing purposes, so the team again adopted the "Chocolate Coeds" name, which it had used previously in 1938.[33]

At the end of January Pickett's team was in Idaho Falls, Idaho, playing as the Chocolate Coeds. The team was pitted against Hart's Bakery and had to play without the services of Helen Smith, who was sidelined with an appendectomy the day of the game. Given the handicap, the team kept the final score surprisingly close, 42–36. In the postgame write-ups on these contests sportswriters often sounded disappointed with the girls' performance—probably reflecting the views of the audiences as well—showing the down side of the barnstorming hype used to draw audiences to the games.[34]

This glimpse of the world of barnstorming in the early 1940s, which Tidye Pickett was experiencing, reveals that it could be a degrading experience. To draw gullible small-town crowds to the contests, the Coeds were presented almost as freaks (their race was made a part of their beyond-normal description), with P. T. Barnum–type exaggeration of their achievements and athletic abilities. One wonders what Pickett thought as she played under the name Chocolate Coeds, gave a demonstration of her sprinting ability on a basketball court, and heard herself being described as the "fastest girl runner in the world." Was it pride in getting recognition in her sports career or a bit of humiliation at being put on display like a circus sideshow act? The Globetrotters and Indianapolis Clowns baseball team also had to effect such guises to find a niche in the sports market, and Jesse Owens was relegated to racing against horses and even leading his own barnstorming basketball team (managed and promoted by Dick Hudson) to make a living after his monumental successes the 1936 Olympics.[35]

Pickett, during her barnstorming years, was married, having wed Gail Russell Eldredge in October 1939. He was thirteen years older than Pickett and worked as a janitor in the Chicago Public Schools. The 1940 census had Pickett and her husband living in a residence along with Eldredge's two children from a previous relationship, her brother and his family, and her mother, Sarah Hagans, who had apparently remarried. Pickett was listed as having completed three years of college and of having earned $480 for twenty-six weeks of work for the previous year. She was not listed as being employed anywhere, and the amount of income probably reflected some or much of her basketball earnings.[36]

### Becoming an Educator

Pickett ended her basketball career after the 1940–41 season, ending her competitive sports career and her identity as a sports figure. She settled down as a housewife, soon to become a pregnant housewife. She had her first child from the Eldredge marriage in August 1942. Sometime in the 1940s Pickett returned to school to get a degree in teaching, graduating from Pestalozzi Froebel Teachers College. In her personal life she ended her marriage with Gail Eldredge, and she married one of her teaching colleagues, Frank Phillips and raised three daughters.[37]

In 1956 Pickett earned an MS degree in education from Northern Illinois University. In September 1957 she joined the teaching staff at the Cottage Grove Elementary School in East Chicago Heights (later Ford Heights), a small, impoverished African American community in the south suburbs. After one year of teaching at Cottage Grove, she moved to Woodlawn School in the same district to serve as principal. Pickett served as principal of Woodlawn School for twenty-three years.[38]

Pickett's legacy is seen in the various awards and recognitions she received over the years. In 1973 Illinois State University (formerly Illinois State Normal University) inducted Pickett into the school's Athletic Hall of Fame. Of the thirteen inductees that year one other was of African American heritage, football player Roosevelt Banks. In 1980, upon her retirement from Woodlawn School, the school was renamed the Tidye A. Pickett School. An organization called FUTURE Foundation, which sponsors a scholarship program in the south Chicago suburbs called FUTURE Foundation Dollars for Scholars, has named one of its awards the Tidye Pickett Memorial Scholarship.[39]

In August 1984 the United States hosted the Olympic Games at Los Angeles, the city of the 1932 Olympics, and Chicago's two local papers, the *Chicago Tribune* and the *Chicago Sun-Times* used the occasion to write a human interest story on Tidye Pickett. The papers obtained Pickett's views on both the 1932 and 1936 Olympics. She recounted the bigotry of the 1932 games and the disappointing injury of the 1936 games, but the *Sun-Times* story captured the gist when it reported that she was rooting for the United States while watching the 1984 Olympics although in 1932 it was "hard for her to feel so patriotic." After some years of failing health, Pickett died a little more than two years later, on November 22, 1986, at the age of seventy-two.[40]

Tidye Pickett is remembered fondly as a pioneer in African American achievement. Along with Louise Stokes she ranks as one of the first black women from the United States to be selected for an Olympic team in 1932, and she alone ranks as the first African American female to participate in the Olympics when she competed in the 1936 Games. Pickett neatly summed up her legacy to the *Sun-Times* as follows: "The girls who came on later didn't have to face the same things. They had a lot to thank us for. We took a lot for them. We really opened the door for them, but I was glad it was opened."[41] On perhaps a lesser, but no less important, scale, Pickett's abilities enabled her to incrementally crack the racial boundaries that allowed Jackie Robinson's entry into MLB a decade later.

### Notes

1. Bureau of the U.S. Census, *Fourteenth Census of the United States, 1920*; Census Place: Chicago Ward 30, Cook (Chicago), Illinois; Roll: T625_347; 6A; Enumeration District: 1858; Image: 956.

2. *Purple and White 1932* (Chicago: Englewood High School, 1932), 149–56; *Purple and White 1933* (Chicago: Englewood High School, 1933), 126–32.

3. Gerald R. Gems, *Windy City Wars: Labor, Leisure, and Sport in the Making of Chicago* (Lanham MD: Scarecrow Press, 1997), 102–10; Benjamin McArthur, "The Chicago Playground Movement: A Neglected Feature of Social Justice," *Social Service Review* 49, no. 3 (September 1975): 382–84; "Anderson Playground to Enter Girls in Chicago American Meet," *Chicago Defender*, June 8, 1929.

4. Doris H. Pieroth, *Their Day in the Sun: Women of the 1932 Olympics* (Seattle:

University of Washington Press, 1996), 32; "Girl Ties World's Track Mark," *Chicago Defender*, February 6, 1932.

5. "History of the U.S.S. Athletic Association," in *1927 Intercollegian Wonder Book or 1779—The Negro in Chicago—1927*, ed. Frederic H. Robb (Chicago: Washington Intercollegiate Club of Chicago, 1927), 76; "Church Girl Cagers Open Season, Feb. 5," *Chicago Defender*, January 18, 1930.

6. "Church League Girl 5s in 3 Fast Tilts," *Chicago Defender*, February 8, 1930; "Women's Sports," *Chicago Defender*, March 1, 1930; Edward Ervin, "Women's Sports," *Chicago Defender*, February 7, 1931; "Pilgrim Boys, Girls Lead in Race for Sunday School Flag," *Chicago Defender*, February 6, 1932; "Leaders Win as Church Teams Near Final Round of Tourney," *Chicago Defender*, March 5, 1932; "Sunday Schools Start Cage Play," *Chicago Defender*, December 17, 1932; "Pilgrim Girls Win Church Basketball Title; Unbeaten," *Chicago Defender*, February18, 1933; "Church Cagers Near Finals," *Chicago Defender*, February 25, 1933; "Pilgrim Girls Reach Cage Finals," *Chicago Defender*, March 18, 1933.

7. "Pilgrim S. S. Five Stages Game Monday," *Chicago Defender*, February 11, 1933; "Pilgrim Girls Reach Cage Finals," *Chicago Defender*, March 18, 1933; Leo Fischer, "Chicago American Cagers Continue Thrillers in American Title Play," *Chicago American*, March 9, 1933; Leo Fischer, "Five More Title Games End Cage Meet Tonight," *Chicago American*, March 18, 1933; "Pilgrim Girls Reach Cage Finals," *Chicago Defender*, March 18, 1933.

8. "Graduates of the High School Department: Englewood, Four-Year Courses," *Proceedings of the Board of Education, July 12, 1933, to July 3, 1934* (Chicago: Board of Education, 1934), 1502; "YMCA League Stages Hot Tilts," *Chicago Defender*, December 23, 1933.

9. A. S. "Doc" Young, *Negro Firsts in Sports* (Chicago: Johnson Publishing, 1963), 186–99.

10. Betty Eckersall, "New Playground Star Ties National 60 Yard Record," *Chicago Tribune*, January 31, 1932; "Girl Ties World's Track Mark: Tidye Pickett Equals Record Set by Filkey," *Chicago Defender*, February 6, 1932; Jimmie Williams, "Ralph Metcalfe, Miss Pickett Steal Show in Track Meet Here," *Chicago Defender* (nat. ed.), March 6, 1932; Wins Dash Event," *Chicago Defender*, March 5, 1932; "Runs Next Week," *Chicago Defender*, June 11, 1932.

11. "Sprint Stars Win in Olympic Tryouts," *Chicago Defender*, July 23, 1932; "Chicago Girl in Olympics," *Chicago Defender*, July 23, 1932.

12. Pieroth, *Their Day in the Sun*, 43–46; "Miss Didrikson the One-Girl Track Team, Heads U.S. Squad of 16 Named for Olympics," *New York Times*, July 18, 1932; "Girl Clerk to Lead Women's Olympic Team," *Cumberland Sunday Times*, July 17, 1932; "Babe Didrikson, One Girl Team, Captures Meet," *Chicago Tribune*, July 17, 1932.

13. Cindy Himes Gissendanner, "African American Women Olympians: The Impact of Race, Gender, and Class Ideologies, 1932–1968," *Research Quarterly for Exercise and Sport* 67, no. 2 (June 1996): 173–74; Pickett quotes from Pieroth, *Their Day in the Sun*, 47; Jody Homer, "Pioneer from 1932 Remains Undaunted:

U.S. Team's 1st Black Woman," *Chicago Tribune*, August 10, 1984; Toni Ginnetti, "Ex-Track Star Recalls Racism at '32 Games," *Chicago Sun-Times*, August 5, 1984.

14. Peiroth, *Their Day in the Sun*, 110–11; Pickett quoted in Homer, "Pioneer from 1932 Remains Undaunted"; King quoted in Gissendanner, "African American Women Olympians," 173–74; Rita Liberti, "'As Girls See It': Writing Sport on the Margins of the Black Press," in *Race in American Sports: Essays*, ed. James L. Conyers Jr. (Jefferson NC: McFarland, 2014), 5–20.

15. Gerald R. Gems, email to the author, September 16, 2014.

16. Peiroth, *Their Day in the Sun*, 111; Louise Mead Tricard, *American Women's Track and Field: A History, 1895 through 1980* (Jefferson NC: McFarland, 1996), 183–84; Eric L. Cowe, *Early Women's Athletics: Statistics and History*, vol. 2 (self-published, Bingley, England, 2005), 131.

17. David K. Wiggins, "The 1937 Olympic Games in Berlin: The Response of America's Black Press," in David K. Wiggins, *Glory Bound: Black Athletes in a White America* (Syracuse NY: Syracuse University Press, 1997), xvi and 64; Helen Jefferson Lenskyj, *Gender Politics and the Olympic Industry* (New York: Palgrave MacMillan, 2013), 71; A. D. Emerson, *Olympians against the Wind: The Black American Female Difference* (Miami Beach FL: Darmonte Enterprises, 1999), 9–10.

18. "Algonquin Athletic Club Feted by Vice President," *Chicago Defender* (nat. ed.), November 5, 1932; "Modern Miss Rivals Brother at South Park," *Chicago Tribune*, February 5, 1933; "U.S. Track Honors to Chicago Women," *New York Times*, February 26, 1933; "IWAC Takes Women's Title with 42 Points," *Chicago Tribune*, July 1, 1933; "Phil Edwards Beaten in AAU Half-Mile Event," *Chicago Defender*, July 8, 1933; "Tennis Stars Meet and Form Club to Entertain Guests," *Chicago Defender* (nat. ed.), August 12, 1933.

19. "Tidye Pickett Will Compete in Girls Hurdle Races Now," *Chicago Defender* (nat. ed.), January 20, 1934; "Bring Championship to Chicago," *Chicago Tribune*, April 16, 1934; "Tidye Pickett Sets New Mark for 40 Yards," *Chicago Defender*, May 5, 1934; Tricard, *American Women's Track and Field*, 216–17.

20. "Chicago Girls Win in Toronto Games," *New York Times*, July 3, 1934; "Tidye Pickett Smashes Canadian Track Mark," *Pittsburgh Courier*, July 14, 1934; "Tidye Pickett Is Star of City Track Meet," *Chicago Defender* (nat. ed.), August 11, 1934; "Lincoln Park Girls Win Two Track Titles," *Chicago Tribune*, August 5, 1934; Cowe, *Early Women's Athletics*, 147.

21. "Tydie [*sic*] Pickett Stars As Locals Win Track Meets," *Chicago Defender* (nat. ed.), March 30, 1935; "Betty Robinson Wins Dash in CAAU Meet," *Chicago Tribune*, August 11, 1935; "Winnipeg Girl Is Holder of Two Canadian Records," *Winnipeg Free Press*, November 20, 1935; "Tydie [*sic*] Pickett to Be Honored at Big Benefit," *Chicago Defender*, July 6, 1935; "Tydie [*sic*] Pickett Will Be Tendered Testimonial," *Chicago Defender*, July 27, 1935.

22. "Three Titles Won by Miss Stephens," *New York Times*, February 13, 1936; "Helen Stephens Ties World Sprint Mark in AAU Meet," *Chicago Tribune*, March 26, 1936; "Tydie Pickett Wins in Women's AAU," *Chicago Defender*, June 20, 1936.

23. Tricard, *American Women's Track and Field*, 229.

24. For a detailed and illuminating discussion of the black press treatment of the 1936 Olympics, see Wiggins, "The 1936 Olympic Games in Berlin," 61–79; "Latest Hitler Edict Seeks to Keep German Blood 'Pure,'" *Chicago Defender*, October 14, 1933; "U.S. Defends Jews in the Olympics; How about Race?," *Chicago Defender*, November 25, 1933; "Hitler Attacks the Louis and Schmeling Battle," *Chicago Defender*, April 18, 1936.

25. Joe Jefferson, "Olympic Stars Given Welcome in Berlin; Prejudice Missing as Athletes Arrive," *Chicago Defender* (nat. ed.), August 1, 1936; Wiggins, "The 1936 Olympic Games in Berlin," 73; David Clay Large, *Nazi Games: The Olympics of 1936* (New York: W. W. Norton, 2007), 234.

26. Large, *Nazi Games*, 228–34.

27. Cited in Homer, "Pioneer from 1932 Remains Undaunted"; Tricard, *American Women's Track and Field*, 226–27.

28. Homer, "Pioneer from 1932 Remains Undaunted."

29. "Tidye Pickett, Normal Girl, Shows Real Form," *Pantagraph*, February 13, 1936; "Bloomington Walther Lutheran Cops Tournament with 70 Points," *Pantagraph*, May 31, 1936; *The Index*, vol. 47 (Normal: Illinois State University, 1937), 77, 288; *The Index*, vol. 48 (Normal: Illinois State University, 1938), 11, 149, 211; Frank A. "Fay" Young, "What Has Become of Our U. S. Olympic Heroes?," *Chicago Defender* (nat. ed.), September 9, 1939.

30. "Basketball," *Chicago Defender* (nat. ed.), December 1, 1934; "Will Play Colored Girls," *Estherville Daily News*, January 29, 1935; "Girls Basketball Team Will Meet Lucerne Club," *Logansport Pharos-Tribune*, January 7, 1938.

31. "Hilbert Cagers Win Two Games," *Sheboygan Press*, December 19, 1939; "Girls' Colored Team Plays Northern at Rapid Tuesday; Merchants Meet Rock," *Escanaba Daily Press*, December 31, 1939; "All Star Negro Girls Will Appear Tuesday," *Monticello Express*, January 18, 1940; "For the Good of Golf," *Chicago Defender* (nat. ed.), June 29, 1940; Henry Brown, "Crude, Unscrupulous Matt Bivins Was Known as Playboy of Policy," *Chicago Defender* (nat. ed.), September 13, 1952; Nathan Thompson, *Kings: The True Story of Chicago's Policy Kings and Numbers Racketeers, an Informal History* (Chicago: Bronzeville Press, 2003), 104, 139, 231.

32. "Jacks Play Negro Girls Tonight," *Lethbridge Herald*, January 18, 1941; "Cardston Leafs Beat Negro Girls," *Lethbridge Herald*, January 20, 1941; "Raymond Trounces Negro Co-eds 53–33," *Lethbridge Herald*, January 21, 1941.

33. "Hilbert Cagers Will Meet Girl Basketeers," *Post Crescent*, March 24, 1938; "Dyer," *Hammond Times*, December 18, 1938; Ty Cobb, "Inside Stuff," *Nevada State Journal* 9 (March 1951); "Colored Basketball Champs Will Meet Local Team Here," *Winslow Mail*, January 9, 1953; Pamela Grundy and Susan Shackleford, *Shattering the Glass* (New York: New Press, 2005), 104–5.

34. "Harts to Battle Chocolate Coeds in Tuesday Tilt," *Post-Register*, January 27, 1941; "Harts, Surgeons Win Cage Tilts," *Post-Register*, January 29, 1941.

35. "Jesse Owens to Appear Here in Person Tuesday," *Freeport Journal Stan-*

*dard*, March 10, 1938; William J. Baker, *Jesse Owens: An American Life* (Urbana: University of Illinois Press, 2006 [1986]), 141–42, 152–53.

36. "Indiana, Marriages, 1811–1959," index and images, *FamilySearch*, https://familysearch.org/pal:/MM9.1.1/QV9M-6H4V (accessed July 25, 2014), Gail Russell Eldredge and Tidye Anne Pickett, 23 Oct 1939, citing County; FHL microfilm 002416447; "United States Census, 1940," index and images, *FamilySearch*, https://familysearch.org/pal:/MM9.1.1/KWTB-VZ8 (accessed July 25, 2014), Gail Eldredge in household of Sarah Hagans, Ward 5, Chicago, Cook, Illinois, United States; citing enumeration district (ED) 103-306, sheet 14A, family 324, NARA digital publication of T627, roll 930.

37. "Honored at Shower," *Chicago Defender* (nat. ed.), August 15, 1942; Homer, "Pioneer from 1932 Remains Undaunted"; Pieroth, *Their Day in the Sun*, 134.

38. Bernita D. Lucas, "Tidye Pickett Biography," FUTURE Foundation Dollars for Scholars, http://www.future.dollarsforscholars.org (accessed July 26, 2014); Homer, "Pioneer from 1932 Remains Undaunted."

39. "ISU to Induct Ten [*sic*] in Hall of Fame Ceremony," *Chicago Defender*, September 15, 1973; Lucas, "Tidye Pickett Biography."

40. Homer, "Pioneer from 1932 Remains Undaunted"; Ginnetti, "Ex-Track Star Recalls Racism at '32 Games."

41. Cited in Ginnetti, "Ex-Track Star Recalls Racism at '32 Games."

# ELEVEN

# Harold "Killer" Johnson

*Making a Career in the Popular Culture*

JAMES COATES

The American sporting and leisure culture is littered with individuals who have made significant contributions to its history and development. Whether as athletes, coaches, managers, trainers, agents, confidants, or entrepreneurs, these individuals have helped to shape the American culture in one domain or another. Before Jackie Robinson integrated Major League Baseball and the American society itself became more openly accepting of integration, men of color participated in some aspect of interracial sport within the country and internationally under the American flag. One of those men, Harold "Killer" Johnson, participated in the sporting industry in every one of the capacities noted above, before, during, and after the career of Robinson. Yet few people know of him, and even fewer know of his contributions.

On February 4, 1912, on a Napoleonville, Louisiana, sugar cane plantation, Thomas and Lillie Johnson eagerly awaited the tenth member of their family. That member, to whom Lillian gave birth, was a boy given the name Harold. Harold Johnson was one of the eleven children that his parents were to eventually bring into this world, five girls and six boys, including one set of twins among the eleven siblings.

Thomas was a sharecropper on the plantation, and Lillie worked as a seamstress for the plantation owner. In fact the entire Johnson family worked on the plantation. For black sharecroppers on the majority of southern farms and plantations, life was not easy, and financial gains were very rarely seen by these workers. The Johnson family's experience was no different. They struggled on a daily basis, but unlike the slavery experience of their ancestors, they managed to stay together as a family unit. Lillie's primary responsibility was to make denim overalls for the plantation workers. At times her hands literally would be ripped apart from the needles used to sew the material together. It was painful and tedious work, but it helped the family and sometimes provided a bit of joy in an otherwise dreary life. One of Lillie's favorite tasks included making the plantation's outfits for Mardi Gras. Her skill as a seamstress was passed along to each of her daughters in the hope that they might be able to find gainful employment.[1]

In 1919 things began to drastically change for the family. The family's matriarch, Lillie, died on the sugar cane plantation. She had provided love and care, and her death created a major strain on the entire family. The members struggled trying to remain together but to no avail. Thomas, unable to provide for the entire family, was forced into some painful decisions. So some of the children, including Harold (who was then eight), were sent to Chicago to live with Mary Etta, one of his twin sisters; the twins were older than Harold, and both had already migrated from Napoleonville to the larger city. Like so many others, they had learned of the more abundant opportunities in the northern big cities and had become part of the Great Migration of the era.

It must have been both a daunting move and one from which much was expected. Other migrants who had returned to visit their southern roots "talked about all the money they were making . . . about the skyscrapers and streetlights, the dance halls, the parties, and the boulevards paved where the colored [sic] people lived."[2] The train trip must have been exciting for Harold, full of exhilaration and expectation. Isabel Wilkerson captured the feeling in her splendid documentation of a journey north: "For a time in the 1920s, the ride to Chicago was interrupted after the train crossed the Ohio River into Cairo. . . . Once over the river and officially in the North, the colored cars had to be removed in a noisy and cumbersome uncoupling and the integrated cars attached in their place to adhere to the laws of Illinois. Colored passengers had to move, wait, reshuffle themselves, and haul their bags to the newly attached integrated cars."[3] Even this otherwise bothersome process for black passengers must have provided a sense of greater freedom and liberation.

Due to various circumstances, including financial considerations, the family intended for Harold to attend specific schools in Chicago. Chicago public schools provided free, integrated, and better education than that available in the South. The family's main choice was Frances Willard Elementary, but in order for Harold to attend this school he had to live in that particular school's district. Not having immediate family members in that area with the resources to allow Harold to go to Willard, the sisters turned to one of their cousins, Chester Reasons, for assistance. Chester decided that he and his family would legally adopt Harold and his sister Mildred. Such communal support patterns exemplified black family life and proved to be one means to address the otherwise overwhelming obstacles presented by racist attitudes and white social practices, which greatly limited employment and income for non-whites. This adoption solved the immediate issue of schooling and provided temporary stability in Harold's life. After Harold had been at Willard for a year or so, Mary Etta was in a better financial position, and she retrieved him from her helpful cousin. Harold then attended Doolittle Elementary School.

By this time Mary Etta had married Walter Smith, and the three of them lived in an apartment at the corner of Forty-Ninth Street and Cottage Grove in the burgeoning "black belt" on the South Side of Chicago. While Harold had been required to do very little (if any) work on the sugar plantation because of his age, this change of address was the beginning of a drastic transformation in his life. First and foremost, the change from a rural plantation to the second-largest city in the entire country was overwhelming for many people, let alone an eight-year-old boy. Because of his young age, however, Harold was quickly able to adapt to his new surroundings. It took some time for Harold to acclimate to the climate change, from the hot weather of Louisiana to the extreme cold of Chicago winters. One of the more significant changes that would be a major part of Harold's persona for the rest of his life was his contact with the Olivet Baptist Church. In addition, Mary Etta was applying the skill she had learned from her mother as a seamstress to earn money in Chicago. She particularly enjoyed making church choir robes, and the growing black population in Chicago at this time filled an increasing number of black churches. The Olivet Baptist Church alone counted ten thousand members by 1920, making it the largest black church in the country.[4]

The sheer size of some of the churches with their massive congregations disoriented some southern migrants. One claimed that in her first trip to Olivet it was so overcrowded that she could not even get in to the service, complaining that "we'd have to stand up. I don't care how early we'd go, you wouldn't get in." Another grumbled that she couldn't understand the pastor and the words he used and that she "couldn't get used to the singing" at Olivet, which she felt was too "proud-like."[5]

The birth of Gospel music in the city spawned a desire for church choirs, so Mary Etta had ample opportunity to utilize her sewing skills. With this talent she always made sure that the clothing Harold wore fit perfectly and was very stylish. The clothing that he had worn on that far off plantation was gone forever. In Chicago Harold would be known for his dapper appearance throughout his life.

In the post–World War I era the explosive growth of Chicago's black population also fostered a vibrant popular culture that revolved around music, nightlife, and sports. Harold's growth and development on the South Side led him to an interest in athletics. From the time he attended Frances Willard and Doolittle Elementary Schools and then went on to Hyde Park High School (now Hyde Park Academy), Harold was actively engaged in sports. The ability to attend Hyde Park School represented a measure of social capital for students. Located west of the segregated black community known as Bronzeville, the affluent Hyde Park was the location of the renowned University of Chicago with its white students, professors, and scientists.

By the time he was fourteen Harold had grown to be very tall, and he was still rapidly growing each day. At this point his brother-in-law, Walter Smith, told him that it was time for him to get a job during the summer. From Walter's perspective any job Harold had would help to bring money into the household. At that time few adolescents, black or white, completed a high school education. In black and poor immigrant families, children were often expected to contribute to the family welfare as soon as possible.

One day while contemplating what to do with his time during the summers of his high school years, Harold decided to accompany Walter to his workplace at the Chicago stockyards, a major employer in the city that penned livestock awaiting the slaughterhouses. Harold was eager to show that he could work. Yet he was very apprehensive about the type of labor he knew awaited him at the stockyards. Harold's task for the day was to pluck chickens. He did so for the entire day, but upon arriving home, he told Walter to look at what had happened to his hands from just one day of work. His hands were swollen. There were cuts, scratches, and stains, and Harold decided that the stockyards were not the kind of place he'd want to seek employment. He returned to working on his first love, his athletic skills, with dreams that he might be able to earn some money in the burgeoning popular culture in the city. Rube Foster had created a professional baseball circuit for black players that was headquartered in Chicago; barnstorming basketball players eked out a living, and even a few black football players managed to earn an income in the nascent National Football League.[6]

While attending Hyde Park High School, Harold became so proficient in his athletic skills that he became a member of both the baseball and basketball teams. The local Chicago papers carried almost weekly stories of Harold's athletic exploits in either baseball or basketball, depending upon which season was current at the time. The large African American population in the city even supported a separate black newspaper, the *Chicago Defender*, which gave extensive coverage to black athletic activities and was disseminated by black porters on the national network of railroads that was centered in the city. In his senior year of high school at Hyde Park, Harold was named as one of the twenty-five best basketball players in the city of Chicago, and he was placed on the All Stagg Team, chosen by the esteemed and nationally famous coach Amos Alonzo Stagg at the

University of Chicago.[7] This team was listed in the *Chicago Tribune*, a paper that was geared toward serving the needs and interests of the majority white community. Harold, in fact, was one of only four African Americans to achieve that honor in Chicago in 1929. Chicago, like the rest of the country at that time, had a very racially divided culture. Although athletic teams engaged in interracial competition, real estate redlining practices produced and enforced residential segregation. Consequently African Americans lived in Bronzeville, south of the downtown region. They would later migrate to a second neighborhood, displacing the Jews and other ethnic groups on the West Side. The selection of black athletes as the best by the white media was extremely rare, as whites assumed their own intellectual and physical superiority. Black athletes began to dispel such notions with increasing frequency, and Harold Johnson would make his own contribution to that process. Harold, because of his deadly shooting skills in basketball and clutch game changing baskets, was given the nickname "Killer," a pseudonym that he carried for the rest of his life.[8]

Harold's interscholastic exploits in the athletic arena of baseball and basketball led to his being offered opportunities on the college level from the University of Chicago, Wilberforce College, and Virginia State College. Both Wilberforce College and Virginia State College are still listed among the approximately 110 historically black colleges and universities (HBCUs) in the United States today. Athletic competition and the skill levels of the black athletes at such institutions were among the best to be found in the United States, but the HBCUs were rarely allowed to encounter white teams. Today they still compete in separate intercollegiate conferences in both the North and the South.

Johnson was not immediately able to accept any of the offers for academic or athletic pursuits. As was the case with many other youngsters during that Depression era, he tried to find work to help his family survive the economic crisis. The Depression was even more devastating to black families, and with employment even more scarce for black applicants, they had to seek sustenance by any means.

Bronzeville offered myriad opportunities. Isabel Wilkerson described Bronzeville as follows:

[It was] a city within a city, rolled out from the sidewalk, the streets aflutter with grocers and undertakers, dressmakers and barbershops, tailors and pressers, dealers of coal and sellers of firewood, insurance agents and real estate men, pharmacists and newspapers, a YMCA and the Urban League, high steepled churches—Baptist, Holiness, African Methodist Episcopal practically transported from Mississippi and Arkansas—and stacked-heeled harlots stumbling out of call houses and buffet flats.

There were temptations a southern sharecropper couldn't have known existed and that could only catch root when so many people were packed into one place, the police could be bought, and the city looked away: reefer pads, card sharks, gangsters and crapshooters. The so-called mulatto queen of the underworld running poker games. Policy kings running the numbers racket, ready to take a migrant's newly earned dollar fresh from the slaughterhouse. The migrants could see Ma Rainey at the Regal or just melt into the neon anonymity of city life without a watchful uncle or jackleg preacher knowing about it.[9]

Black nationalist Marcus Garvey had migrated from Jamaica to New York and preached the need for a separate black economy and black pride until the federal government deported him for his radical views, but Bronzeville was not quite what Garvey had in mind.[10] The writers and artists of the Harlem Renaissance of the 1920s also advocated an appreciation of African American culture and pride in its accomplishments, and the restricted nature of residential opportunities forced the black middle and upper classes to inhabit the same urban spaces as their less fortunate brethren and the newcomers, as was the case in Bronzeville.[11] "The color line in Chicago confined them to a sliver of the least desirable blocks between the Jewish lakefront neighborhoods to the east and the Irish strongholds to the west, while the Poles, Russians, Italians, Lithuanians, Czechs, and Serbs, who had only recently arrived themselves, were planting themselves to the southwest of the colored district."[12] Such locations made the disparity of wealth and status obvious, but they also exemplified the opportunities for social mobility available in the North.

Within such communities some preyed on the weak, the poor, and the gullible. Johnson learned quickly, determined not to be any of the above, and used his wits and his skills to improve his own livelihood. Some of the work he had was not always within the accepted legal parameters of that era. One of his jobs included working with and for the policy racketeers. Policy operators, as they were then known, were the kingpins of illegal lotteries. In many black communities these individuals were known as "numbers runners." Many blacks had little to lose, so gambling on sports events, in card games, or in picking the winning "numbers" became a regular strategy to meet their needs. In some black communities policy kings used their sizable profits to field baseball teams, while less fortunate others simply hosted "rent parties," which provided liquor, food, and dancing for the price of admission. Concurrent poker games allowed the host to take his/her cut of the pot, thus enabling such neighborhood entrepreneurs to pay their monthly rent.[13] Harold had become friends with a group of such entrepreneurial brothers in high school who were involved with "policymaking." These were the Jones brothers, who were engaged in various enterprises of dubious legality.[14]

The Jones brothers' primary family business was running a funeral home and religious activities, although their entrepreneurial activities extended to a tailor shop, music interests, and gambling. Their father was an ordained Baptist minister who held a Doctorate of Divinity degree, but his friendship with this family led Harold into relationships with individuals who worked on what is often called the seedy side of American society. Many African Americans found solace in religion, a need exploited by the less scrupulous. Many "preachers" without the credentials of Dr. Jones simply opened storefront "churches" and enticed patrons with their oratorical skills to donate money to their professed cause.

Religion merged with popular culture through sports, as the larger churches sponsored their own athletic teams, practicing a form of social control that not only kept youth off the streets but also marketed their services.[15] Aside from playing in the Chicago high school leagues, Harold further enhanced his reputation in basketball by obtaining his church league union card. This allowed him to participate with any team within the church league. He chose to play for the Olivet Baptist Church, and his reputation grew to magnificent levels within the organization. The sports fans of Chicago began to look for Harold's feats on a regular basis. As noted, from 1929 to 1931 Johnson starred on the Hyde Park High School basketball and baseball teams. His white teammates even elected him captain of the latter squad, a signal honor. Harold "Killer" Johnson seemed well on his way to honing his knowledge and skills to the point of becoming one of the great contributors to the sporting culture of American society. Yet to this day Johnson's contributions are relatively unknown.

Johnson had planned eventually to attend New York City College. Harold arrived in New York, but due to some unknown circumstances he never attended the school. Without the social contacts in New York that had assisted him to make his way in Chicago, Johnson yearned for his former roots. Speculation is that the life that Harold had begun to develop with the Jones brothers was still deep in his blood. That is, while working for and with the brothers, he developed a great taste for the nightlife of the big city—specifically alcohol, women, money, and status. As a young lad Johnson had already established a reputation as a well-dressed individual. He also became notorious as a "ladies man." Even before high school he had girls of all races walking him home from school and carrying his books. So while the nickname "Killer" referred to his athletic skills, it could very well have been earned via his ability to charm his way with the girls and women that he encountered in sports, entertainment, and high society.[16]

Basketball had already merged with nightlife by the 1920s, as dance halls in both New York and Chicago imported basketball teams to entertain their patrons during intermissions. Both the New York Renaissance Five and the Harlem Globetrotters got their starts in such a fashion. The Globetrotters started out in the Savoy Ballroom in Bronzeville.

Aside from his nightlife activities, Johnson traveled around with several road teams (a term used to describe barnstorming basketball teams of that era) before heading off to New York. Among his first post–high school traveling teams was a stint with the Harlem

Globetrotters. The Globetrotters were still a young organization at the time, and the financial incentives were minimal at best, and Killer soon quit the team. Upon being asked why he had done such a thing, he responded, "I got hungry enough to start my own traveling pro club." Of course the Globetrotters went on to become world famous. Harold did not.[17]

Upon leaving the Globetrotters, Johnson did form his own team, the Famous Trotters, who traveled throughout the West playing games. The Trotters may have been the first black team to participate in integrated games in both Texas and Oklahoma. One of their most noted foes was the Olson Swedes of that region. Each time the Trotters played against the Swedes, attendance was the largest the western and southwestern towns had ever seen for any basketball game.[18] The Trotters' feats were truly remarkable at the time for many reasons, the least of which was that very few venues were willing to accept black teams in their facilities, especially those trying to play against white teams. Integrated activities of any sort between blacks and whites were strictly forbidden in most venues in the South and Southwest. Such restrictions made it extremely hard to maintain any consistency in formulating playing schedules.

One of the other teams on which Killer made a name for himself while playing basketball was the Crusaders, owned by the Jones brothers. This was another instance where the relationship between the brothers and Johnson was solidified. In other words, the school friendships, the tailor shop relationship, the sporting industry relationship, the brothers' musical backgrounds, and of course the policy relationship led to an exceptional business partnership between Killer and the brothers. For the most part, it can even be stated that Mack Jones, one of the brothers, was a major role model for Johnson in many ways.

Although they were close in age, Killer admired Mack Jones. They both had exceptionally good taste in dress at all times. Both men were extremely popular with women, who would do just about anything for them, including carrying gambling notes from customers placing their chosen numbers for the policy games. One newspaper, the *Pittsburgh Courier*, once referred to Mack as a "pro-basketball playing playboy."[19] It continued, "[He] popped into Chi looking like a million dollars."[20] A number of women succumbed to Johnson's charms as well, and he used his wiles to employ them as vulnerable sex workers. Pimping represented the conflicted nature of black masculinity, whereby black men relied on visible symbols of physical prowess, in addition to sports and music, when limited or no advancement seemed possible in other economic spheres.[21] But the most powerful influence Mack had on Killer was that he too was an athletic-minded individual. Although Mack did not participate any longer himself, his interest in sports showed Johnson that one could do multiple things and still participate in a love of athletics, and all such interests mixed naturally in the street culture of Bronzeville.[22]

Killer combined his street life with his athletic abilities to make a living throughout the Depression, playing with teams known as the Gladiators and simply the Cagers (an anachronistic term that labeled basketball players who were once confined to playing within chicken wire enclosures to shield them from unruly and sometimes aggressive fans who antagonized barnstorming teams). Johnson, and his brother, Robert, played with a team or teams, such as the Famous Globe Trotters or New York Globe Trotters, which masqueraded as the more famous and genuine Harlem Globetrotters, as they barnstormed through Iowa in the 1937–1938 season. In one such game with a team in Davenport the game ended in a brawl over the rules, and five players, including the Johnson brothers and their manager, were arrested. Black players in white towns playing in games against white teams and with white referees often faced arbitrary calls by the officials. The following season Harold Johnson stayed closer to home, forsaking the New York Globe Trotters and playing closer to home with another contingent known as the Savoy Big Five.[23]

During his travels Harold once met with a newspaper sports reporter who was covering one of Killer's former high school teammates, Al Johnson. Al at that time was playing for the New York Rens, an all-black team from New York's Harlem neighborhood. The Rens, as historian Susan Rayl has documented, were the best draw in basketball prior to the popularity of the Harlem Globetrotters. Harold told that particular reporter that he was headed for the coast to play for a baseball team sponsored by Bill "Bojangles" Robinson. Robinson was one of the finest and most popular black entertainers in the entire country, especially noted for his dancing ability.[24] Although Johnson was to obtain his personal post–high school honors in basketball, his first love in sports was always baseball. One journalist credited Johnson with his play for the Chicago Giants, a renowned black team in the city. A columnist for the *Chicago Defender*, one of the most prominent of the nationally known black newspapers, wrote, "If Killer wasn't the finest first base prospect discovered in Chicagoland a lot of professional scouts and managers were fooled. Yet Killer never moved out into the pros, rather electing to do something he liked better. The same was true of the ... baron [Johnson's] prospects in basketball."[25]

Johnson's contribution to the larger sporting culture would include more than his playing career, which reached a level of national notoriety. His skills as a manager, trainer, businessman, and entrepreneur were to bring him even more of a global identity. With his own athletic participation declining, Johnson turned to other pursuits. In 1942 he began his long career as an upper-crust entertainment baron. He began as the maître d' of the 411 Club in Chicago, owned and operated by Mack Jones and Ily Kelley. The club was well known as a gamblers' haven, offering roulette, craps, betting on horse races, slot machines, card games, and policy wheels. A variety of entertainment was also available each night. Within such an environment Johnson honed his amiable social skills and business networks throughout World War II.

Nightclubs represented a visible sign of social and economic capital for managers and owners and a means to social mobility. Frequented by movers, shakers, and aspirants to the upper classes, they clearly offered more than the juke joints and saloons to which the working classes were confined.[26]

In 1949 Johnson opened the famous Archway Lounge on the South Side of Chicago, which attracted black celebrities such as Nat "King" Cole, Sammy Davis Jr., and Lena Horne.[27] He made the acquaintance of heavyweight champion Joe Louis through the Jones brothers, and that led to a relationship with Truman Gibson, an African American lawyer with connections to professional boxing. Gibson would gain notoriety in the 1950s for his partnership with the gang-sters Frankie Carbo and Frank "Blinky" Palermo, who, with the help of sports promoters James Norris and Arthur Wirtz, monopo-lized professional boxing championship bouts and venues by coer-cion and intimidation.[28]

Johnson parlayed his friendships into more lucrative sporting ventures. Joe Louis invited him to a bowling party where he met Sugar Ray Robinson, the world welterweight champion. Robinson and Louis had become friends as they toured army posts and gave boxing exhibitions during their time in the military in World War II. Robinson had won the middleweight championship by 1950 and even challenged for the light heavyweight title as he won recognition as the world's greatest fighter. Killer had already become a strong member of Ray's entourage, serving as his confidante, and he accom-panied Robinson on trips to places like Las Vegas, as well as cruises on the ocean liner *Liberty*, which took them to Europe in May 1951. Johnson was also furthering his notoriety during the time he man-aged Sugar Ray. According to one reporter, Killer never met a cam-era he didn't like. The reporter was referring to times when Killer would not allow photographers or reporters into Robinson's locker room unless they took his picture before entering. Johnson became the only nonofficial actor in Ray's life story, "Pound for Pound."[29]

Killer Johnson had solidified a friendship with the champion, and he was offered a role as one of Robinson's management team mem-bers in 1954. Johnson accepted this offer and officially became a major force within the Robinson camp, traveling throughout the United States and Europe and assuming a greater management role by 1956. Johnson extended his management activities to other boxers, rang-ing from lightweights to heavyweights.[30] His further involvement in the music industry extended to investment in Chicago-based Chess Records, a white-owned company that promoted black artists.[31]

With his growing economic and social capital Johnson began to reflect more seriously about his role in the community, and he became more involved in the civil rights movement. Chicago had been a cauldron of racial discontent since the race riot of 1919, but by the 1950s a concerted effort to restrict black housing assumed new proportions as city officials and urban planners marked African Americans for public housing tenements. Even blacks with sufficient income to afford houses in white neighborhoods or suburbs faced vehement backlashes that included fire bombings.[32] In the wake of such campaigns Johnson assumed a more strident role in the NAACP on the local level. He used his extensive network of friends to promote fund-raising activities and was very generous with his charitable contributions to the South Side Boys Club and other organizations. In 1958 Killer was elected chairman of the membership drive of the sport committee for the Chicago branch of the NAACP.

Johnson's last endeavor with the nightclub and entertainment industry came in 1962, when he, in partnership with Truman K. Gibson, operated the Sutherland Lounge. This establishment was known as a South Side Chicago jazz emporium, a fitting memorial to Johnson, who died on January 3, 1966, survived by his wife, Barbara, and a teenaged son.[33]

While there are many more details still being uncovered about the career of Harold "Killer" Johnson, one thing is very clear. He led a fascinating life, participating in all aspects of the interlocking sport and entertainment industries at a time when most African Americans were prohibited from engaging in some of the simplest venues in American society. Johnson's skills and persona were not enough to overcome racial exclusion at all levels, but touring with teams such as the Harlem Globetrotters, the Famous Trotters, and the Crusaders enabled him to see much of the country. His relationships with other athletes, such as Sugar Ray Robinson, permitted him to travel beyond the dreams of most Americans of the era. Johnson utilized his athletic and social skills to fashion a career that earned him a measure of celebrity within African American society and a full, if only a brief, life. From his humble roots on a Louisiana plantation to the pinnacle of the athletic world, he reinforced a belief in American meritocracy despite the harsh realities of persistent racism in American society.

### Notes

1. Harold Johnson family memoirs (currently in the possession of Phyllis Courtney, great niece of Harold); death certificate of Harold Johnson (copies in pos-

session of the author), December 2014; Howard Pulley, "Personality Spotlight," *Chicago Defender*, December 26, 1959, A5.

2. Isabel Wilkerson, *The Warmth of Other Suns: The Epic Story of America's Great Migration* (New York: Random House, 2010), 93–94.

3. Wilkerson, *The Warmth of Other Suns*, 200.

4. Christopher Manning, "African Americans," in *The Encyclopedia of Chicago*, ed. James R. Grossman, Ann Durkin Keating, and Janice L. Rieff (Chicago: University of Chicago Press, 2004), 5–7.

5. Cited in Wilkerson, *The Warmth of Other Suns*, 288.

6. See Gerald R. Gems, "Blocked Shot: The Development of Basketball in the African-American Community in Chicago," *Journal of Sport History* 22, no. 2 (Summer 1995): 135–48; Kevern Verney, *African Americans and U.S. Popular Culture* (New York: Routledge, 2003), 1–30.

7. Howard Pulley, "Personality Spotlight," *Daily Defender*, December 16, 1959, 13.

8. "Restaurateur 'Killer' Johnson Dies at Age 53," *Chicago Daily Defender*, January 4, 1966, 1.

9. Wilkerson, *The Warmth of Other Suns*, 268–69.

10. Martin Summers, *Manliness and Its Discontents: The Black Middle Class and the Transformation of Masculinity, 1900–1930* (Chapel Hill: University of North Carolina Press, 2004), 69–110.

11. Nathan Irvin Huggins, ed., *Voices from the Harlem Renaissance* (New York: Oxford University Press, 1995).

12. Wilkerson, *The Warmth of Other Suns*, 270.

13. Wilkerson, *The Warmth of Other Suns*, 270–71, 277–80. See Michael E. Lomax: *Black Baseball Entrepreneurs 1860–1901: Operating by Any Means Necessary* (Syracuse NY: Syracuse University Press, 2003), and *Black Baseball Entrepreneurs: The Negro National and Eastern Colored Leagues 1902–1931* (Syracuse NY: Syracuse University Press, 2014), as well as Adrian Burgos, *Cuban Star: How One Negro League Owner Changed the Face of Baseball* (New York: Hill and Wang, 2011), on baseball team ownership.

14. Nathan Thompson, *Kings: The True Story of Chicago's Policy Kings and Numbers Racketeers* (Chicago: Bronzeville Press, 2003); Johnson family memoirs.

15. See Gems, "Blocked Shot," on the women's team of the Olivet Baptist Church.

16. Howard Pulley, "Personality Spotlight," *Daily Defender*, December 16, 1959, 13; Johnson family memoirs.

17. Cited in "Restaurateur 'Killer' Johnson Dies at Age 53," *Chicago Defender*, January 4, 1966, 1.

18. "Restaurateur 'Killer' Johnson Dies at Age 53," *Chicago Defender*, January 4, 1966, 1.

19. Earl J. Morris, "Grand Town: Day and Night," *Pittsburgh Courier*, April 27, 1935, A8.

20. Earl J. Morris, "Grand Town: Day and Night," *Pittsburgh Courier*, April 27, 1935, A8.

21. Summers, *Manliness and Its Discontents*, 174–75.

22. Verney, *African Americans and U.S. Popular Culture*.

23. *Fort Madison (IA) Evening Democrat*, December 22, 1937, 2; *Freeport (IL) Journal-Standard*, December 12, 1938 (clipping).

24. Austin Rhea Johnson, "News in the Sports Realm," *Metropolitan Post*, November 12, 1938, 10.

25. Howard Pulley, "Personality Spotlight," *Daily Defender*, December 16, 1959, 13; Ole Nosey, "Everybody Goes When the Wagon Comes," *Chicago Daily Defender*, January 10, 1966, 11 (quote).

26. Summers, *Manliness and Its Discontents*, 175.

27. "Restaurateur 'Killer' Johnson Dies at Age 53," *Chicago Defender*, January 4, 1966, 1.

28. Gerald R. Gems, *Boxing: A Concise History of the Sweet Science* (Lanham MD: Rowman and Littlefield, 2014), 41.

29. "Pound for Pound," *Chicago Defender*, May 1, 1956, www.boxrec.com (accessed December 16, 2014).

30. Johnson's close relationship with Robinson led to a lawsuit filed by comanager Ernie Braca; it was settled in 1958 with Braca receiving a settlement of $18,000. See "Ray Settles Suit for $18,000," *Afro-American*, May 22, 1958, 13.

31. Robert Pruter, *Chicago Soul* (Champaign: University of Illinois Press, 1991).

32. Wilkerson, *The Warmth of Other Suns*, 372–78.

33. "Restaurateur 'Killer' Johnson Dies at Age 53," *Chicago Defender*, January 4, 1966, 1.

# TWELVE

# Continuing the Struggle

*Teddy Rhodes and Professional Golf*

RAYMOND SCHMIDT

Historical commentary that credits the eventual ending of racial segregation in American sport to Major League Baseball's breaking of its color barrier with the signing of Jackie Robinson to a contract has always failed to recognize that the condition continued well beyond 1946. Major League Baseball itself could not point to the integration of all its teams until the end of the 1950s, while many primarily southern universities continued to practice racial segregation in their athletic teams into the early 1970s. Despite Jackie Robinson many black athletes continued to be adversely affected by the white resistance of certain teams, officials, schools, and organizations to the integration of sport.

Seldom recognized is the institutional racial discrimination practiced in American men's professional golf by the administration of the Professional Golfers' Association (PGA) and the hardships it imposed on qualified black golf professionals. The PGA had practiced racial exclusion since its forming in 1916, and the organization continued to use every tactic available through the civil rights movement of the 1950s and into the 1960s to exclude non-white golfers from becoming PGA members and playing in its increasingly lucrative tournaments. One sport historian has written that nowhere was white resistance to the integration of blacks into sport more complete than in golf, continuing on that "golf was the last major sport to remove formal racial barriers to black participation at the professional level."[1]

Almost from its earliest inception in America, golf had been a sport for the social upper class, and until the opening of municipal golf courses it was even difficult for the average upper-middle-class sportsman to play. For decades at the country clubs, especially in the South, African Americans were excluded, relegated to working for the golf clubs in a variety of labor jobs such as caddying or course maintenance, and they were rarely allowed to actually play golf on any regular courses.

This restrictive racial environment surrounding golf ensured that African Americans would be regarded by the white memberships as what cultural historian Marvin Dawkins calls "permanent golf course servants." Despite any talent or success African American golfers might somehow achieve as players, there would be little chance of earning a living from the sport as professionals without access to the lucrative PGA tournaments and the club pro jobs that were available only to PGA members.

The exclusion of African Americans from eligibility for country club membership, along with racial segregation that was practiced even at many of the municipally owned public courses that were built, eventually drove groups of African American golfers to join together to form a national organization to promote golf for blacks. Soon local tournaments and a national championship—most with a division for black pro golfers—were being held annually to provide competitive opportunities for the African American membership, and so was created a separate sporting world to that of white golf clubs. By the 1940s there were a number of excellent players among the African American golf pros, and a small group of these men believed that they were good enough to compete against the white professionals of the PGA. Soon they began to seek entry to the white "major league" golf tournaments wherever possible, and most were ready to challenge continued racial exclusion in the courts if necessary. Yet this struggle would continue for nearly twenty years after the signing of Jackie Robinson.

One of these top-flight African American golf professionals who sought to gain entry into the regular PGA membership, and so fashion a career and living from the links sport, was Ted Rhodes. Many golf historians regard him as the greatest African American golfer before the arrival of Tiger Woods decades later, and he was one of the pioneers who helped to end the racial segregation of the PGA.[2]

### Early Years of the Struggle

Teddy Rhodes was born on November 9, 1913, in Nashville, Tennessee, to a laborer, Frank Rhodes, and his wife Della (Anderson). He was the youngest of nine children in the family, having seven sisters and one brother. At an early age he was given the nickname "Rags," not all that surprising considering the difficult conditions in which the family lived. When Teddy was eight years old and had reached what would be about the equivalent of fifth grade, he dropped out of school and began to work as a caddie at the Belle Meade Country Club, attracted by the game of golf and the chance to help support his family.

In those days none of Nashville's public or private courses allowed black players, so with Rhodes' quickly wanting to spend all his free time learning to play the game, he and a few friends began practicing whenever possible, primarily at Douglas Park on the east side of Nashville or sometimes in one of the other public parks. If the grass was a little long, they would bring over a lawn mower to make a few makeshift greens and then stick tree branches into their self-dug holes to serve as flag sticks. The boys would then play with improvised golf clubs and golf balls found at the country club. Eventually, in spite of the physical barriers he faced, Rhodes began to demonstrate an aptitude for golf, and the caddie master began to help him to improve—including sometimes allowing him to play on the Belle Meade course very early in the morning.

As Teddy grew older, his reputation as both a highly sought-after caddie and one of the better golfers in the Nashville area—although one not allowed to play in local tournaments—brought him some better work opportunities at Belle Meade. While still playing and practicing at every opportunity, Rhodes served for a time as the assistant caddie master, worked in the locker rooms, and filled in at other jobs around the course where help was needed. As his golf game improved, Teddy also began gambling on his playing whenever he had a little cash to spare or some others wanted to back him in a money game. While all these golf-related activities generated income for Rhodes, the situation was a classic illustration of the principle that without the chance to be a full member of the PGA with its potential benefits, there was a definite limit on the income he could realize from the sport and his ability to earn a living.[3]

In the late 1930s Rhodes joined the Civilian Conservation Corps (CCC) and temporarily left his job at the country club, although not giving up his hopes for golf. The CCC was a New Deal organization set up by the Roosevelt administration to provide unemployed single men a chance to earn a wage. While it is not known exactly what Rhodes did, the CCC basically provided unskilled manual labor jobs that were involved with forestry management and the conservation and development of natural resources—definitely outdoors jobs. By 1940 Teddy had discovered the United Golfers Association (UGA), and his appointment with golf history was approaching.[4]

The UGA was formed in early 1925 at a meeting of respected African American men at Washington DC's Twelfth Street YMCA. Led by Dr. George Adams and Dr. Albert Harris, both physicians in the nation's capital, the meeting sought to create a national organization that would gather together all African American golfers and golf associations under one group. Of major interest was the sponsoring of regional and national tournaments for the membership, along with the provision of a social, competitive, and cultural experience for those participating that would be far beyond what local club events normally provided.

Here was yet another example of African Americans' having to create a parallel sporting existence in the face of unrelenting racial discrimination, a situation very similar to that of baseball's Negro leagues. Among the other goals of the UGA was the expansion of golf to introduce more potential black men and women players to the game and provide venues for the better African American golfers to demonstrate and improve their skills. By the third annual UGA National Open in 1928 the competition included a men's professional division that featured a modest amount of prize money for the top finishers, along with the formal addition of an amateur division.[5]

Exactly how long Rhodes worked for the CCC is unclear as in an interview two decades later he said that he was back working at golf by the start of the 1940s. Although his financial resources were still a problem that prevented him from a good deal of wide-ranging travel to UGA golf tournaments, in 1941 he was able to play in the club's Chicago Open and another far more important tournament in Detroit that would eventually make possible his greatest days in golf after the war.

Joe Louis, an African American boxer, reigned as the world heavyweight champion from 1937 to 1949 and is considered to be one of the greatest fighters of all time. Moreover, by 1940 Louis was considered a national hero, and he was a black athlete who commanded respect from most of the white population and white mainstream media, along with the obvious adulation he received from African Americans. Not only was the "Brown Bomber" (his most famous nickname) a personable individual, but he had also earned the appreciation of much of the country because of his title fight destruction of Max Schmeling of Germany in 1938.

When Schmeling had defeated Louis in their first match in 1936, Adolph Hitler and the Nazi party had trumpeted the result as clear evidence of the superiority of the Aryan race, which was preparing to threaten the world, and what its war machine was capable of. When Louis trounced the German in less than one round of their rematch, much of the American population saw the result as revenge and payback to Hitler for what it believed was rudeness toward track star Jesse Owens and other Americans at the 1936 Olympic Games in Berlin, and the American fighter became a symbol of anti-Nazi sentiment.

Around 1936 Louis had become interested in the game of golf and began to practice as much as his boxing schedule allowed. As his playing skills improved, the champion eventually hired a series of personal instructors from among the top African American golf professionals; by 1940 his teaching pro was Clyde Martin of Detroit. Although Louis could freely move among most of white society, he was fully aware of the parallel golf world that had been forced upon African Americans by racial discrimination. Looking to provide more opportunities for black athletes, Louis hit upon the idea of sponsoring an annual UGA golf tournament in Detroit that he believed would do much to publicize the playing skills of top African American professionals. So in 1941 the first Joe Louis Open was held at Detroit's Rackham Park municipal course. The tournament would come to be regarded as the second major event on the UGA schedule each season; it always attracted all the top African American players and would be played between 1941 and 1951—suspended only during the war years of 1942–44.[6]

In August 1941 Teddy Rhodes was able to make it to Detroit to enter the first Joe Louis Open, and there he surprised the experienced UGA golf pros by qualifying and then finishing in a tie for third place that brought him a decent prize check. More important, he met Joe Louis and made a favorable impression upon the boxer. Rhodes then returned to Nashville and worked around various golf clubs, supplementing golf jobs with a part-time job as an entertainer–soft shoe dancer at a local night spot in 1942.

Late that summer of 1942 Rhodes learned that Louis, already serving in the U.S. Army and making appearances around the country for the war effort, would be playing at a UGA tournament in Dayton, so he traveled to the Ohio city and entered the event. Rhodes played well, but more important, he again met and impressed Louis with his golf game. Louis was then preparing to take a short leave in New York to work on his golf game, so he invited Rhodes to come along and give him some playing lessons.

Once in New York, Louis bought Rhodes his first real set of golf clubs, golf shoes, and other needed equipment. The playing lessons went very well, and, with Louis wanting to develop his golf game as far as possible even while in the army, he offered to hire Rhodes to travel around with him and work as his personal teaching pro. The Nashville golfer quickly accepted and always considered this to be the start of his career as a professional golfer.

Rhodes traveled and played golf with Louis until 1943, when he decided it was time to join the U.S. Navy. Not much is known of his military service except that for a time he was stationed in the Chicago area (most likely at Great Lakes Naval Station) and then later in California. The end of his navy days is also the subject of some confusion as, according to a longtime Nashville friend, Rhodes served only a short time and was discharged early because of a "kidney problem," a health issue that would plague him occasionally the rest of his life. Yet in a 1961 interview a comment by Rhodes implied that he had served through the end of the war.[7]

### Into the Golf Wars

With the war over and Louis discharged from the army in late 1945, the boxer again hired Rhodes to be his personal golf pro and playing partner as they traveled around the world—a partnership that continued until 1951. But first—apparently anticipating the gambling on big money golf games in which the two would often be involved—Louis sent Rhodes out to California for a time to take lessons and work on his game with white professional Ray Mangrum, the brother of a very good touring pro, Lloyd Mangrum. Able to now concentrate on golf without financial worries, Rhodes quickly polished his natural golf skills and was soon a top-flight player. Through the years of their association Rhodes would repay Louis by teaching the boxer much about golf and helping him to improve his game substantially.[8]

When 1946 arrived, Teddy Rhodes had his golf game ready to serve as playing partner for Joe Louis in whatever money games the boxer might arrange on his travels, to take on the best African American pro golfers in the country in what served as the major tournaments on the UGA's annual "tour," and to try qualifying at the few white pro tournaments that would allow him to enter. This last possibility for playing was going to be even more difficult than before, as in 1943 the PGA had revised its constitution to restrict membership and playing privileges to only white pros with the incorporation of its infamous Section 1, Article III "Caucasian only" amendment, which allowed only "Professional golfers of the Caucasian Race, over the age of eighteen years, residing in North or South America."[9]

In January 1946 Rhodes was able to come up with an invitation to try qualifying in the prestigious Los Angeles Open of the white pro tour. Until the early 1950s there were generally only three tournaments on the white PGA tournament circuit with the prestige and political "clout" to get away with inviting whatever players they chose, without regard to the PGA's "Caucasian only" membership clause—the Los Angeles Open, the All-America Open in Chicago promoted by businessman George S. May, and the Canadian Open. By the end of the 1940s May had launched a fourth tournament with very lucrative prize money called the World Championship, and it was added to those white pro events that refused to practice racial discrimination.

Rhodes failed to qualify for the 1946 Los Angeles Open, but later that summer he qualified for the All-American Open at Tam O'Shanter Country Club outside Chicago, and as the only African American player in the field, he surprised everyone by finishing in forty-third place and earning a prize check of $150. Yet the really big news was his breakthrough in the UGA tournaments that year as he won several of the smaller tournaments. The high points of his play in 1946 came in the two most important UGA events as he first won the Joe Louis Open in Detroit with its top prize of $750. Quickly he followed this up with a second-place finish in the UGA National Open at Pittsburgh, as he came up just two shots behind the winner, Howard Wheeler. This tournament began the rivalry that would continue through the rest of the decade and into the 1950s between Wheeler—who had won two UGA Nationals in the 1930s—and Rhodes, who had already become recognized as one of the most highly regarded black pro golfers after his performances in 1946.[10]

By late 1946, after all his travels with Joe Louis and the tournament successes compiled that year, Rhodes had developed his personal "style" of dressing and the golf game that would eventually be admired by many of the pros on the white PGA tour. He was 5-foot-11 and weighed about 150 pounds, and in pictures he appears quite slim. Friend and fellow golf pro Charlie Sifford described Rhodes as a "handsome guy, tall and light skinned," continuing that he was "one of the fanciest dressers on any tour." George S. May's daughter remembered him as the "classiest, flashiest guy you've ever seen."[11]

As much as Rhodes always impressed others with his style and dress, it was his golf game that stood out as that of a player with all the tools to succeed in the game. He was always accurate hitting his tee shots and an excellent iron player on the fairways. Such success all came about from the smooth, fluid, and rhythmic pass (swing) he always made at the ball—representative of the many hours of practice spent on his game. In addition, Rhodes had an outstanding short game, as he combined his accurate short iron play with terrific chipping and putting to produce what Sifford called the "best short game I've ever seen."[12]

Rhodes came back in 1947 with an impressive season on the UGA tour, reeling off seven consecutive tournament titles leading up to the UGA National. Beginning in June he won the Houston Open, the Chicago Open, the Miami View Open in Dayton, the Courier-Yorkshire Open, the Sixth City Open in Cleveland, and the Eastern Open. He played excellent golf in the entire series, including shooting a course record 66 at Seneca Park in Cleveland and a five under par total for the Eastern, where he left Wheeler in second place. Rhodes then tuned up for the National by defending his title in the Joe Louis Open as he won the $1,000 first prize check with an eight under par total for the tournament that held off Wheeler and a top-flight field of other African American golf professionals. But his streak ended the next week in Philadelphia when Wheeler defended his UGA National Open title with a four-shot victory, while Rhodes finished in a disappointing fifth place.[13]

Rhodes looked ahead with considerable confidence to his 1948 tournament plans, never realizing that he was about to become involved with two major and highly publicized disputes with the PGA over the group's aggressive discrimination policies. In January, after playing in the Los Angeles Open and finishing in a tie for twenty-first place, which according to the rules automatically qualified him for the next week's PGA tournament, Rhodes and two other black golfers—Bill Spiller and Madison Gunter, who also believed they had qualified for the upcoming Richmond Open—headed north to Oakland for the following event. After paying their entry fees and playing a couple of practice rounds, they were approached by a PGA official who informed the three that they would not be allowed to play in the tournament as they were not PGA members.

After a stormy confrontation—Spiller was one of the most aggressive and outspoken black golf pros seeking to overturn the blatant discrimination of the white tour—the trio retained an attorney named Jonathan Rowell and filed a $250,000 lawsuit against the PGA and the Richmond Country Club. For Rhodes, being actively involved in a confrontation such as this was totally opposed to his basic personality, and clearly it was driven by Spiller's views on how to address the problem. The Nashville golfer wanted to play on the PGA tour with his every fiber, but his fundamental personality was easygoing and non-combative, and he believed, all evidence to the contrary, that gains could be made through negotiation, compromise, and friendship with the PGA and that nothing could be accomplished by stoking the flames of hatred.

The attorney attempted to broaden the attention focused on the lawsuit by approaching the NAACP for assistance, yet this organization gave only limited attention to the golfers as it clearly was more focused on larger national issues, such as attempting to desegregate schools and public facilities, as part of the gathering civil rights movement. Meanwhile, the PGA had denied all charges of discrimination in the Richmond case, yet the organization was growing concerned behind the scenes over the increasingly bad publicity the white tour was receiving and the growing opposition to its obvious segregation policies.

Before the end of 1948 the lawsuit was dropped after an out-of-court settlement that provided the trio of black golfers no financial damages, the PGA promising to review the "Caucasian only" provision in its constitution. It was also agreed that the tournaments' host organizations would be allowed to "invite" black golfers to enter their events if they desired; very few ever did, and when an invitation was tendered to a black player, the PGA would quickly step in and pressure the local group into retracting its offer. Many black golfers viewed the settlement as a significant step toward eliminating the exclusion of black golfers from white professional tournaments, yet the PGA really did nothing about ending its segregation policies.[14]

So Rhodes returned to playing UGA tournaments and attempting to enter PGA events whenever possible. Early in the summer of 1948 he managed to qualify for the U.S. Open, the most prestigious tournament in American golf, which was being played in Los Angeles in 1948. He opened the tournament with a 70 over the lengthy Riviera cc course that left him just three shots out of the lead, but after finishing out of the money, Rhodes again returned to the UGA tournaments, where he was continuing to have success. That summer there was a new tournament on the UGA schedule as another boxer, "Sugar" Ray Robinson, decided to begin sponsoring an event. In August Rhodes won the first Ray Robinson Open at the Engineers Golf Club on Long Island, and then he headed to the Midwest, where he understood that the PGA's St. Paul Open would accept his entry.

With the California lawsuit against the PGA still pending, Rhodes and another black pro, Solomon Hughes, submitted their entries for the St. Paul Open, which was to be held at the publicly owned Keller Golf Course. The expectation of being accepted into the tournament was encouraged by recent events that included the fact that a baseball Negro Leaguer, Roy Campanella, had played for the St. Paul Saints that season and that the mayor of Minneapolis, Hubert Humphrey, had delivered a dramatic speech on civil rights at the recent Democratic National Convention. Yet the Minneapolis–St. Paul area was actually home to a very small African American population, and these people were the objects of various unofficial segregation policies relative to housing, employment, and restaurants.

It still was somewhat surprising when the entry fees were returned to Rhodes and Hughes on August 8 by the St. Paul Jaycees, sponsors of the tournament. At first the chairman of the tournament committee said that the two golfers had not been invited to play because of an "oversight," but this statement was soon amended to stress that the pair were not PGA members and were therefore not eligible. Immediately the *Minneapolis Spokesman*, a weekly African American newspaper, began to highly publicize the controversy and criticize the PGA's discrimination, while also attacking the mainstream Twin Cities newspapers for saying little about the affair.

Whitney M. Young, a young official of the St. Paul Urban League and an eventual major civil rights leader nationally, quickly became involved and sought to bring considerable pressure on the St. Paul Jaycees. Still the PGA refused to allow the Jaycees to accept the entries from the two golfers, with Tom Crane, the executive secretary of the PGA, even telling the mayor of St. Paul that if they were allowed to play in the tournament, it would jeopardize the PGA in the pending lawsuit in California. Ultimately the Jaycees, while publicly against the segregation policy of the PGA, gave in on the issue rather than risk losing the golf tournament, which was a major event for the St. Paul business community.[15]

After being involved in two highly publicized controversies with the PGA in 1948, Rhodes was glad to get back on the golf course. After winning the UGA's Gotham Open, he had a fourth-place finish in a minor pro tournament called the Santa Anita Open, and then he headed back to Detroit, where he captured his third consecutive championship in the Joe Louis Open. The last major event on his 1948 schedule was the UGA National Open at Indianapolis. Again it was a showdown between Rhodes and defending champion Howard Wheeler. Rhodes was two strokes behind his archrival heading into the final round, and then he struggled to a 39 on the first nine holes that seemed to all but finish his chances. But on the final nine holes of the tournament the Nashville golfer pulled out all the stops and fired a blistering 32 that left him just one shot behind Wheeler after the final green with a total of 288 for the tournament.[16]

### Moving Up in Class

The stage was now set for 1949 and what would later be considered as perhaps the greatest year of Teddy Rhodes's competitive career in golf. After qualifying for the Los Angeles Open early in the year, he finished out of the money, but then his personal life took center stage in California as he married Claudia Oliver. In 1950 their daughter, Deborah, was born, and the couple would later have a second daughter named Peggy. When Rhodes returned to the UGA tour, he won the Houston Open early in the season, and then over the July Fourth weekend he captured the Sixth City Open in Cleveland along with the $400 prize money.

After defending his title with another victory in the Gotham Open, Rhodes finally finished July with a trip to New York for the second annual Ray Robinson Open on Staten Island, which was marked by occasional outbursts of heavy rain and typically scorching hot weather. Apparently not always as soft-spoken as usual, early in the tournament Rhodes actually firmly asked Robinson—a middleweight champion—to leave his gallery as the presence of the popular boxer was causing considerable distractions for the Nashville golfer.

Rhodes found himself five strokes behind his nemesis, Howard Wheeler, after thirty-six holes of play, but then his game came around in the final two rounds. Over the last thirty-six holes of the Robinson Open Rhodes combined blazing tee shots with deadly putting and fired a dazzling 62 in the third round, and then followed this up with a 68 to finish with a thirteen under par total of 275 that left Wheeler in second place, six shots behind. For his brilliant play Rhodes took home a nice $800 prize check.[17]

In early August 1949 Rhodes was in Chicago to play against the white professionals in the All-American tournament, with a chance to qualify for the World Championship at Tam O'Shanter Country Club. Rhodes was one of seven black pro golfers invited to play in the All-American tournament and quickly proved he belonged there by shooting a brilliant 68 in the first round. He struggled in the last three rounds but still won a prize check that qualified him for the next week's World Championship. Against a top-flight field of PGA players, Rhodes shot impressive scores of 71-69-71 over the last three rounds to tie for fourteenth place and earn a check for $300.

After his success in Chicago an increasingly confident Rhodes traveled to Detroit for the 1949 UGA National championship, still looking for his first title in the event. This year he was not to be denied as he played consistent golf while shooting rounds of 69, 69, 70, and 69 for a total of 277 and a ten-shot margin over the second-place finisher. Rhodes collected a check for $750 for his victory, while his rival, Howard Wheeler, finished in fourth place. The following week the Joe Louis Open was played over the same Detroit course, and again Rhodes finished on top in the tournament for the fourth consecutive year, posting a total of 283 that was good for the winner's check of $1,100. Originally Rhodes had intended to skip the Louis tournament as he had received an invitation to play in the PGA's Cedar Rapids (Iowa) tournament. Yet just days later he was informed by a PGA official that the invitation had been sent "by mistake," so he quickly entered the Louis Open and successfully defended his title.[18]

As the 1950s dawned, the UGA was still providing tournament competition for African American pro golfers; the 1950 schedule included fifteen approved UGA tournaments, while the Los Angeles Open and Tam O'Shanter continued to provide chances to play against white PGA pros. Although the number of UGA events offering prize money would soon decline, the organization itself would remain the mainstay of golf for the many African American amateur players, both men and women.

Rhodes started off 1950 with a nice nineteenth-place finish in the Los Angeles Open that was good for a check of $160, and then later in the summer he won both the UGA's Houston Open and the Dayton Fairway Open. His streak of wins in the Joe Louis Open ended as he took second place and a check for $300, finishing behind a white pro named Al Besselink. But in the all-important UGA National Open, played in 1950 in Washington DC, Rhodes successfully defended his title with a two-shot win with a total of 280, which produced a check of $750. He trailed Charlie Sifford after the first round but then came blazing down the stretch with three sub-par rounds—including a brilliant 67 in the third round that featured a 31 on the first nine holes.

The 1951 season opened for Rhodes as he won $220 at the PGA's Los Angeles Open with a sixteenth-place finish, and he then returned to the UGA tournaments. This was the last year that the Joe Louis Open was held—the former heavyweight champion by now incurring the financial problems that would plague him for years—and Rhodes finished in third place, despite shooting three rounds in the 60s, as Howard Wheeler captured his first-ever win in the tournament. Yet when the UGA National Open was contested at Cleveland's Seneca Park course, Rhodes captured his third consecutive title in this most prestigious tournament in African American golf as he posted a total of 280, which was good for a six-shot victory and a check of $700.[19]

The 1952 golf season was to eventually stand out as a major turning point in Ted Rhodes's competitive career on the links. He opened the year with a good performance at the Los Angeles Open, where he tied for fifteenth place and won $230. Although eligible to enter the qualifying for the PGA's San Diego Open, Rhodes decided not to join Joe Louis, Bill Spiller, and Eural Clark in attempting to play there and so missed out on the largest controversy yet with the white golf organization.

When the three African American golfers arrived in San Diego, they learned that despite the fact that the sponsors of the tournament had "invited" Joe Louis to play, the PGA had stepped in and ruled that none of the three could play in the event. Since the PGA had avoided the 1948 lawsuit with an out-of-court settlement, it had done absolutely nothing in the intervening four years to honor its commitments or take any other constructive action. But in 1952 the PGA miscalculated the national attention that would be drawn to San Diego when it kicked an American cultural and sporting hero like Joe Louis out of the tournament in yet another obviously racially motivated decision.

Almost instantly the San Diego golf controversy was the focus of national media attention and commentary—none of it favorable to the tournament or the PGA—and the pressure began to build. Attempting to ward off the unwanted attention to its discrimination efforts, the PGA finally allowed Joe Louis to play in the San Diego Open as an amateur yet still excluded the two black golf pros. In an act of incredible hypocrisy, the PGA again promised to review its "Caucasian only" policy, only this time no one was buying it, and the national public criticism only escalated.

Finally the PGA installed a new program to ensure the entry of some qualified African American pro golfers into its tournaments on a controlled basis, with the announcement of the formation of a committee of top black golfers—of which Rhodes was to be a member. They would be allowed to designate a few players for "approved entry" into any PGA tournament where the local club and sponsor were agreeable, without PGA interference. Obviously this ruling was going to exclude all the tournaments in the South, where racial discrimination in golf was still a fact of life, yet there were enough tournaments elsewhere around the country so that a few black golfers would be able to enter approximately ten to twelve events each year. It was a major step forward for the African American golf pros, yet the institutional racism of the PGA and its continued resistance to African American golfers' gaining full membership continued unabated despite the pressures of the civil rights movement years.[20]

For the rest of 1952 Rhodes played both in UGA tournaments and PGA events where he was allowed to enter. The new "approved entry" policy was a major benefit to those black golf pros with the financial capability to travel to PGA tournaments, as in recent years the prize money available on the UGA circuit had declined precipitously. In 1951 only four of the fourteen UGA tournaments had a division with prize money, while in 1952 there were only three black tournaments that offered prize money for the pros. Increasingly Rhodes and a few other of the best African American golf pros would turn to the PGA events open to them in search of income.

For the rest of 1952 Rhodes played in another seven PGA tournaments, where he survived the thirty-six-hole "cut," although not winning prize money in any of them against large fields of top white players. He had quickly started to limit his UGA tournament play, and that summer he won a small event in Chicago called the Windy City Open.

In late August 1952 Rhodes traveled to Pittsburgh, where he won his fourth consecutive UGA National championship with an eight under par score of 280 over the South Park course, finishing six shots ahead of runner-up William Mays and earning a prize check of $650. Forty years later, with the beginnings of a growing number of books and articles that would be written on all aspects of African American sport, the records of UGA golf history would be widely distorted after black golfer Charlie Sifford claimed in his autobiography to have won the 1952 UGA National, the former pro not even correctly remembering where the tournament had been played. This major error relative to the 1952 UGA tournament's winner was somehow picked up and included in the table of UGA champions from 1926 to 1962 in the widely consulted book by Dawkins and Kinloch (*African American Golfers during the Jim Crow Era*). The erroneous information from Dawkins and Kinloch was then obviously picked up and propagated by other writers; hence the widespread mistakes in UGA records.[21]

## Competition Gets Tougher

The 1953 season saw Rhodes increasing his play on the PGA tour. He made the cut in six tournaments and took home prize checks at the St. Paul Open, the Canadian Open, the Fort Wayne Open, and the LaBatt Open in Montreal. At the LaBatt he posted a sparkling total of 272 and tied for fourth place, good for a check of $1,300—which would prove to be his best finish ever in PGA play. Since the previous summer Rhodes had believed that the increased chances to play in the top-flight competition of the PGA tour were improving his golf game significantly. There was evidence of this belief in 1953 as he shot quite a few outstanding scores in PGA events, highlighted by rounds of 66 at St. Paul, Montreal, and Fort Wayne.

Yet 1953 also brought a major happening in the UGA career of Rhodes. In midsummer he had won the Houston Open and then later in August had taken second place in the UGA's South Bend Open, after which he drove north into Canada to play in the PGA's lucrative LaBatt Open in Montreal. As mentioned, he played very well and earned a big prize check; however, his late finish caused him to stay in Montreal until Sunday night. Unfortunately the UGA National championship—where Rhodes was the four-time consecutive defending champion—was being held the next week in Kansas City, and there was not enough time to make the drive there by the event's opening. Reluctantly yet possibly influenced by the way he was playing and the big prize check he had just won, Rhodes decided to not attempt to make it to the UGA and instead stayed in the East, where he played in the PGA's Insurance City and Eastern Open tournaments—finishing out of the money in both.

Rhodes would have been a heavy favorite to win his fifth straight UGA National crown at Kansas City in 1953, but he had decided that even limited chances at the PGA tour were better financial prospects for him and his family. He would stick to this decision and would also not play in the UGA National championships of 1954–56. Late in the 1953 season Rhodes won a small tournament called the St. Louis Public Links Open, but while driving to Chicago afterward, he became seriously ill with what was reported as a kidney condition—similar to the problem he had encountered while in the service. Increasingly he would now face occasional health issues that began to affect his golf game. Evidence of such issues could be occasionally seen when he would post two or three good rounds in a tournament, only to struggle in with a mid-to-high 70s score in one of the later rounds that would result in his just missing a prize check.[22]

The golf seasons of 1954–56 saw Rhodes still playing in the occasional UGA tournament yet placing his major attention on the PGA tour, where he regularly received invitations to play. He opened 1954 by winning a small check in the Los Angeles Open, but then late-tourney struggles quickly followed at the PGA's San Diego and Phoenix events, where an 81 and a 76 respectively in the last rounds dropped him just out of the money. Despite his winning $485 with an impressive twelfth-place finish at the Motor City Open, 1954 on the PGA tour was an ongoing struggle for Rhodes.

It was more of the same in 1955 and 1956 as Rhodes continued to play on the PGA tour wherever he was allowed to enter. In 1955 he won a check for $155 at the St. Paul Open, but then despite playing well for most of the summer, he failed to win a prize check in six PGA events—each tournament marked by a round of 75 or 76 that kept him just out of the money, three times by three shots or less. During the 1956 season Rhodes made the thirty-six-hole "cut" in eleven of the PGA tournaments he was able to enter, although he won prize checks at only the Los Angeles, St. Paul, Western, and Imperial Valley events. He failed to win cash at the Rubber City (Akron) and Phoenix tournaments by just one shot in each, final rounds of 76 and 75 respectively costing him greatly.

Rhodes had not lost touch with the world of African American golf though, as early in 1956 he finished in second place at the UGA's popular North-South Open in Miami. The major respect that Rhodes was still accorded in the UGA was evident in 1956, when he was signed to a position on the advisory staff of Burke Golf Sales of Newark, Ohio. A company official said that "Ted is a fine golfer and very much a gentleman and will reflect the same credit to our organization as he has to golf and sportsmanship in general."[23]

While this position and all of Rhodes's appearances on the PGA tour signified that someday the widespread discrimination in the sport of golf might actually end, there was still plenty of evidence that it was going to continue longer. Even though the PGA now offered "approved entry" of African American players into some of its events, it was always clear in the 1950s that it had every expectation of continuing to prohibit black golfers from membership despite the growing progress toward full integration in other professional sports. Moreover, despite the civil rights movement and the growing pressures for the ending of segregation in America, many organizations and cities continued to believe that they could maintain discrimination in their golf-related activities and at their municipal golf courses. Yet by the second half of the 1950s many of them had been legally forced to discard such practices. For example, in early 1956 the city of Los Angeles banned a local men's club from using municipal golf and meeting facilities because of its "Caucasian only" policy, and in early 1957 the Southern California Public Links Association was forced to drop its "Caucasian" policy if it expected to be able to continue playing on Los Angeles area municipal courses.[24]

### Heading Back Home

Now living in St. Louis, Rhodes struggled through much of the 1957 season as health issues still cropped up occasionally and apparently affected his stamina at times. In PGA events he only made the thirty-six-hole cut in three tournaments, and in each of them he finished just one shot away from winning a prize check because of final round scores of 74 or more. With his limited record on the PGA tour in 1957, he continued to play in the few UGA events that still had a section for professionals, and he supplemented these meager earnings with his long-standing practice of playing "money games" whenever he could line up willing opponents.

The biggest moment of 1957 came when Rhodes turned up in Washington DC at the East Potomac course and entered the UGA National Open—his first appearance in the tournament since he had won his fourth consecutive title in the event back in 1952. His long-ago rival Howard Wheeler was still near the top of UGA pro golf, but in 1957 the chief rival for Rhodes was Charlie Sifford. After the first two rounds Rhodes was trailing by one shot, but then in the last two rounds he came roaring back with scores of 69 and 65 for a ten under par total of 276 and his fifth UGA National title. His seven shot win over Sifford brought him a welcome prize check of $500, and the black media heralded his return to the tournament and his fifth crown—the *Chicago Defender* even providing a listing of his four previous wins of 1949–52.

Buoyed by his 1957 UGA national title, late in the season Rhodes won nice prize checks in a pair of small PGA tournaments, finishing in third place for $450 at the Pomona Valley Open and seventh place for $240 at the Montebello Open. The following season, 1958, Rhodes began to slightly reduce the number of PGA events he was entering, the financial demands of traveling widely on the tour with only limited success no doubt a major factor. In 1958 he made the midway cut in seven PGA events but only cashed in two of them, his seventh-place finish in the Jamaica Open producing a $325 prize. In UGA tournaments Rhodes won the Gotham Open and the Peoria Progressive title, although in the UGA National he struggled to a ninth-place finish as Howard Wheeler won the prestigious black championship for the sixth time.[25]

The 1959 season would prove to be the last attempt of any consequence at the PGA tour for Rhodes, as he finished out of the money in three tournaments—missing by three shots in each because of a poor score in the final rounds—and won a decent check at the Canadian Open. In UGA tournaments he finished in second place at the North-South Open and tied for fourth at the UGA National. In 1960 Rhodes played a tournament in Havana at the invitation of the Cuban government, but for that year his name only appears for one final time in the PGA record book—that for winning $100 in the Rheingold Invitational.[26]

Although he would still continue to play golf—and play it well— for the rest of his life, by 1961 Rhodes had finally come to realize that his health problems would no longer permit the wide-ranging tournament schedules he had pursued for so many years. He finally returned to live again in Nashville but first tried unsuccessfully to qualify for the Los Angeles Open, which had been so loyal to African American golfers over the years. In Nashville he began to work at whatever kind of jobs he could find that would occasionally allow him to play in a nearby UGA tournament, and he began to give golf lessons. In 1962, when it was learned that Rhodes was recuperating from surgery at the VA Hospital in Nashville, the Chicago UGA club and others held fund-raising events for the legendary African American golfer.

### A Lasting Sport Legacy

After leaving the hospital Rhodes would increase his golf teaching, his most prominent student being Lee Elder, who would eventually be a full member of the PGA and was the African American golfer who finally shattered the last symbol of racial discrimination in professional golf in 1975, when he qualified for the Masters tournament. Meanwhile, the PGA had continued stalling throughout the 1950s, and it had voted to retain the "Caucasian only" clause at its 1960 meeting after attempting yet another bluff earlier in designating Charlie Sifford as an "approved tournament player"—despite the legal pressure that was building around the country behind the leadership of California attorney general Stanley Mosk and the NAACP.

Finally it became clear to the PGA leadership that it was chancing major financial consequences for its organization and members in continuing to avoid the inevitable, so at its November 1961 annual meeting the removal of the "Caucasian" clause from the PGA constitution was approved. In 1965 Charlie Sifford would finally become the first African American pro golfer to earn full PGA membership, but all of this was too late for Teddy Rhodes. After continuing as a popular teaching professional and watching the gains finally achieved for African American pro golfers—and still playing a good game himself despite his fragile health—Rhodes at last passed away on July 4, 1969, in Nashville, where he was still residing. He was fifty-six years old.[27]


The dapper Teddy Rhodes had compiled a marvelous competitive golf record in African American tournaments over nearly two decades. In particular, the successes he realized on the PGA tour in the 1950s, along with his marvelous golf swing and friendly personality, all combined to demonstrate that there were some very capable African American golf professionals around, so he had made a significant contribution toward ending segregation in pro golf.

Recognized by many as one of the true pioneers of African American golf, Rhodes was in all ways a perfect and respected ambassador for the many black golf pros who were struggling to earn a living from the game outside of the PGA. Golf historian Calvin Sinnette has described Rhodes as a "cult" figure, and certainly during the 1950s and beyond that is an accurate portrayal of the reputation he earned and that in fact continues into the current world of professional golf.

Yet Rhodes never let all his golf titles and days playing on the PGA tour change the person he was. A soft-spoken gentleman, he believed until the end of his playing days that the African American golfers were making progress toward eventually being eligible for PGA membership, despite some of the rough treatment he acknowledged receiving from white PGA players. In 1961 Rhodes explained to an interviewer that an overriding love of the sport and the search for some security were what motivated him and the other African American golf pros to endure the discrimination and abuse they regularly encountered. He said, "We will be content to be allowed to make a living at the thing we do best—play golf. We will always be happy to find a place to eat and sleep where we will be welcome."[28]

When his competitive playing days were over, Rhodes still never lost sight of the quest of African American professional golfers to gain the opportunity for membership in the PGA. While hoping he could still help young black golfers who were following behind him, he modestly told an interviewer, "I think I've contributed a little something to the struggle to have my people given a fair break in golf."[29]

In an act of recognition that was long overdue in arriving, Teddy Rhodes and two other long-ago African American golf professionals were awarded full membership posthumously in the PGA in 2009.

### Notes

1. Marvin P. Dawkins, "Race Relations and the Sport of Golf: The African American Golf Legacy," *Western Journal of Black Studies* 27, no. 4 (2003): 231–32.

2. Marvin P. Dawkins and Graham C. Kinloch, *African American Golfers during the Jim Crow Era* (Westport CT: Praeger, 2000), 7, 153; Dawkins, "Race Relations," 232; Marvin P. Dawkins, "African American Golfers in the Age of Jim Crow," *Western Journal of Black Studies* 20, no. 1 (1996): 39–40.

3. Alison M. Gavin, "Ted Rhodes," in *African Americans in Sports*, vol. 2, ed. David K. Wiggins (Armonk NY: M. E. Sharpe, 2004), 299; Robert Joseph Allen, "The Odyssey of Ted Rhodes," *Golf Magazine*, February 1961, 19, 46; Lenwood Robinson Jr., *Skins & Grins: The Plight of the Black American Golfer* (Evanston IL: Chicago Spectrum Press, 1997), 83; John H. Kennedy, *A Course of Their Own: A History of African American Golfers* (Lincoln: University of Nebraska Press, 2005), 46.

4. Calvin H. Sinnette, *Forbidden Fairways: African Americans and the Game of Golf* (Chelsea MI: Sleeping Bear Press, 1998), 85; Alan Lawson, "Civilian Conservation Corps," in *Dictionary of American History*, 3rd ed., ed. Stanley I. Kutler (New York: Charles Scribner and Sons, 2002), 220.

5. Kennedy, *A Course of Their Own*, 21–22; Pete McDaniel, *Uneven Lies: The Heroic Story of African Americans in Golf* (Greenwich CT: American Golfer, 2000), 50–51; Sinnette, *Forbidden Fairways*, 57–58; Dawkins and Kinloch, *African American Golfers during the Jim Crow Era*, 44.

6. Allen, "The Odyssey of Ted Rhodes," 19; Dawkins and Kinloch, *African American Golfers during the Jim Crow Era*, 67–75; David Clay Large, *Nazi Games: The Olympics of 1936* (New York: W. W. Norton, 2007), 231–33. One of the features of the Joe Louis Open for years was the staging of an exhibition match at the end of the tournament between a team of two of the top African American professionals and a pair of local white golf pros. This was clearly done to showcase further the playing talent of the black pros and to demonstrate that the two races could coexist in golf competition. In the later years entry to the tournament was also opened up to white professionals, making the Joe Louis Open one of the earlier pro tournaments with a mixed racial field, demonstrating further that coexistence on the golf links was possible.

7. "Champ Is Put Out Early," *Chicago Defender*, August 23, 1941; Allen, "The Odyssey of Ted Rhodes," 46; Kennedy, *A Course of Their Own*, 46–47.

8. Sinnette, *Forbidden Fairways*, 85; Kennedy, *A Course of Their Own*, 47; Robinson, *Skins & Grins*, 83.

9. Dawkins and Kinloch, *African American Golfers during the Jim Crow Era*, 153.

10. Allen, "The Odyssey of Ted Rhodes," 46; "Louis Ups Golf Monies," *Chicago Defender*, May 31, 1947; Dawkins and Kinloch, *African American Golfers during the Jim Crow Era*, 58, 76.

11. Kennedy, *A Course of Their Own*, 47; Charlie Sifford with James Gullo, *Just Let Me Play: The Story of Charlie Sifford, the First Black PGA Golfer* (Latham NY: British American Publishing, 1992), 48–49.

12. Sinnette, *Forbidden Fairways*, 87; Kennedy, *A Course of Their Own*, 109; Sifford with Gullo, *Just Let Me Play*, 45.

13. "Joe Louis Wins Eastern Amateur," *Chicago Defender*, August 16, 1947; "Joe Louis Open," *Chicago Defender*, August 30, 1947; "Wheeler Wins National Title," *Chicago Defender*, September 6, 1947.

14. *Official PGA Tournament Record Book: 1941–1949* (Chicago: Professional Golfers' Association, 1950), 66; Sinnette, *Forbidden Fairways*, 126–27; Kennedy, *A Course of Their Own*, 50, 61–62; Dawkins and Kinloch, *African American Golfers during the Jim Crow Era*, 59, 78, 154.

15. *Official PGA Tournament Record Book: 1941–1949*, 75; Thomas B. Jones, "Caucasians Only," *Minnesota History*, Winter 2003–4, 383–93.

16. Sinnette, *Forbidden Fairways*, 86; "Wheeler Wins Golf Tourney," *Chicago Defender*, September 4, 1948.

17. Sinnette, *Forbidden Fairways*, 87; "Golf Crowns," *Chicago Defender*, July 16, 1949; "Teddy Rhodes Sets New Mark," *Chicago Defender*, August 6, 1949. A note of interest is that the Ray Robinson Open, like the Joe Louis Open, allowed white players to enter the tournament, fifteen of them competing in the 1949 event.

18. "Demaret Ties Palmer at Tam," *Chicago Tribune*, August 15, 1949; "Rhodes Wins UGA," *Chicago Defender*, September 3, 1949; *Pittsburgh Courier*, September 10, 1949; Sinnette, *Forbidden Fairways*, 86.

19. Dawkins and Kinloch, *African American Golfers during the Jim Crow Era*, 59; *Official PGA Tournament Record Book: Consolidated 1950–1958 Supplement* (Chicago: Professional Golfers' Association, 1959), 7; "Joe Captures Amateur Title in Ohio," *Chicago Defender*, June 15, 1950; "Al Besselink Wins Crown," *Chicago Defender*, August 26, 1950; "Ted Rhodes, Ann Gregory Win," *Chicago Defender*, September 2, 1950; *Official PGA Tournament Record Book: Consolidated 1950–1958 Supplement*, 27; "Wheeler Winner of Louis Open," *Chicago Defender*, August 4, 1951; "Ted Rhodes Fires 280 to Win Pro Crown," *Chicago Defender*, September 8, 1951.

20. Dawkins and Kinloch, *African American Golfers during the Jim Crow Era*, 81–85, 154–55; Jones, "Caucasians Only," 390–91; "How Louis Upset PGA Race Barrier," *Chicago Defender*, January 26, 1952.

21. Dawkins and Kinloch, *African American Golfers during the Jim Crow Era*, 60–62; *Official PGA Tournament Record Book: Consolidated 1950–1958 Supplement*, 44–58. This new essay accurately credits Teddy Rhodes with five UGA National Open championships during his career. This information is the correction of a major error relative to the 1952 tournament's professional division winner that is included in the table of UGA champions from 1926 to 1962 in the widely consulted book by Dawkins and Kinloch, *African American Golfers During the Jim Crow Era*. Their table incorrectly lists Charlie Sifford as the winner of the 1952 UGA National Open and thus credits him with winning the tourney six times during his career, including consecutive victories from 1952 to 1956. The correct facts—that Teddy Rhodes won the 1952 UGA National in the tourney that was played in Pittsburgh, while Sifford finished in sixth place—were discovered in the *Chicago Defender*'s coverage of the tournament while I was doing research for this article. Confirmation was obtained in the 1952 tournament coverage of the *Pittsburgh Cou-*

*rier* and another Pennsylvania newspaper, while other eastern papers were seen to also correctly report Rhodes as winning the 1952 UGA event. Also, in following years several references were found that correctly named Rhodes as the 1952 champion and mentioned how many national titles each man had won. Coverage of Rhodes's winning the 1952 UGA National Open can be seen in "Ann Gregory Upset in Finals," *Chicago Defender*, September 6, 1952; "Only Two Champions Survive Tough Play in 1952 Nationals," *Pittsburgh Courier*, September 6, 1952; "Ted Rhodes Again Wins Golf Title," *Bradford Era*, August 30, 1952. Also see Sifford with Gullo, *Just Let Me Play*, 43, 60.

22. *Official PGA Tournament Record Book: Consolidated 1950–1958 Supplement*, 76–81; "Eural Clark and Gregory Win Crown," *Chicago Defender*, August 20, 1953; "Rhodes Seeks Fifth Straight Golf Title," *Chicago Defender*, August 20, 1953; "Rhodes Will Not Defend UGA Title," *Chicago Defender*, August 27, 1953; Sinnette, *Forbidden Fairways*, 89.

23. *Official PGA Tournament Record Book: Consolidated 1950–1958 Supplement*, 84–101, 130–32; "Sifford, Clark Sawyer Walk Off with North-South," *Tee-Cup Magazine*, February–March 1956, 4; "Ted Rhodes on Burke Golf Advisory Staff," *Tee-Cup Magazine*, February–March 1956, 2 (quote).

24. "Los Angeles Bars Club at Muny Course," *Tee-Cup Magazine*, April–June 1956, 2; "Golf Bias Is Canned," *Tee-Cup Magazine*, February 1957, 2. Some of the municipalities that waged court battles in the 1950s and early 1960s before being forced to yield on their segregation of public golf courses include Houston, Miami, Greensboro, Tallahassee, Nashville, and Atlanta. For an excellent article on the battles over segregation on public golf courses, see George B. Kirsch, "Municipal Golf and Civil Rights in the United States, 1910–1965," *Journal of African American History*, Summer 2007, 371–91.

25. *Official PGA Tournament Record Book: Consolidated 1950–1958 Supplement*, 157, 175; "Rhodes and Brown Win Titles," *Chicago Defender*, September 14, 1957; "Rhodes, Brown, Gregory Capture UGA Crowns," *Tee-Cup Magazine*, August 1957, 2, 10; "Light As a Feather," *Tee-Cup Magazine*, October–December 1957, 5; *Official PGA Tournament Record Book: Consolidated 1950–1958 Supplement*, 191–221; Sinnette with Gullo, *Just Let Me Play*, 89; "Howard Wheeler Wins 6th UGA Title," *Tee-Cup Magazine*, February 1959, 10.

26. *Official PGA Tournament Record Book: Consolidated 1950–1958 Supplement*, 29–33; "Thomas, Botts, Funches UGA Winners," *Tee-Cup Magazine*, April–August 1959, 6; Sinnette with Gullo, *Just Let Me Play*, 89; *Official PGA Tournament Record Book: Consolidated 1950–1958 Supplement*, 80.

27. Allen, "The Odyssey of Ted Rhodes," 47–48; Sinnette with Gullo, *Just Let Me Play*, 89. There are several available accounts of the final battle that eventually forced the PGA to join the rest of the professional sports world in ending racial discrimination. See Dawkins and Kinloch, *African American Golfers during the Jim Crow Era*, 157–59, and McDaniel, *Uneven Lies*, 88–90. "Ted Rhodes, Golfer, Dead; First Negro in Pro Tour," *New York Times*, July 6, 1969; "Ted Rhodes," *Chi-*

# CONTRIBUTORS

**James Coates** completed his graduate degrees at the University of Maryland, College Park, and is an associate professor in the Professional Program in Education at the University of Wisconsin, Green Bay. His work focuses on teaching; cultural studies; and sport, leisure, and recreation in the African American community. Coates has lectured, consulted, presented, and published articles and essays on sport, education, and African American history. He is currently working on further research and understanding of the career of Harold "Killer" Johnson.

**Sarah Jane Eikleberry** completed her MA and PhD in health and sport studies at the University of Iowa and is an assistant professor in the Department of Kinesiology at St. Ambrose University in Davenport, Iowa. Her research and teaching are located at the intersection of sport studies, sport history, and physical education. Her work focuses on the structures, ideologies, and interventions that influence access and experiences in sport and physical activity settings. Her work has been published in the *Annals of Iowa* and the *Journal of Sport History*.

**Gerald R. Gems** is a full professor in the Kinesiology Department at North Central College in Naperville, Illinois. He is a past president of the North American Society for Sport History, the current vice president of the International Society for the History of Physical Education and Sport, and a Fulbright scholar. He is the author or editor of over two hundred publications, including seventeen books that address race, religion, ethnicity, gender, and social class in sports. He is the book review editor for the *Journal of Sport History* and also serves on the editorial boards of several international journals. Gems is a frequent speaker at national and international conferences.

**Bieke Gils** is a sociocultural kinesiologist with an interest in the history of the gendered and racialized female body. She recently earned her PhD degree from the University of British Columbia, Vancouver, Canada. In it she explored histories of female aerialists, including trapeze flyers and pilots who performed around the turn of the twentieth century in both North American and European contexts. Gils is currently involved in a research project on women's pioneering work in the history of movement education in North America and Europe, also at the University of British Columbia.

**Michael E. Lomax** is an independent scholar and former associate professor of sport history in the Department of Health and Human Physiology at the University of Iowa. His primary research focus is on the African American experience in sport and the rise of sport entrepreneurs. He has written several articles on race and sport, labor relations in sport, and Major League Baseball's expansion era. His first book, *Black Baseball Entrepreneurs 1860–1901: Operating by Any Means Necessary*, examines the ways in which African American entrepreneurs transformed baseball into a commercialized amusement. His second book, *Black Baseball Entrepreneurs: The Negro National and Eastern Colored Leagues 1902–1931*, traces the forces that led to the rise and decline of the Negro National and Eastern Colored Leagues.

**Pellom McDaniels III** is the curator of African American Collections in the Manuscript, Archives, and Rare Book Library at Emory University and an assistant professor in Emory's Department of African American Studies, where he specializes in sports history, visual culture and performativity, and black masculinity. McDaniels's research and publishing on the African American athletes includes

"The Strong Men Keep a Coming On: African American Masculinity, Athletic Performance and the Philosophy of Resistance," in *The Olympics and Philosophy* (University Press of Kentucky, 2012); "Body and Soul: History, Memory and Representations of Black Masculinity," in *What's Up with the Brothas* (Men's Studies Press, 2010); and "'As American As . . .': Filling in the Gaps and Recovering the Lost Narratives of America's Forgotten Heroes," in *All Stars and Movie Stars: Sports in Film and History* (University Press of Kentucky, 2008). His most recent book, a biography on the African American jockey Isaac Burns Murphy titled *The Prince of Jockeys: The Life of Isaac Burns Murphy* (2013), was funded by the National Endowment for the Humanities Fellowship.

**Murry Nelson** is professor emeritus of education and American studies at Penn State University. He is the author of short biographies of Bill Russell (2005) and Shaquille O'Neal (2007); three volumes on pro basketball history: *The Originals: the New York Celtics Invent Modern Basketball* (1999), *The National Basketball League: A History, 1935–49*, and *Abe Saperstein and the American Basketball League, 1960–63* (2013); and editor of two encyclopedias on sport and American history: *A History of Sports in America* (2009) and *American Sports; A History of Icons, Idols and Ideas* (2013). He is writing a two-volume history of Big Ten basketball.

**James E. Odenkirk**, an educator for over fifty years, is professor emeritus from Arizona State University, where he taught twentieth-century American history, including sports in the United States. He is active in the North American Society for Sports History, NINE, and the Society for American Baseball Research. He has written numerous refereed articles and three books, including a political biography, *Frank J. Lausche: Ohio's Great Political Maverick*, and *Tribes and Tribulations: A History of the Cleveland Indians*. He resides in Chandler, Arizona.

**Robert Pruter** is the reference and government documents librarian at Lewis University, Romeoville, Illinois. His work in sport history concentrates on the pre–World War II recreations and sports in the high schools and amateur ranks. His articles and reviews have appeared in the *Journal of Sport History, International Journal of the History of Sport, Sport History Review,* and NISHIM: *A Journal of Jewish Women's Studies and Gender Issues.* He has contributed essays for many reference books, notably *A Companion to American Sports History* and *Sports in America from Colonial Times to the Twenty-First Century.* Pruter is the author of *The Rise of American High School Sports and the Search for Control, 1880–1930* (Syracuse University Press, 2013).

**Susan J. Rayl** is an associate professor in the Kinesiology Department at the State University of New York College at Cortland. She teaches introductory courses in physical activity and upper-level courses in the history of sport. Her doctoral dissertation delineated the history of the New York Renaissance professional black basketball team, and her research focuses on the African American experience in sport in the twentieth century. Her article "African American Ownership: Bob Douglas and the Rens" was published in *Basketball Jones* in 2000; "Arthur Ashe, Jr." was published in *African American Icons of Sport: Triumph, Courage, and Excellence* in 2008; and "'Holding Court': The Real Renaissance Contribution of John Isaacs" was published in the *Journal of Sport History,* Spring 2011.

**Raymond Schmidt** is an independent sport historian now retired from his career in computer systems. He has studied and written on the history of several major sports, with college football as a primary interest, and is the author of four books and numerous sport history articles for journals and reference works. Schmidt has served as editor of the College Football Historical Society's journal for twenty-seven years and now lives in Ventura, California.

# INDEX

CPSIA information can be obtained
at www.ICGtesting.com
Printed in the USA
LVOW11s1303140317
527168LV00001B/216/P